RESILIENT
ADULTS

RESILIENT ADULTS

ADULTS

Overcoming a Cruel Past

Gina O'Connell Higgins

Jossey-Bass Publishers
San Francisco

Substantial discounts on bulk quantities of Jossey-Bass books are available to corporations, professional associations, and other organizations. For details and discount information, contact the special sales department at Jossey-Bass Inc., Publishers. (415) 433–1740; Fax (415) 433–0499.

For international orders, please contact your local Paramount Publishing International office.

Manufactured in the United States of America. Nearly all Jossey-Bass books and jackets are printed on recycled paper containing at least 10 percent postconsumer waste, and many are printed with either soy- or vegetable-based ink, which emits fewer volatile organic compounds during the printing process than petroleum-based ink.

The passage in Chapter Six from FRIED GREEN TOMATOES AT THE WHISTLE STOP CAFE by Fannie Flagg, Copyright © 1987 by Fannie Flagg, is reprinted by permission of Random House, Inc., and David Higham Associates (for Vintage Books).

Remaining credits are on p. 373.

Library of Congress Cataloging-in-Publication Data

Higgins, Gina O'Connell, date.
    Resilient adults: overcoming a cruel past / Gina O'Connell Higgins — 1st ed.
      p. cm.
    Includes bibliographical references and index.
    ISBN 1-55542-673-5
      1. Problem families—Psychological aspects. 2. Adult children of dysfunctional families—Psychology. 3. Abused children—Psychology.
    4. Resilience (Personality trait)   I. Title.
    HV697.H54   1994
    362.82'4—dc20   94-7283
                                                 CIP

FIRST EDITION
HB Printing   10 9 8 7 6 5 4 3 2 1   *Code 9490*

For my youngest brother,
Gordon,
to buttress your flickering but fundamental faith in benevolent
possibility

and

the shattered scarecrow,
who loved us, crushed some, and died young,
and thus, through a twisted grief,
gave the last gift,
a second chance to live

and, not least,

Jim, Caitlin, and Taryn –
the second chance

Contents

*Three passions, simple but overwhelmingly strong,
have governed my life: The longing for love, the search
for knowledge, and unbearable pity for the suffering of
mankind. These passions, like great winds, have
blown me hither and thither, in a wayward course,
over a deep ocean of anguish, reaching to the very
verge of despair . . . I have sought love, first, because
it brings ecstasy so great that I would often have
sacrificed all the rest of life for a few hours of this joy.
I have sought it, next, because it relieves loneliness –
that terrible loneliness in which one shivering
consciousness looks over the rim of the world into the
cold unfathomable lifeless abyss. I have sought it,
finally, because in the unions of love I have seen, in a
mystic miniature, the prefiguring vision of heaven that
saints and poets have imagined. This is what I sought,
and though it might seem too good for human life, this
is what – at last – I have found.*

–Bertrand Russell[1]

Preface

What are the silken threads that hold a web of hope in a gale of hate? How is good salvaged from evil? Continually impressed by the human capacity for decency in the face of hurt, I began exploring psychological resilience nearly twenty years ago. Given my training as a psychologist and my work with atrocity and trauma, I had certainly learned that those who are emotionally undercut stumble. Unfortunately, in a field dominated by pathology, I had learned little about how they call on their resilience to right themselves. Yet some severely traumatized individuals do overcome unthinkable horrors and live fulfilling lives. This book is meant to delineate and celebrate the strengths of the traumatized and to demonstrate that many people have a robust capacity to love despite exposure to hate.

Can resilience be cultivated? *If I did not believe this, I would not have written this book.* Although some aspects of resilience may be genetically graced, many others are not. Regardless, genes do not *determine* behavior but *influence* it, leaving a strong role for individual motivation as well as for environmental impact. Because resilience is a multifaceted phenomenon influenced by both natural and nurturant factors, my emphasis remains on what we can do to promote it. Clinical work with the less hardy traumatized may be turtle therapy, but with competent intervention, the motivated *do* recover. Most of my subjects invested in therapy as adults, and all reported that teachers, neighbors, friends, young love, or chance events had changed the course of their earlier lives. With good company—and determined to beat the odds—they evolved over time, devoting their lives to growth and change. Yet even the resilient need to be reminded of their strengths. Although our interview sessions had explored the worst aspects of their pasts, they reported feeling steady yet uplifted in the following days because we had also examined *what went right*. If the resilient benefit from this emphasis, so should their less recovered counterparts. Thus, while I refer to them as "the resilient," you can read this as "individuals who exemplify and amplify resilient capacities that inhere in us all." (The former is a bit tidier.)

A detailed summary of the research design and major findings is included at this end of this book (see Resources for Researchers). However, the following brief discussion of the enterprise and its guiding assumptions is integral to an understanding of the findings, which form the infrastructure of the text.

In order to find forty resilient people, I contacted more than thirty seasoned clinicians in the Greater Boston area in the spring of 1984 and again in the fall of 1992, including both licensed psychologists and licensed independent social workers. All had a decade or more of intensive clinical experience. First, I conveyed a clinical picture of resilience. Then, defining the phenomenon more formally, I emphasized that resilience implies that potential subjects are able to negotiate significant challenges to development yet consistently "snap back" in order to complete the important developmental tasks that confront them as they grow. Unlike the term *survivor, resilient* emphasizes that people do more than merely get through difficult emotional experiences, hanging on to inner equilibrium by a thread. Because *resilience* best captures the active *process* of self-righting and growth that characterizes some people so essentially, I chose it in preference to other descriptions.

In addition, each clinician reviewed specific screening criteria to help me determine whether or not each subject not only had confronted extraordinary early challenges but currently maintained good mental health. With their help, I located forty adults clustering around age forty with a history of multiple, significant stressors during childhood and adolescence, including serious illness in themselves or their families, low income, chronic family discord or parental fighting, parental substance abuse, persistent and harsh parental discipline, or prolonged parental absence. Additionally, more than half of the subjects had a history of repeated physical and/or sexual abuse. Because combined risk factors potentiate one another, their negative effects are multiplied rather than simply added. Thus my subjects were sorely challenged. While their troubles varied, all subjects were judged to have grown up in severely, extremely, or catastrophically stressful families. They had one parent (and usually two) with major psychopathology who functioned at either a poor, very poor, or grossly impaired level during the subjects' childhoods. Despite these backgrounds, all subjects were deemed by various measures to be psychologically mature and healthy.

These forty subjects were also chosen because they love well. Each clinician understood the following operational definition of those who "love well" and ensured that all subjects met the definition:

- They establish and maintain relationships marked by a high degree of reciprocity and concern for the other as well as the self.

- They develop and actively participate in relationships that can withstand (or even thrive on) conflict, disappointment, frequent anger, and frustration when the needs of either person in the relationship are not met. These conflicts are actively and successfully negotiated throughout each relationship.

- They relate to others in a way that, in general, does not

sacrifice the accuracy and empathy with which they perceive other people; that is, they make consistent and generally successful attempts to recognize the needs and characteristics of others and to differentiate those needs from their own.

Each subject sustained a satisfying intimate love relationship for an average of twelve and a half years in the 1984 group ($n = 23$) and eighteen years in the 1992 group ($n = 17$). Five of the original subjects were reinterviewed in 1992 to ensure that their resilience had endured; their additional years in primary relationships are reflected in the first figure. The second group were chosen in part because they had been in committed love for so many additional years.

Although there were no specific screening criteria for "working well," the clinicians understood that a strong work identity (which can, and in this case usually did, include parenting) and job satisfaction were essential. All subjects met these criteria.

My subjects' backgrounds are typically associated with posttraumatic consequences and compromised adult functioning, although the literature on trauma and resilience reviewed in the introductory chapter suggests that positive outcomes *do* occur under these circumstances and thus warrant thoughtful consideration. In almost all cases, the referring clinicians noted that they had always puzzled over the considerable mental health of their subjects. Since all of us had become familiar with the devastating effects of abuse on so many of our clients, our explanations for their strengths seemed unsatisfying and thin. Thus both clinicians and subjects were generally eager to participate, finding the project intriguing and hopeful.

It is also worth noting that these mental health criteria are rather rigorous. Several of the clinicians, chosen for their own psychological balance, sheepishly doubted that they would meet them. Happy eighteen-year relationships, for example, do not abound even among those with an Ozzie and Harriet childhood. My emphasis on rigorous criteria is deliberate, however. I felt that finding extremes of early turbulence and current mental health in midlife adults would establish resilience as a legitimate phenomenon. I also thought it might help us understand the mechanisms that propel growth under less drastic circumstances and, most crucially, among the abused who are *not* surmounting difficulties as well.

As is evident throughout the narrative, I am at pains to point out that finding some healthy traumatized individuals does *not* mean that abuse is acceptable. I am determined to maintain what Judith Herman calls "moral solidarity" with those struggling more fundamentally with trauma, because they are most in need of hope and least in need of another reason to feel bad about themselves. Abuse is anathema. No one in this study wishes her or his past on anyone else, and virtually all of us have respectfully devoted our personal and professional lives to preventing abuse or to repairing its effects on the limping majority of abused individuals.

While this study has many quantitative components, it is predominantly qualitative in design. I interviewed each person for 4 hours, totaling 180 hours ($n = 45$, including the reinterviewed subjects). The themes emerging strongly during the twenty-three interviews completed in 1984 were pursued in depth during the subsequent twenty-two interviews in 1992. While I made provisions to disconfirm the hypotheses generated in my original research, the uniformity of these subjects' responses remained remarkable. Thus I am reporting on the repeated themes, well aware of the dangers of any academic Procrustean bed. Since many of these findings are consistent with the variables reported in the academic literature on resilience, I will attend more fully to the *process* by which resilience develops.

I have several reasons for taking a more phenomenological, clinical approach. First, there is little systematic knowledge about resilient *adults*, let alone the resilient capacity to *love*. Second, my analysis is placed in a developmental framework, for which there was no precedent in this population. When little is known about a phenomenon, it is important to explore it in a relatively open manner in order to isolate relevant variables for future quantitative analyses. Semistructured interviews allow for gathering some consistent data while granting subjects greater latitude to offer unanticipated perceptions and analyses. Third, my intended audience includes clinicians, educators, the educated lay public, and especially any traumatized person determined to heal. The personal narrative of these pages seems most closely attuned to the language traumatized people commonly speak. I am determined to write about *subjects* rather than *objects*, in thick and telling detail. If the voices of my subjects resonate with yours or those you are helping to heal, and if my analysis of the motifs makes sense in your own lived experience, then the work is more likely to be useful. I offer it to buttress your faith in the human capacity to overcome.

What will you find here? Chapter One considers the prevalence and effects of abuse, briefly summarizes what is generally known about resilience, and introduces the characteristics and dynamics of the resilient subjects in this research. Chapter Two portrays two resilient lives in some detail, weaving in the more prominent motifs explored in later chapters. The third chapter takes a developmental approach to the unlikely evolution of the capacity to love among my subjects, focusing on the locus of hope that sustained them in childhood despite the significant neglect or even hatred that they encountered. Chapter Four investigates the later loci of hope in their lives, especially those adolescent "adoptive" families and settings that can foster growth in the maltreated so effectively. The fifth chapter explores the firm role of faith and vision in sustaining resilience, demonstrating that faith is inherently relational and that symbolic imagery can preserve people even when they are enduring dramatic insults to their developmental integrity. Chapter Six looks at the fierce social and political activism among these resilient adults, suggesting that their altruism is both an outgrowth and the continuing wellspring of their effectiveness in overcoming. Chapter Seven winds the struggles of the resilient around the metaphor of Odysseus passing the Sirens. It underscores the seductive appeal of less resilient solutions to the inescapable challenges presented by abusive families. The final chapter summarizes the strongest recommendations made by my resilient subjects based on what they feel was most helpful to them in surmounting their own abuse. Its aim is to amplify the central leitmotifs rather than to develop a new score, since most of what really made a difference to them is fundamental, far easier to say than to do, and yet essential.

I include a variety of other "voices" in the text very deliberately. They include psychological theory and research, extensive quotes from my own subjects (pruned very reluctantly, as they are the most direct source of data), my own organization and analysis of the qualitative accounts, and a large measure of metaphor. The last seems important for a number of reasons. First, it is simply how I generally think (and the form of thinking that I most enjoy). Second, there are now many sources of quantitative research on resilience, but not many that convey the depth and poetry of the lives of the resilient. Third, since I assert that imagery and symbolism are pivotal to overcoming, it seems reasonable to employ them to convey the phenomenon itself. I try to make the literal truth distinct while moving beyond exactitude to *symbolic* truth through the use of allusion, just as the resilient lift themselves from *their* actual plight through the substantial use of imaginative mastery.

What was it like to participate in these interviews? An uncanny experience, akin to that of a guest conductor stepping up to the podium to face a collection of virtuosos, all having arrived belatedly from the airport with no opportunity to review the score. With some invested but generic gestures from my baton, the orchestra suddenly swelled into a coherent symphony, each with its own voice but firmly connected to an articulate whole. While there were certainly variations within each instrument's part, a

series of leitmotifs emerged in the data. I intend to offer that
remarkable symphony so that you can savor the sound of the piccolo and the oboe yet feel the collaborative harmony guiding hard
lives lived well.

The emotional range of these subjects is especially noteworthy.
Most reported, exclaimed, laughed, sighed, wept, stilled, saddened,
and beamed during the interview. One moment, tearful and
poignant, they might explore some of their deeper anguish; the
next, they might be matter-of-fact and jocular. They were often
truly hilarious. Since I probed the great highs and lows of their
lives, their affect was appropriate rather than labile. I mention this
range because it is a good demonstration of their capacity to restore
their own emotional equilibrium. Thus throughout this book you
will hear a considerable spectrum of affect and observation from
them and from me, including our humor, as we attempt to capture
the affective and cognitive complexity inherent in resilience. The
humor may also help you see that we refuse to let a terrible past get
in the way of having a good time.

What sustains my intense interest in this work? At Harvard I
once heard someone remark that all dissertations are veiled auto-
biographies. Perhaps this is true of all committed professional work,
varying mostly in the transparency of the veil. I certainly know
how hard-won are the quiet victories of a reclaimed life. While
many of my subjects endured far worse, and I make no exaggerated
claims for my own mental health, I do bring an informed subjectivity to my work. While I believe that this kind of past is deeply
unacceptable, I also know that it allowed me, fueled by stamina
and considerable luck, to be far more than I might have been
otherwise. In my clients' and subjects' lives, I have learned to hear
beyond the levels at which this is rationalization or denial and grasp
its convictional roots: a faith in the promise of a kinder life. While
I have gone to great efforts to ensure as much objectivity as
possible in the analysis, frequently exposing it to the exacting eyes
of other researchers, clinicians, and reliability observers, my

comprehension of these phenomena is certainly enriched by my own experience. I am motivated in the manner of many of my subjects: if only a few lives are inspired by our legacy of "good enough overcoming," then I am well pleased with the entire effort.

Salem, Massachusetts   Gina O'Connell Higgins
June 1994

Acknowledgments

Many people are important to the evolution of this work. I will mention them roughly in the order of their appearance in my life rather than in the hierarchy of their importance, since everyone here deserves acclaim.

Jim, Caitlin, and Taryn Higgins, to whom this book is dedicated, deserve my deepest thanks for teaching me that one can live well within resilient love for a long time. Fondest recognition belongs to Jim for freely extending steadfast encouragement and considerable yeoman's work—giving me stamina and the time to write—and for being my dear friend for so many years. I feel an odd gratitude toward my brothers and parents for the admixture of love and anguish that forged my own resilience, such as it is. I am happily indebted to my brother Gordon, who let me be his locus of hope. Anne Nicodemus Carpenter's surrogate love during my adolescence and beyond ignited my faith in forging extended family ties. Zella Luria and Mitchel Rose at Tufts University became her intellectual successors; the harmonics of their humanity are still in my work.

Sharon Parks sponsored this book by telling Jossey-Bass about it. Without her generosity of spirit and action, it might not have been published. She, Robert Kegan, and George Goethals were exceptionally respectful doctoral thesis advisers and remain inspiring intellects. William Rogers at Harvard was also a mentor, encouraging me to pursue a path with heart. Jane Jacobs, Jane Hanenberg, and Margery Gans served willingly as reliability observers (and far more). Without their collective vision, I would not have been able to study the capacity to love while I was at Harvard.

Becky McGovern, senior editor of the Jossey-Bass Social and Behavioral Science Series, shepherded this project with quiet grace and unobtrusive wisdom. Without her even-keeled openness, the poetry of these resilient lives would not have been heard. Evelyn Lesch typed all the transcripts, while Alta D'Oleo and Esther Tibbetts helped with life's pragmatics—indispensably and kindly. Nancy Vasilakis, Kerry Galm, and Rosemary Levesque generously assisted in obtaining materials for the literature review.

Carol Taylor and Dennis Norman offered steady kindness, penetrating intellectual companionship, and unflagging faith in this project. They read all the chapters one or more times and gave solid evaluative feedback throughout the project. Many subjects, who unfortunately cannot be named, read chapters and verified their accuracy. The members of the Clinical Developmental Institute in Belmont, Massachusetts, also collaborated well on my behalf. They include the delightfully irreverent Laura Rogers, whose attentive focus made *me* look harder; Robert Kegan, whose warm messages buoy my days; and the equally helpful Sharon Parks, Robert Goodman, Gil Noam, Ann Fleck-Henderson, Elizabeth Speicher, and Michael Basseches. Other sustaining friends and colleagues also read portions insightfully: Dan Boynton, Andrea Celenza, Susan Eisen, Ellen Fisher, Susan Gere, Franny Hall, Jane Hanenberg, Jane Jacobs, James Manganiello, Gordon O'Connell, Richard Olivo, Charlie Sorrentino, Diane Smith, Russell Vasile, and Ron Jenkins. I am especially grateful to Ron for deepening my laughter in the wake of his having what he refers to as "a little brain surgery."

I also honor the gifted givers who graced the lives of the resilient in this study as they moved through the midst of winter. Know that you are among the silent guardians of human hope.

My final remarks go to those to whom I am ultimately most indebted. You are, of course, the resilient adults whose voices shaped this work. As you might recall, I asked if you had any heroic figures who influenced your vision of the person you are or want to be. Now I will answer the same question. You enabled this research to evolve, but you also offered me new ways to live in the light of your own inspiring lives. Your integrity, hilarity, and passion are now part of my own sustenance. You offered the sturdy companionship that propelled this work from its inception and compelled me to its end, certain that your voices needed to rise above the darker din and speak of love kindling in hate's ashes. While I see your struggles, even the turmoil that you occasionally negotiate, *you are doing it—and well*. Bearing witness to your overcoming firmly anchors my faith in resilience itself, renewing me on dimmer days and convincing me that I can continue to offer an outstretched hand to those who still struggle. If one can be said to be in a state of grace, then I am in a state of gratitude to each one of you. While I can never change your past—which will always make me sad—I hope that my efforts to understand you will soften your future.

Without you all, I would be a lesser woman.

G.O.H.

The Author

Gina O'Connell Higgins is a licensed psychologist in private practice in Salem, Massachusetts. She is an instructor at Harvard Medical School and a staff psychologist at Massachusetts General Hospital in Boston, as well as a fellow at the Clinical Developmental Institute in Belmont, Massachusetts.

Higgins received her bachelor's and master's degrees (1972 and 1974, respectively) from Tufts University and then completed her doctoral degree (1985) at Harvard University. She was a faculty member at Lesley College Graduate School for many years and taught at Tufts University. She continues to teach for the Harvard Programs in Professional Development with other members of the Clinical Developmental Institute. Her formal academic work on resilience began during her studies at Harvard, but her childhood and adolescence—as well as her subsequent clinical experiences with traumatized clients—provided (and still enriches) her primal understanding of the process.

CHAPTER ONE

The Challenge of Resilience

Clinical psychology and psychiatry typically study the dire, the deadly, and the derailing. We admire or envy—but rarely puzzle over—dazzling psychological success. Although a lot is known about the genesis of illness and dissolution, the origins of mental health are often ignored. Moreover, even less is known about the origins of healthy *loving*, which can develop even when early hopes are repeatedly dashed. Therefore, we need a psychology of the development of compassion to deepen our understanding of how human beings effectively integrate the inevitably scarring experiences that they encounter. Perhaps we can begin to form this psychology by studying individuals who have surmounted even the most turbulent pasts in order to love well, work well, struggle well, and expect well in the present. We might then understand how most of us acquire our largely uncelebrated resilient strengths.

Resilience implies that potential subjects are able to negotiate significant challenges to development yet consistently "snap back" in order to complete the important developmental tasks that confront them as they grow. Unlike the term *survivor, resilient* emphasizes that people do more than merely get through difficult emotional experiences, hanging on to inner equilibrium by a thread. Because *resilience* best captures the active *process* of self-righting and growth that characterizes some people so essentially, I have chosen that term in favor of other descriptions. In addition, while *resilience* embraces many of the aspects of this process, no other labels (particularly the term *invulnerability*) adequately convey the hurt and even anguish that the severely psychologically challenged negotiate as they emerge from their turbulent pasts. Thus my research assumes that an additional strength of the resilient is their ability to acknowledge and experience significant psychological pain and still maintain their ability to love well. I do *not* assume that the resilient love perfectly or that they are without normal human shortcomings. But they trouble themselves more than they trouble anyone else, and the size of their hurts is now small.

More pointedly, human faith is inevitably assaulted, sometimes with indescribable savagery. Yet in the wake of such assaults, we frequently remain kinder and gentler than anyone would imagine. Our capacity for concerned action often flourishes despite—perhaps even because of—vicious assaults on our developmental integrity. Not a few of us hold another's fate in hand and make a noble choice, for a moment or a lifetime. Many of us love when we might lie and maim, as the following brief review of the literature on abuse and resilience will attest. It is time for us to understand why so many emerge from abuse *without* becoming abusive.

It is also essential for us to stop subordinating the study of health to a pathologically oriented, reimbursement-driven medical system that does not encourage us to fully explore the wellsprings of individual strength. If we do not firmly understand the psychological nourishment that fuels an individual's growth beyond what we might otherwise predict, how can we know what potentials to encourage as we help that soul arise? The abused are often so many shattered stained-glass windows, each shaped with at least some integrity and spectral grace, awaiting a collaborative, restorative partnership. How can we consider ourselves effective cathedral conservators if we do not understand the origins of their saturated hues and tensile strength? And how do we explain those elaborate resilient panels emerging with only minor stress fractures, essentially intact when the cathedral is shattered?

Psychologists—in fact, many people—assume that children require unconditional love, attention, respect, security, and safety in order to become mentally healthy. By contrast, we historically see "maladaptive" or "defensive" behavior as a nearly inevitable outgrowth of compromised family life, especially when interpersonal stressors are extreme. That is, we assume that assaults such as parental alcoholism, gross neglect, systematic shaming, and sexual intrusion will derail development. The following discussion of the effects of abuse creates a sobering picture of the potential devastation. Yet even trauma researchers, understandably committed to discouraging the minimization and denial of abuse, note that people react differently to the same stressors and that some even respond relatively well. When people emerge from difficult circumstances and still demonstrate particular psychological strengths, they challenge the prevailing wisdom among developmental and clinical psychologists regarding the ways that personality strengths evolve—or *devolve*. Thus clinical and empirical emphasis is now being placed on individuals whose functioning is *not* significantly compromised by major stress. In fact, some of these people demonstrate unusually good adaptive capacities.

My own study explores why some individuals who are treated assaultively throughout most of their formative years emerge "loving well" in adulthood. I explore the resilient person's capacity to *love* well since that capacity is the least expected outcome of a hateful past. In addition, it is one of the central preoccupations of the human race—sought and cherished, lost and mourned, inspiring sparkling imaginative leaps and shattering defeats, focal to most of us and yet only dimly understood. I hope that studying resilience and love will help us identify and foster adaptive strengths in anyone trying to forge a future in hate's ashes. In fact, given the average expectable pain we encounter in our lives, it becomes equally (if not more) compelling to explore the mechanisms that propel the strength of human hope, especially when it is repeatedly challenged.

A few central questions guide this work. What are the mechanisms that spur ongoing resilient capacities? Are there identifiable themes in people's lives that tell us how some people surmount cruelty so effectively? Can convincing theoretical explanations be proposed for the initial formation of resilience and its subsequent evolution? I assume that resilience is not a collection of traits but a *process* that builds on itself over time. My subjects also acknowledge this process: many pointedly reminded me that they would not have met all (or even most) of the "resilient" criteria during earlier chapters in their lives. Yet they always had several core dynamic capacities, and these launched them beyond their more fundamental struggles into their current level of overall psychological health. Centrally, they see themselves as people who have continually and self-consciously *worked* on growing. They remind me of the words of W. H. Auden, who was thought to be an inwardly free man. In describing his own personal evolution, he captures theirs: they gradually squeezed a slave out of themselves, drop by drop.

Understanding how health flourishes in apparently barren developmental soil may help us understand ways to identify and nourish resilient capacities even in those who are still struggling significantly with a potentially overwhelming past. I press this point so early and so earnestly because this book is ultimately not only for those who are doing far better than they (or anyone else) might have predicted on the basis of either their tumultuous childhood or their faltering during early and late adolescence. It is ultimately, and most essentially, meant for those who are still suffering, those with whom the resilient are most deeply politically and personally allied. It is imperative to understand that I do not mean to define and serve a new developmental elite while abandoning those who are currently in a partial eclipse. I particularly honor the unsung songs who faded before they, too, might become hymns of resilient love. To use this work *against* the abused would be a miscarriage of the very justice we are trying to restore. At the same time, by identifying how the more resilient surmount abuse, perhaps we will find ways to help the daunted launch beyond the trauma that confines their tattered spirits.

Let me add, as an impassioned caveat, that by studying the resilient I do not intend to deny or minimize the overwhelming social compromises that so many people face. Nor am I minimizing the anguish that many people inevitably negotiate as they grow. Personal and social complexities frequently undercut even the sturdiest spirits if they accumulate too early or too fast. Many people cannot help themselves because they are denied essential resources such as food, shelter, and respect. Many are too firmly under the heels of social powerlessness to stride forth. To blame the disenfranchised for their plight without thoroughly recognizing the numerous social forces that bind them is to perpetuate cultural abuse. Thus we need to understand and replicate the community resources that encourage the more resilient to flourish rather than to perpetually blame and abandon the less hardy.

In sum, it is a travesty to use the findings of this or any similar study as ammunition to reblame the victim; likewise, we cannot cancel social welfare programs simply because a few people thrive after the onslaught. Instead, I hope to delineate some of the natural "holding environments" that promote the growth of these resilient individuals during childhood and adolescence so that more, not fewer, organized community and governmental efforts can be mounted to buttress the lives of the less strong. At the same time, recognizing the faithful, gritty determination of the resilient and understanding the process by which they ascend with grace maintains the hope of educators, clinicians, and other compassionate people working with the maltreated—as well as the abused themselves.

This book should be relevant to any clinician, educator, informed layperson, or developmentalist interested in the emergence of human adaptive capacities. It is particularly aimed at thoughtful practitioners of any stripe who sustain a curiosity about the interior lives of the unpredictably strong, because I am most intrigued by the ways in which resilient capacities might be constructed, maintained, and revised *internally* throughout the adult years. Perhaps a deeper understanding of the emergence of unexpected strengths will help us refocus on adaptation rather than deterioration in our clinical and educational work and will encourage us to appreciate the developmental integrity that guides even the most challenged lives.

The Prevalence of Abuse

This section presents a condensed literature review of the dismal prevalence of abuse and its destructive impact, followed by a brief summary of the more hopeful empirical work on psychological resilience. Those who are familiar with the consequences of abusing children and adults might move ahead to the resilience literature review. Those who prefer to draw their own conclusions from clinical data and analysis can turn to Chapter Two, which contains case studies of two resilient adults.

Just how prevalent is abuse? While estimates vary, depending on the way that abuse is defined and how the data are gathered, a few well-respected studies report astounding rates of maltreatment in our culture. While this empirical evidence is meant to be representative rather than exhaustive, it builds a sobering scaffold. For example, to determine the incidence of sexual victimization, human rights activist and sociologist Diana Russell interviewed 930 women of diverse ages and backgrounds in the San Francisco area, using random sampling techniques.[1] Russell's interviews were face to face and in-depth. She found that one woman in three reported having been sexually abused during childhood and one in four reported being raped. Judith Herman, who analyzed results from five studies published between the 1940s and the early 1980s, discovered that 20 to 30 percent of the women reported an unwanted sexual encounter with a male during childhood.[2] John Wodarski and

Sandy Johnson reported a similar incidence of 25 to 38 percent.[3] However, women are not the only targets of sexual assault: 8 to 9 percent of college men in David Finkelhor's study reported being the target of a completed or attempted rape.[4] The incidence of sexually abused men in the general population is likely to be even higher than this, though, because men are widely thought to underreport their own abuse to an even greater extent than women. College *women* in Finkelhor's study, as well as in the work of Mary Belenky, Blythe Clinchy, Nancy Goldberger, and Jill Tarule,[5] reported a lower rate of sexual abuse than the population at large (one out of four or five women rather than one out of three). Yet few of these assaults are reported to the criminal justice system, and fewer than one out of four victims are seen by professionals.[6] Sexual abuse is frequent, yet it is usually undisclosed and untreated when it occurs.

Physical abuse is also a considerable problem. A recent compendium entitled *Child Maltreatment,* edited by Dante Cicchetti and Vicki Carlson, offers a lucid and thorough exploration of the causes and consequences of child abuse (particularly physical abuse) and neglect. The editors open their book by noting that "the American Association for Protecting Children tallied 1,727,000 reports of suspected child maltreatment in 1984. Forty-two percent of these reports were substantiated. A national survey reported that 10.7 percent of parents admitted to having perpetrated a 'severe violent act' against their child in the previous year."[7] Composing a similarly chilling collage of corporal punishment in the American home, Edward Zigler and Nancy Hall note the following:

> The most widely accepted incidence figures are those prepared by the National Committee for the Prevention of Child Abuse, which estimates that over 1 million children are "seriously abused" and 2,000 to 5,000 deaths occur each year. . . . Ninety-three percent of all parents practice some form of corporal punishment. One survey revealed that 25 percent of mothers spank their infants in the first

six months of life; nearly half spank their babies by the end of the first year. [Fathers were not mentioned.] A survey by Viano revealed that 66 percent of teachers, police, and clergy expressed approbation for striking a child with the hand; 10 percent condoned physical punishment with belts, brushes, and straps; . . . 52 percent of one group of adolescents had been physically punished or threatened with physical punishment during their senior year in high school.[8]

Spousal abuse is likewise prevalent. Murray Straus, Richard Gelles, and Susan Steinmetz found that 16 percent of marital partners reported violent interactions between them in the past year, while 28 percent cited similar violence between them at some time in the marriage.[9] Nor are children protected from bearing witness to abuse: many children reported seeing violence between their parents without any adult attempts to shield them from it.[10]

Apparently, by the end of childhood only a minority escapes traumatic exposure. Susan Gere summarizes two surveys of posttraumatic stress disorder in undergraduates that support that finding.[11] The first—a survey conducted by Shirley Segal and Charles Figley—found that 80 percent of 281 college women and men reported experiencing one, usually two, highly stressful events by age eighteen.[12] Similarly, Dean Lauterbach and Scott Vrana, in the second survey, assessed the incidence of traumatic events of sufficient intensity to cause potential posttraumatic symptoms among a sample of 440 college students.[13] "They found a surprisingly high incidence of traumatic experiences. . . . Only 17 percent of the respondents reported experiencing *no* traumatic event. . . . [They also found that] these traumatic events often resulted in significant psychological symptoms and that those experiencing multiple events appeared to increase the risk of specific post-traumatic reactions, depression, and anxiety."[14]

Because alcohol is an enabler of both sexual and physical abuse as well as neglect, it is crucial to note that roughly 10 percent of adults in the United States grew up in alcoholic homes.[15] Many children also grow up in abject poverty, and half of all children in divorced households receive no financial support from their non-custodial parent (usually the father) five years after the divorce.[16] Low-income status can be considered intrinsically abusive, as it exposes children and adolescents to many other associated stressors, such as poor nutrition, community violence, and substandard housing and health care. Obviously, trouble is not in short supply.

The Effects of Abuse

Now, just why is abuse bad? The reasons are painfully self-evident to the abused as well as to those who love and work with them. "An Early Silence" speaks to one enduring grief in a multitude. It is my own, written to my brother. He ultimately killed himself in reaction to his prolonged sexual abuse as a child.

> This morning,
> beyond a tidal pool
> dappled with rocks, the sleek onyx heads
> of proud seals,
> I slipped your coffin
> into the waves.
>
> A skeletal boy,
> your waxen face in sculpted solitude.
> Yet glints, a troupe of russet angels,
> dance from your hair into the light
> above the sea.
>
> You rest in a soft curve,
> knees drawn to your chin,
> a thin undershirt stretched over your legs,
> as it was when we perched
> on the edge of a sun-baked morning,

encircled in buoyant laughter,
a sister and a brother joined
before the frost.

A Trojan
slipped quietly into the chaos of our youth
offering the fatherhood we had lost,
pressing himself into your fragile frame instead.
Your promise rises into the mist above the seal's head stones.

You drift quietly offshore now,
cradled by the ebbing tide,
while I reach,
straining beyond my hand,
yearning to run my palm
along your still, small back,
and soothe you into
an early silence.

However, I am eternally reminded of our culture's ambient climate of minimization, social apathy, and outright denial of abuse that renders even well-intentioned, educable individuals uninformed about its effects. Illustratively, the New York Times reported on a recent Roper Organization poll sponsored by the American Jewish Committee.[17] The pollsters, who surveyed 992 adults and 506 high school students, discovered that 22 percent of the adults and 20 percent of the adolescents said it seemed possible that the Nazi extermination of the Jews never took place. Another 12 percent said they did not know if it was possible or impossible that the Holocaust occurred. If such uncertainty exists in the face of organized, abundantly documented evil, no wonder less centralized abuses are overlooked. Most of the traumatized bear no remaining physical manifestations of their abuse and have no witnesses; the culture is just beginning to see the numbers tattooed on their souls. Therefore, a brief review of the prominent findings regarding the aftereffects of abuse will remind us that it does *indeed* exist, occurs frequently, and often devastates people.

In assessing the effects of abuse, it is important to look at abuse histories among those who come to our clinical attention seeking mental health services *because* they are struggling. Simultaneously, since many of the maltreated never come for help, it is also important to mention specific subgroups subjected to similar traumatic events who remain outside the mental health system. These include "captive" populations—veterans of heavy combat, rape victims arriving at emergency rooms, kidnapped children, Holocaust victims, and children living in community and familial war zones. The capsule review that follows will help us get a better sense of how gravely so many suffer after abusive episodes or abusive lives— whether they seek treatment or not—creating an explanatory puzzle regarding those who seem to do better. As you read, remember that these and similar forms of abuse are the ones that were inflicted upon the forty subjects in this study of resilience.

Trauma became the renewed focus of clinical and empirical attention in the past decade, just as I completed the first stage of this study. Judith Herman's articulate and courageous efforts to resurrect abuse from what she terms "periodic cultural amnesia" deserve particular mention here. Her sophisticated recent volume, *Trauma and Recovery*, provides a highly competent analysis of the similar impact of widely varying *forms* of abuse.[18] Crucially, Herman shifts our attention away from the troubles we have to the *origins* of our troubles. By scrutinizing etiology and deemphasizing the implicitly victim-focused—thus often accusing—process of diagnosis, Herman returns abuse to the limelight.

For example, Herman reviewed numerous studies of people receiving both inpatient and outpatient treatment for symptoms such as depression, anxiety, panic, and somatic complaints. She found that somewhere between 50 and 75 percent of patients revealed a history of childhood trauma upon careful interviewing.[19] (Indeed, childhood trauma is one of the central reasons that any-

one seeks help.) When more disruptive diagnoses (such as borderline personality disorder) are considered, the incidence of reported
abuse climbs to over 80 percent. And in the case of multiple personality disorder—perhaps the most severe psychiatric disorder—
Herman notes that Frank Putnam found histories of major trauma
in 97 of 100 patients he studied. "Extreme sadism and murderous
violence were the rule rather than the exception in these dreadful
histories. Almost half the patients had witnessed the violent death
of someone close to them."[20] Herman also notes that people institutionalized for mental illness have a frequent history of sexual
abuse. "While only a small minority of survivors, usually those with
the most severe abuse histories, eventually become psychiatric
patients, many or even most psychiatric patients are survivors of
childhood abuse."[21]

More clinically based works also capture the anguished voices
of women and men, notably *The Courage to Heal: A Guide for
Women Survivors of Child Sexual Abuse*, by Ellen Bass and Laura
Davis, and *Victims No Longer: Men Recovering from Incest and Other
Sexual Child Abuse*, by Mike Lew.[22] These voices, along with those
arising from grass-roots support groups across the country, leave little doubt about the anguishing effects of abuse. In fact, my many
traumatized clients typically report that they can read only a few
pages of these books at a time because the narratives are so painfully
accurate and powerfully evocative. As if illuminated by a blinding
sun, they can gaze directly into it for only a few moments before
looking away. Yet even these moments are affirming, warming
chilled soil and stirring renewed growth.

Although abuse is often associated with a spectrum of
disruption, ranging from milder symptoms of distress to pervasive
personality difficulties, it frequently causes posttraumatic stress
disorder as well. Posttraumatic stress disorder is a response to trauma
in which people alternately experience "fight or flight" hyperarousal
symptoms, such as anxiety, irritability, distractibility, panic, hypervigilance, nightmares, flashbacks, or intrusive memories of stressful

events. By contrast, they may also experience numbing, dissociation, social withdrawal, constricted affect, and/or a shrunken sense of the future. Oscillation between these states of autonomic hyperreactivity and emotional underreactivity are common. For the sufferer, posttraumatic stress disorder is unwanted and unpleasant, if not completely debilitating. Because posttraumatic stress disorder accurately—albeit implicitly—emphasizes the hammer blows that create so much psychological disruption, I yearn to see some version of this diagnosis as the overarching rubric under which most other disorders are subordinated. Since so many forms of distress originate in assault, we need to refocus on what is disruptive to people rather than obsessively categorizing those who are disrupted. Perhaps this would reorient clinical treatment to how and why people become organized (or disorganized) around past experiences. It might also remind us that we all come by our ways honestly, even if our coping strategies are daunting or unlivable for others.

It is also essential to take an integrative approach to posttraumatic stress disorder, alcoholism, and mental disorders, since trauma makes people more vulnerable. The estimated lifetime prevalence rate of alcoholism is 13.5 percent, and more than a third of alcoholics evidence a comorbid (simultaneous) mental disorder.[23] Since many of these mental disorders (depression, anxiety, and antisocial personality, for example) are themselves strongly associated with past trauma, abuse certainly seems to play a significant role in the etiology of a significant percentage of alcohol abuse and dependence. Judith Herman also cites several studies linking trauma and substance abuse problems directly.[24] She notes that among 100 combat veterans with severe posttraumatic stress disorder, Herbert Hendin and Ann Haas found that 85 percent developed serious alcohol and other substance abuse problems when they returned home.[25] Just 7 percent of these veterans were alcohol-dependent before they went to war. Another large-scale study, the National Vietnam Veterans Readjustment Study, reported similar rates of substance abuse.[26] Francis Hall, a clinical social worker who has been working with alcoholics in Lynn, Massachusetts, for twenty-five years, confirms a high incidence of early abuse—emotional, physical, and sexual—among substance abusers, most notably female substance abusers.[27] Open testimony in self-help organizations across the country suggests that this connection is axiomatic. Many victims are presumably attempting to anesthetize trauma's painful effects, although substances certainly have a life of their own and *create* symptoms of depression, anxiety, and impairment over time.[28] While alcohol amounts to poor alchemy for transforming posttraumatic stress symptoms, for many it is an understandable (albeit destructive) response to intolerable experiences.

Abuse also predisposes victims to subsequent trauma at the hands of others or oneself. Diana Russell's study revealed that two-thirds of the women reporting childhood sexual abuse were raped in adulthood.[29] For these women, rape becomes an independent, although additive, insult. For example, Ann Burgess and Lynda Holmstrom interviewed and counseled ninety-two women and thirty-seven children presenting at Boston City Hospital's emergency room in the aftermath of rape.[30] "They observed a pattern of psychological reactions [in everyone] which they called 'rape trauma syndrome.' They noted that women experienced rape as a life threatening event, having generally feared mutilation and death during the assault."[31] Herman also notes that persistent posttraumatic stress disorder symptoms were often present years later among rape victims. Similarly, 75 percent of veterans of heavy combat remained symptomatic in the years following the ending of the Vietnam War, and over a third qualified for the diagnosis of posttraumatic stress disorder fifteen years afterward.[32] Even more grave, "Survivors of the Nazi concentration camps . . . reported tenacious and severe intrusive symptoms" after *forty* years.[33] Obviously an *internal* cease-fire takes far longer. Thus forms of recognition such as the Vietnam War Veterans Memorial and the Holocaust Museum in Washington, D.C., serve a crucial function in dignifying the continuing struggles experienced by so many of the traumatized.

Finally, direct attempts at self-injury are also highly prevalent in the traumatized. Herman reports that women battered as adults (who, as I just noted, were frequently abused as children) reveal entrenched self-destructiveness—reportedly as high as 42 percent.[34] Prisoners of war also have elevated mortality rates from suicide, homicide, and suspicious accidents. As Michael Rutter understatedly concludes a recent literature review, "Apparently adverse life experiences make it more likely that people will act in ways that create threatening situations for themselves."[35]

Hostile family climates and marital discord are also associated with poor mental health.[36] For example, John Bowlby looked at attachment in children whose parents had a diminished capacity for empathy, low tolerance for frustration, low self-esteem, and heightened dependency and concluded that these factors contribute to insecure attachment patterns.[37] Sadly, parental emotional unavailability, depression, alcoholism, and somatic preoccupation are linked cyclically with past trauma, perhaps accounting for those families that perpetuate abuse across generations. Marital discord is also a firmly established factor in the emergence of conduct disorders and delinquency.[38] Actual abuse and hostile home lives are also being recognized more widely as causing (rather than being caused by) learning disabilities, cognitive deficits, and hyperactivity.[39] In her psychiatric interviews with the children buried in a school bus at Chowchilla, California, Lenore Terr found that virtually all of them had cognitive dysfunctions not present before the kidnapping, including visual hallucinations, distortions of visual and auditory perception, and a strong superstitious belief in omens.[40]

The consequences of abuse go beyond individual suffering. Abuse is also expensive for all of us. Dante Cicchetti and Vicki Carlson emphasize that "the economic and human costs of maltreatment in American society are astronomical. It is likely that billions of dollars are spent in treatment and social service costs and lost in lessened productivity for a generation of maltreated children. . . . The human costs are a litany of psychological tragedies.

Maltreated children suffer from poor peer relations, cognitive deficits, and low self-esteem among other problems; moreover, they tend to be more aggressive than their peers, as well as having behavior problems and psychopathology. . . . The emotional damage due to maltreatment may last a lifetime."[41]

Thus when people develop symptoms of distress in adulthood and come to clinical attention, a history of trauma is heavily implicated in their troubles. Few face extreme hurt at the hands of trusted others without hearing the wail of the soul betrayed. Given that, how do we explain that so many surmount their strafed pasts and more insular concerns, frequently helping their partners in peril? In fact, *many* of us seem to avoid the plague of the House of Atreus, wherein the sins of the parents are forever passed on to their children. Although the intergenerational transmission of abuse has become a popular assumption, a recent literature review indicates that most maltreated adults do *not* assault their own children.[42] While the assumption that we are fated to repeat the curse may serve to keep receptive parents on their ethical toes, it also causes them unnecessary and often extreme anxiety about repeating the past. More specifically, Edward Zigler and Nancy Hall note that when "Hunter and Hilstrom . . . employed a prospective rather than a retrospective technique, they found that 82 percent of the parents they followed who had themselves been abused were able to break the cycle of abuse. Similar results were obtained by Egeland and Jacobvitz, who found that even in what might traditionally be considered a sample of parents at high risk for abusing their children, 70 percent were able to avoid doing so."[43] A well-controlled study of a nonclinical population of offspring of Holocaust survivors found that they, too, have adjusted well as a group despite their parents' horrific histories.[44] Thus not only are their offspring unabused, but many survivors have been successful at raising psychologically *intact* children. This is characteristic of my forty subjects as well. Why is their quiet heroism unhailed?

Unless we understand the determined forces leading so many

abused children to protect their children (often becoming effective trauma workers in the bargain), driving maligned social workers to reenter fearsome tenements, and compelling Gentiles to rescue Jewish people during Nazism despite threats to their own lives,[45] we cannot understand how to perpetuate and expand our capacity for sustained human concern. Once again, why do some love so well despite such hate?

The Incidence of Psychological Resilience

Although we must not minimize the crucial and terrible findings in the field of trauma, we can counterbalance them with the more emblematic findings in the rapidly growing academic literature on risk and protective factors—that is, literature on the research into why some children, demonstrating remarkable resilience, do not succumb to the significant assaults that they endure in childhood and adolescence. This field burgeoned after I completed the first stage of my study in 1985, although there is still a paucity of findings about *relational* competence in resilient adults from a developmental perspective, which is the focus of my research. Further, there is at present no standard definition of either *resilience* or *risk*, which creates difficulties in comparing study results. Although the field, like any other, is fraught with methodological and conceptual debate, the findings do have some encouraging consistency. Competent literature reviews and empirical research abound.[46] Recently, clinical researchers such as Sybil and Steven Wolin are offering more usable clinical substance to a popular audience in an effort to make this field more accessible to those who most need it.[47] All of these contributions potentially infuse the maltreated with essential hope.

What does all this research reveal about how often resilience occurs? By defining *resilience* broadly for the moment and calling it the ability to function psychologically at a level far greater than expected given a person's earlier developmental experiences, there are many studies that suggest that resilience occurs often in groups at high risk for the development of psychopathology. The figure frequently cited is approximately 10 percent of the population under scrutiny (although because definitions of *resilience* differ across studies, it is difficult to know what this figure represents). Emmy Werner and Ruth Smith's thirty-year study of 700 insular, low-mobility, ethnically diverse subjects in Kauai, Hawaii, yielded a 10 percent resilient subgroup, although most of these subjects often had effective parenting amidst the strain of impoverishment.[48] Another low-income, thus vulnerable, group of 818 children in which 10 percent were found to be exceptionally competent both behaviorally and educationally also had supportive, interested, and positive parents.[49] Thus subjects in both studies were similarly economically challenged in comparison to my subjects, but they lacked the particular developmental insult of parental psychopathology and/or abusiveness. Earlier studies by E. J. Anthony and Michael Rutter and by C. Kaufmann and colleagues researched resilient offspring of mentally ill parents and found a similar incidence of 10 percent who demonstrated unusual talents in the face of adversity.[50] More recent works, such as William Helmreich's 1992 study of 211 Holocaust survivors, suggest far higher percentages of successful outcomes, with 83 percent of Helmreich's subjects sustaining stable marriages (in contrast to 62 percent of American Jews of the same ages).[51] Despite persistent symptoms of distress, these survivors had a multitude of strengths and derived great satisfaction from their lives; criminality was virtually absent among them. In fact, upon a careful review of the literature on risk, researchers Stuart Hauser, Marie Anne Vieyra, Alan Jacobson, and Donald Wertlieb, citing their own research and the work of others such as E. J. Anthony and Norman Garmezy, conclude that "only a minority of children at-risk experience serious difficulties in their personality development. . . . The majority of children exposed to various forms of adversity grow up to enjoy productive, normal lives."[52]

At first glance, these figures seem to contradict the findings on the consequences of abuse. Remember, however, that the data on mental disorders are generally derived clinically, which leaves the incidence of more and less shattering outcomes in the general population less well understood. Since rates of serious mental disorders are far lower than the nationwide incidence of abuse, many people are summoning substantial strengths and courage to play well when they are dealt a bad hand. Recall that two-thirds of the people who were abused in childhood are *not* abusing their children. Perhaps what we are seeing in the resilience literature is a focus on the strengths and successes that commingle with some symptoms of posttraumatic stress—strengths and successes that allow many people to love, work, struggle, and expect well *enough* in adulthood. In any case, when we look at groups chosen for their *unusually* high levels of functioning in the face of adversity, a conservative incidence estimate is approximately 10 percent.

Characteristics and Dynamics of the Resilient

What do we know about the resilient thus far? I offer a skeletal summary of my own research first, noting that only a few closely related empirical studies informed my initial study in 1984. At that time, Werner and Smith's aforementioned prospective, longitudinal design was highly relevant, in that Werner and Smith found a smaller subgroup within the resilient 10 percent that remained hardy at age thirty although they had encountered four or more major stresses (such as chronic family discord, absence of the father, death of a sibling, parental divorce and/or remarriage, and chronic poverty).[53] This group also had the additional risk of having a parent with significant psychiatric difficulties. This is precisely the group most interesting and relevant to my analysis, because it is the one that *least* predicts resilience when defined as the ability to *love* well.

The twenty-three adults in my original study,[54] as well as the current group—a combined total of forty—have several characteristics in common. They are above average to superior in IQ; possess exceptional talents, including creativity and other inner resources (and have developed many of these); have obtained higher economic levels than their family of origin; demonstrate high levels of ego development; have sustained empathically attuned, close relational ties in childhood, adolescence, and adulthood (including those they formed with parental "surrogates"); frequently have highly psychologically compromised siblings; and maintain strong political and social activism.

More dynamically, they remain fiercely committed to reflection, new perspectives, and ongoing therapy. In fact, the resilient get unusually good emotional mileage out of virtually any experience they encounter. In therapy they grapple actively, with close personal accountability and tight self-scrutiny. They absorb information well and take most reasonable suggestions readily, although not indiscriminately. Self-propelled, they operate with a firm belief that knowledge is power and that their futures will advance if they are active change-agents in their own lives. Although their own parents were not typically well educated, they themselves are unusually well educated—far more than the national norm and often under their own enterprising steam. Whether they are learning formally or informally, they seize the day. Is it any mystery that others generally find them so gratifying?

I also found that they tend to negotiate an abundance of emotionally hazardous experiences proactively rather than reactively, thus solving problems flexibly; they make positive meanings out of their experiences, actively constructing a positive vision despite emotional disappointments; they effectively recruit other people's "invested regard";[55] and they demonstrate a strong capacity to form and then nurture a vision of an interpersonal world that is more satisfying than the one from which they emerged. This last quality— hardly the least—might be considered a profound form of faith. It is imaginatively sustained through an elaborate system of myths, symbols, and ideals that can survive highly discrepant experiences in the actual world. They have certainly needed it.

Like other observers, I am struck by how friendly these people are and by their authentic rather than manipulative appeal. Their affect is generally positive, if not buoyant, without seeming forced. They move with optimism and energy and seem to have an underlying sense of their own efficacy, faithfully expecting competence and tenacity to *work*. They employ a distant but comprehending and even compassionate view of their families of origin, and they remain committed to a measured perspective on the poisonous aspects of the past. Resolved not to repeat their parents' folly, they have become highly skilled at conflict resolution and dedicate themselves to maintaining emotional clarity with others. Although they struggle with an underlying, nagging sense of their own "basic badness," they simultaneously maintain high self-esteem regarding their own executive and interpersonal competence, believe that they deserve to be loved, and feel that their trials made them far more than they might have been otherwise. These commingling, apparently contradictory convictions capture the complexity that is so characteristic of a resilient life. Over time, these people have become more integrated, reducing their discrepant views of themselves and achieving consistently higher self-esteem. They have also gradually relaxed their initial, overdetermined sense of self-reliance, collaborating more fully with others. Finally, the resilient in my group are marked by a fundamental decency, by integrity, and by ingenuousness amidst great sophistication. All these characteristics are startling when we recall that the resilient came of age stalked by winter's heavy footsteps.

One hazard of resilience research is portraying these subjects as near saints. *They are certainly not.* I do emphasize their considerable strengths throughout this book, however—strengths that are most remarkable because these people were raised in hell. If this emphasis endows them with faint halos, they will probably feel uncomfortable, since they tend to be somewhat preoccupied with their faults. But they are marked only by the same human foibles that characterize any healthy person. I am sure all would readily admit to being sour-tempered at times, hurting or disappointing a partner, fighting over something stupid, or slighting a friend in need. They have all stepped on toes unwittingly, let a child down, missed appointments, or left an unfinished fight to crust over. Focusing on their capacity to love well is *not* meant to imply that they have never had a rude or mean moment. Although they were *chosen* for their unusual psychological strength, all of them acknowledge their many human shortcomings. But these shortcomings are still well within normal limits, and the resilient are more trouble to themselves than they are to anyone else. In fact, the resilient are probably kinder and more decent than others, yet they have far more reason to be cruel than most people.

How do these findings compare to others in the field? Since the first stage of my work was completed, many of the reviews and empirical reports noted above have found similar themes. Remember, however, that the academic literature is still primarily focused on the *traits* (rather than developmental processes) of resilient *children*. In any case, characteristics repeatedly described in the studies of this subject include above-average intellectual competence, cognitive flexibility, information seeking, reflective planning, good school performance, positive appraisal of school experiences, internal locus of control, relational competence with individuals and extended support systems, voluntary and/or mandatory helpfulness in childhood and adolescence, high self-esteem, good impulse control, and possession of special talents and inner resources as well as the capacity to employ them. While many of these characteristics overlap or are highly correlated with one another and are often associated with good mental health and higher intelligence in general, they do not necessarily *predict* either one another or resilience. Some traits may be somewhat inborn, but many of them can be learned and thus promoted. In any case, these are the bricks and mortar of overcoming.

Resilience researchers and clinicians have historically doubted that the traumatized can truly love in adulthood, seeing them as too stifled by the persistent pestilence of parental hate or indifference. Adult loving is certainly the least expected outcome of a hateful past. However, my work, as well as David Quinton, Michael Rutter, and C. Liddle's longitudinal study of women institutionalized in childhood, contradicts such pessimism.[56] Quinton, Rutter, and Liddle found that some of their maltreated subjects essentially obliterated the dire effects of their past by choosing an effective marital partner in early adulthood. Recognizing that his work is still primarily descriptive, Rutter calls for an intensified focus on the protective *processes* that promote growth over the life span.[57]

With all that we now know about the resilient, we are still left with the mystery of *how* people who are tripped, trapped, hit, hated, or left can employ these capacities to help them rise, over time, phoenixlike from the ashes. Therefore, I looked microscopically at those themes undulating across forty adult interviews that suggest how resilient love might unfold over time, emphasizing these adults' interpretations of their own lives. I hope my work illuminates how the maligned emerge with a bedrock faith in a benevolent kingdom, determined to ensure firm citizenship for themselves and others.

CHAPTER TWO

Two Portraits: Shibvon and Dan

And thus, like the wounded oyster, he mends his
shell with pearl.

—*Ralph Waldo Emerson*[1]

Perhaps the most immediate way to convey the challenge, vitality,
and dynamics of resilient lives is to introduce two individuals—
Shibvon and Dan—who exemplify many of these capacities. They
are engaging and decent human beings hailing from opposite ends
of the socioeconomic spectrum. While they do not fully represent
the mosaic of resilience, just as no life captures any single human
pattern, their stories express the essential leitmotifs explored more
focally in later chapters.

Although Shibvon's and Dan's portraits are thoroughly dis-
guised in ways that protect others' right to privacy—criminal and
innocent alike—both these individuals prefer the literal truth.
Independently, each asked me to present the data as factually as
possible. They explained that, while they are circumspect, accuracy helps them heal from their nearly cannibalistic childhoods.
Because lies brutalized them as children, making them feel additionally disoriented and betrayed, they prefer the truth. Thus, after
all the *identifying* data had been altered significantly, Shibvon and

Dan reviewed the vignettes to ensure their essential factual and interpretive accuracy. Although they tidied their own narratives somewhat—eliminating sentence fragments and redundancies, for example—the content remains carefully *un*changed. Unfortunately, it is all quite true.

Reading their impassioned narratives in some detail allows us to hear their agony and their poetry. Since Shibvon, Dan, and most of the other subjects urged clinicians to bear witness to the last shivering scrap of terror among the traumatized, I honor their wishes here. For if abuse is the first horror of an unlucky child's life, enforced silence is certainly the prolonged second. Shibvon and Dan also feel strongly that if even a single person is helped by their disclosures, their own potential discomfort pales by comparison. Through their portraits and subsequent quotes in this volume, I hope to show that ultimate hope lies in our recognizing that, although human cruelty has a long history, so does human fortitude. With a blacksmith's forearm of emotional strength, these souls refuse to shrink in hate's glare.

Shibvon

Shibvon is a gentle, reflective forty-year-old pediatric nurse practitioner who grew up in cold, grinding poverty. At work she ministers to infants in an urban neonatal intensive care unit, a particular passion. Her competent co-workers respect her Calvinism and unflagging integrity. Shibvon is widely seen as the sturdy pillar in any medical crisis, focused and empathic. On many occasions, the hospital requests her presence as an unofficial goodwill ambassador for traumatized patients—a position of respect earned during her two decades in this setting. More often, she assumes this role spontaneously, simply because she values extending herself beyond her own spiritual skin. Shibvon, who married at twenty-one, remains much in love with her husband after twenty years. Despite her history of severe sexual abuse, they enjoy a mutually satisfying sexual relationship (although Shibvon feels that she *created* her satisfaction insistently, refusing to cede her sexuality to past abuse). The task of overcoming her assaultive childhood is not Shibvon's only challenge: she and her husband have three sons who are all afflicted with a genetically based joint disease requiring ongoing medical intervention, including casting, braces, occasional surgery, and parents with the stamina of Job. Her sons' adjustments to these complications have been constantly scrutinized over the past decade by concerned, psychologically astute medical professionals, who have seen no reason to refer the children for counseling. Raising even-keeled children in the face of such significant medical challenges suggests that Shibvon indeed loves them well and probably passed her resilient adaptive repertoire on to them.

Is Shibvon a trouble-free person? Of course not; nobody is. Her primary adult struggles involve an irrational underlying conviction that she is guilty of crimes she never committed, which makes her somewhat more vulnerable to the manipulations of misguided others. However, she grapples with this steadily ebbing experiential subtext with insight, humor, and perspective. She now confronts others in a forthright, precise, and constructive manner despite her former, unfounded fear that she would be transformed into a resurrected version of her harridan mother if she even *approached* the mats. After three years of recent therapy for some depression and anxiety, she is well able to maintain good psychological stride in the face of her past and her unusually demanding present.

How can we best understand Shibvon's resilience? Let me first describe her most challenging *figures*—her parents and her perpetrator—and then describe the daunting *events* of her life more chronologically, so that we can see her adaptive repertoire building progressively over time.

Shibvon's Parents and Her Perpetrator

In her childhood, Shibvon's father was diagnosed with various severe psychiatric disorders in the schizophrenic range and hospitalized repeatedly. He was a benign, ineffectual force, sadly and utterly unable to protect Shibvon. To his dismay, Shibvon and her three siblings depended on welfare benefits throughout her childhood, supplemented by his modest but unflagging financial contributions. Although her father was so personally limited, Shibvon feels that he genuinely cared about her, wishing her well despite his confined capacity to provide for the children either emotionally or financially.

By contrast, Shibvon's mother rejected her relentlessly from birth. A remorseless individual, she pummeled and castigated her first daughter with arctic rage, once forcing Shibvon, at four, to eat a regurgitated meal:

> [I remember] . . . a lot of screaming, a lot of yelling, getting thrown across the room. Even that young, [I knew] that *I* wasn't right, that I didn't do anything right [in her eyes, as if] . . . there was something wrong already with me, that I didn't fit in. . . . [I remember] being older than my years. . . . That was commented on a lot [by adults]. . . . I always feel like I never had a childhood. I don't have any memories of . . . [simply] being on the swing, having a good time, and going in to have supper. . . . Something was *always* wrong; it was Gestapo basically. . . . [My mother] was huge; she was tall, plus her voice was booming. . . . She wasn't gentle. I don't have any memories of my mother hugging me or rubbing my back or sitting on the couch watching TV with me or holding me. . . . I didn't have any of that at all. . . . I don't think it ever happened.

Once, during a marital fight in the family car, her mother shoved her own weight against the door of the quickly moving vehicle, trying to push Shibvon from her lap onto the street. Shibvon was six. Oblivious to her offspring's feelings, she also tied her four tiny children to their beds at night to keep their eyes from her affairs. As an adult, Shibvon slowly awakened to the chilling implications of these and similar assaults. Her mother was not struggling to keep her safe in the car; rather, she was trying to throw

Shibvon out forcibly. And tied at night, there was no dignified way to relieve herself at an age when bladder control nearly defines successful selfhood; more gravely, Shibvon and her siblings had no means of protection from common tenement fires, nor did their mother care. Above all, *there was no escape*. At times Shibvon felt, with good reason, that her mother was trying to kill her; at other times, her mother was simply exhibiting rank heedlessness. In any case, luck prevailed and Shibvon and her siblings survived.

Since her four children continued to exist despite her attempts to erase them psychologically, if not physically, Shibvon's mother twice gave all of them to Catholic orphanages. When she was not in an orphanage, Shibvon was singled out for the lion's share of her mother's brutality. With particular vengeance, her mother frequently reminded Shibvon that she was a failed abortion:

> She started screaming one day that she wished she had aborted me; she had tried damned hard. . . . She took some pills that didn't work, . . . and she did have her abdomen X-rayed [deliberately]. She heard that if you X-rayed your stomach, it would make you lose the baby. So I grew up knowing that she tried to abort me, and she's very up front about it. I wouldn't be here if it had been 1992, not 1952. . . . To marry my father was just to cover this baby, the pregnancy; that's the only reason. Motherhood was not . . . chosen.

Eventually, this mother offered her eldest daughter as a sexual sacrifice to her married lover—Proctor—when Shibvon was nine, in the fifth grade. Apparently, she meant to keep this man involved at a time when he threatened to become more peripheral: Proctor might stay if he could have Shibvon, but not otherwise. Shibvon vividly recalls her mother's shadowy figure at the door to her child's bedroom, ushering in her own paramour. There was no question of her mother's ignorance; she planned and sanctioned her daughter's sacrifice. Shibvon also knew that complaining meant risking her mother's fury; she felt that her mother might have killed her then, and she was right. Thus authorized and protected, Proctor began abusing Shibvon extensively, including regular vaginal and anal intercourse as well as forced fellatio and cunnilingus. Yet Shibvon's worst terror was that Proctor would kill her father if she disclosed her abuse, an oft-repeated threat. Violating her several times a week for over a year, he slowly built a coffin in her heart:

> I remember him starting to touch me. . . . I remember being afraid and crying, "Tell him to leave me alone," and him starting right off [telling me that] if I said anything, he would kill my father. . . . I remember I could never tell my mother he was doing this, because I was afraid she'd hurt me. . . . [Anyway,] *she* had brought him in [to the room], although she'll deny and deny and deny that. I could go to that apartment today and tell you where she stood as she opened the door to let him in. . . . I remember it being a very obvious thing. . . . I felt like it was another way of saying how much she hated me *[spoken very softly]*, and how much I just was a piece of excrement, a sacrificial lamb. . . . I often thought of jumping out the window, but I knew that if I didn't die from the fall, my mother would beat me or kill me, and that was worse. . . .
>
> I remember thinking that I had to do this if I wanted to survive *[weeping]*. That's the part that's bothering me now: I think I felt like I had to do it to live. . . . [My mother] kept referring to me as being crazy like my father. . . . When I started to question things, she'd say, "You've always been a problem. You've never been happy; you're just like your father."
>
> *[You were afraid she would try to hospitalize you?]* Yes. And I felt like no one would believe me, because I *had* [tried to disclose the abuse]. Once Proctor was having oral sex with me in the car at the beach and a police car pulled up near us, but I couldn't cry for help. There were also times when I said something to people, and people

approached my mother [about her beating me], but all that happened was I was beaten more.

A Pivotal Incident

To understand Shibvon's life more chronologically, so that I might see the evolution of her resilience, I asked her, "What really stands out for you as you grew up?" She replied, "Chaos." She recounts a pivotal incident at age seven: "The day the police came when I was cooking hot dogs"—an incident that is the organizing principle for her perceptions of her family and herself. Her mother was in the hospital after a miscarriage from her liaison with Proctor. Overwhelmed, her father decided to attempt death by drowning in February. Hacking at a nearby pond with a shovel but failing to crack the ice, he was sighted by concerned neighbors, who called the police to help him. Shibvon, well aware of the gravity of this day, never fails to laugh at the absurdity of *anyone* trying to drown himself in midwinter. In any case, her father did remember to tell the police there were small children unattended at home, and some officers came to investigate. They found Shibvon cooking lunch.

This marks the last day of Shibvon's living with her father; but it is also the day that her life veered right when it might have careened left or—worst of all—stayed on the same grim trajectory:

> The most vivid memory is the day [the police] came in and took us out. . . . That's the day everything ended. . . . The police knocked on the door. I remember standing on a chair by the stove when they walked in and asked me what I was doing, and I said I was cooking lunch. . . . Jake ran . . . screaming upstairs and hid under the bed. I asked them what was the matter, and they said that I had to go with them, that something had happened to my father. No one would tell me what happened. They just said that my father wasn't coming home, that he was sick, too. They just said he was sick. . . .

There were two big cops and a nice lady in between them, probably the social worker from the Division of Social Services. . . . I went upstairs to try to drag Jake out from under the bed. . . . He had got himself so far under the bed, screaming that he wasn't going anywhere. . . . I didn't fight. . . . They finally got him dragging and screaming, literally. . . . That was the worst part. *[He was five?]* Yes. I was the big sister, and I had to act mature—I don't remember crying, and *he* doesn't remember me crying. He says he remembers me just sitting there. . . . So then they took us in the cop car. That's how we left the house. We never went back to the house, and that's the worst thing. . . .

They did take us to the police station, and we were in a cell—with the door open—but that's where we sat for hours, literally. (My two youngest siblings were taken somewhere else.) I asked Jake [about it recently]; I wanted to make sure. That was a vivid memory—but I [needed to know] that I hadn't imagined this. We didn't go to a placement; we were in a *cell* and listened to people say, "What are we going to do with *them?*". . . This was an emergency pickup; there was no great planning. [The social worker] was in and out all day. She was a lovely lady; we got coloring books, and we got crayons. . . . We weren't in a bad place, but it was obviously a holding cell at that point. . . . We could hear people coming back and forth [trying to decide] where we were going to go, and it was getting dark, and we were scared we were going to sleep there.

Openly acknowledging that she feels she has been abjectly abandoned at this point, Shibvon originates her career as a caregiver at age seven—perhaps younger—by trying to nourish her brother and herself, both literally and more symbolically. She also realizes at the bedrock that *any place* would be a better place than home, since she does not protest her removal and sees some slender shafts of light—"the lady with the crayons"—illuminating her day in a jail cell.

At this juncture, Shibvon knows with great clarity that her life has collapsed, that she has no home outside herself and the sustaining bonds that she might forge with willing parental surrogates. Home alone one moment, peremptorily removed by the police the next, she and her five-year-old brother, Jake, begin an odyssey that takes them through several months of foster care and a year at Mercy Orphanage; an abortive family resurrection effort during her fateful fifth-grade year of Proctor's relentless sexual abuse; four years of respite and benign clergy at Bethlehem Orphanage; and a final tour of duty under constant maternal assault for her three remaining high school years. But first let us return to Shibvon and Jake in the jail cell:

> They [finally] took us to my [paternal] aunt's for the night. That's where we landed up. And my aunt had us for the night, and then we went to foster care the next day. That's the part that bothers me, because I never said goodbye to the house [weeping]. Then we went to foster care, Jake and I. We still didn't know what had happened to my father—[although] we knew my mother was sick. . . . When we went to foster care there was a lady with a ton of kids, all her own, and Jake and I were in her home, in our own room, together, about two months. The setup wasn't perfect, but we were okay. . . . Then the lady was pregnant, and that's when we went to Mercy Orphanage, another change; . . . and [then there was the] fifth grade; . . . and then we went to Bethlehem Orphanage [for four years].

The Loci of Hope

Now, in citing her jagged childhood itinerary, Shibvon mentions "and then there was the fifth grade." She is referring to Proctor's sexual abuse of her, briefly discussed earlier. This phase of her life requires closer inspection now, since it is the most devastating and since—despite the devastation—it coincides with an infusion of light through parental surrogacy and Shibvon's redoubled determination to surmount her circumstances. Let us follow her after the first orphanage stay.

After about a year at Mercy Orphanage, which proved emotionally chilly but adequate, Shibvon and Jake return to their mother and two younger siblings. Here the darkest clouds gather for her. Shibvon's perpetrator, Proctor, tells her that he will kill her father if she tells anyone about the ongoing abuse. Her mother implicitly threatens the same. Repeated anal intrusion renders Shibvon unable to stay in her seat in fifth grade. Ashamed and in chronic pain, she leaves the classroom continually simply to sit on the toilet in the girls' bathroom. Nobody notices, or at least noticing does not lead to any intervention. She volunteers to stay after school every day to clean erasers or run errands, and her young teacher has the wisdom to welcome her presence. Shibvon still remembers this teacher vividly, with cherished gratitude: a novice who knew *something* was terribly wrong, who probably had as few words and fewer images for the unspeakable as Shibvon did. She gave what she had—basic warmth and concern—and it has mattered for *decades*.

Groping for any other slim shaft of sun, Shibvon also comforts herself with a fierce belief that her inescapable ordeal preserves her younger siblings from similar intrusions. Thus, at nine, she infuses her suffering with cherished *meanings*, the only influence she wields. She also recalls her paternal aunt offering abundant food and clothing and her mother promptly giving it all away to the relatively affluent children of her lover, perhaps out of some competitive jealousy with her sister-in-law and a compulsive, gratuitous cruelty toward Shibvon in particular. Thus Shibvon's central family comfort becomes the *indirect* pleasure that she receives from watching her younger siblings gratified, although in adulthood she is more balanced about nurturing herself as well:

> I'd never want to get stuff for me. I'd say, "Buy it for the kids." . . . I stopped getting things, because it wasn't worth it. . . . They'd buy

toys, and my mother didn't seem to mind, . . . but it was too much
if *I* had it. I felt like I didn't belong. . . . [My mother] was always
moaning about having no money and . . . how good of her it was to
take us back. . . . That was her big thing. . . . Something about me
bothered her [*weeping*]. I was the ugly one, the stupid one . . . stupid, stupid, stupid, when you know you're *not* stupid.

Recognizing that lies are an integral part of her hell, Shibvon
also becomes ferociously attached to authenticity. Her intolerance
of her mother's casual, self-serving relationship to the truth becomes
something of a mission early on, despite the grave danger of her
mother's retaliating:

She felt threatened by me. . . . I think somewhere in there, I fought
her a little bit, or I would question. . . . I remember saying a lot,
"What happened to our house? What happened to our house?" And
they said, "It flooded." So, as any normal kid would do, I remember
driving by it when I was in somebody's car and thinking, "My house
is right there! It's fine." . . . They also told me it burned. . . . [In
actual fact,] they lost the house. It was foreclosed. I think I do
remember once saying, "My house is still there. What happened to
it?" and getting whupped, but I always wanted the truth. . . . I think
if you give [kids] the right answer the first time, [they're reas-
sured]. . . . Once the lies start, then you're always questioning.

But how did Shibvon learn to love—let alone love *well*—in the
midst of such mendacity and betrayal? Shibvon's paternal aunt
becomes the locus of hope in her life early on, a beacon of humanity and coherence. Although her contact with Shibvon is infrequent by parental standards, she provides her with steadfast
emotional support, never denigrating Shibvon's mother. Crucially,
she subtly communicates that Shibvon is *chosen* in some fundamental way, special to her and thus undeserving of her withering
plight. Shibvon also understands that her aunt is unable to adopt

her: she is a single, self-supporting nurse anesthetist on frequent night call and without a prayer of obtaining custody of her niece from Shibvon's mother.

> Yes, she would be good; she'd hug you, she didn't tie you to beds, and she always said I was something. . . . Her house was a doll house . . . [with] lots of knickknack stuff. . . . She had a dog; she took care of my grandmother for years, until she died. . . . She had an Oreo cookie jar. . . . I guess what she had is that you could walk in her house and it was the same thing all the time. . . . Until she died there were Oreo cookies: it wasn't that you ate them, but they were always there. . . . She had mugs . . . with animals on the bottom, and that's how we used to always have our milk, so you could find the animal at the end. Even though she was a single woman, she knew what kids liked. . . . She had some friends, nice lady friends who used to come over and visit with us; . . . and she *always* came to the orphanages, wherever we were, and took us out to supper. She was the one, if anybody, who said, "You're okay," and she was always positive about my father to us. [My aunt and her friends] never downgraded my mother in front of us. I think we sensed at times she disagreed a lot, but she never said, "Your mother's a jerk," or something like that, whereas my mother said that my aunt was a jerk; my father was a jerk; everybody was a jerk. . . . I think [my aunt's withholding judgment] gave some dignity to what we were living in.

By contrast, it is difficult to see Shibvon's mother as other than a caricature. She is not unlike a stepmother in a Grimm brothers' fairy tale, actively obstructing good fortune when it promises to soothe her envied and hated daughter. For Shibvon, the juxtaposition of such vicious hatred with her aunt's benevolence becomes the anchoring experience for her intense identification with her aunt's goodness. Strikingly, Shibvon's actual clock time with her aunt is sorely limited. She sees her only once a month throughout her childhood and adolescence. This places a premium on Shibvon's capacity for getting good emotional mileage out of intermittent spiritual fuel, which indeed sustains her. It also suggests that her aunt might be an especially gifted giver or that her love is cast in such bold relief that Shibvon *perceives* her to be peerless. Regardless, Shibvon, a fiercely riveted barnacle in a tempest, cleaves to vivid images of a more noble humanity even though she comes of age predominantly outside her aunt's care.

Critically, Shibvon actively recruits her aunt's high regard despite her mother's hate and continually locates *new* love, capturing odd patches of light in her steel-trap memory and gradually building vivid images of an autonomous, luminous future. This is essential at the next turning point, for when Shibvon's mother's ploy to maintain the lover by sacrificing Shibvon fails, she jettisons the children by telling them they are going to camp in Vermont for two weeks. Shibvon, ten at the time, recalls her spirits deflating when one of the resident orphans reveals the truth—this is an *orphanage*, not a summer camp—just as one would mention the time:

> We got there thinking we were going to summer camp. I remember thinking, "This sure don't look like no camp to me," . . . because, to me, I guess, a camp was [a place with] rustic buildings. . . . There was a pool, but it was way far down from the orphanage. There was a school, and I remember seeing the school and thinking, "Son of a bitch, something's going on." . . . So we got there; we were dropped off. Of course, everybody started crying. Jake was shrieking; Peter was crying. . . . I remember we all huddled around unpacking, and all these kids . . . came, and I remember somebody said, "Well, we're only here for two," or something like that, and I'll never forget this girl, Maggie—God knows, she's probably shot people by now, she was that tough. She was wicked good, though, Maggie, and she said, "Two?" She said, "I've been here five years!" I'll never forget: [the

children] were all in a semicircle lined up giving us their years, and
that's how we found out we were "lifers," or whatever we called ourselves.

That's how we found out. I was hysterical because my father was
supposed to pick us up [at home] that Saturday, . . . and we were
gone. That's his most devastating memory of that. He was never
told. The nuns didn't know that we didn't know. They didn't know
my father didn't know. [My mother] lied; she told the nuns that
everybody knew. But my father drove up there, and he was hysterical by the time he found us. [My mother] landed up in court on that
one. They took her to court, my aunt and my father, but what the
judge decided was that we were placed and we were okay; . . . and
what they did is they transferred my father's [child-support] checks,
and he was allowed his visitation, and that ticked my mother off,
too. The nuns . . . always spoke very highly of my aunt and my
father; they loved them. . . . But my mother lied to them; she's like
that. I guess [the judge] decided this was the best place, that we were
safe there, and that it was better to leave us there. . . . I think once
my father met the nuns and all that, *he* was fine. So my tenth birthday was at the orphanage. . . . We went June 4th, and then we
started school there, so it was another school change; and I never
said goodbye to my friends, and we stayed, and then we liked it.

Thus Shibvon recovers from temporary defeat in the relieving
absence of her perpetrator and by attaching to a sturdy flotilla of
benevolent nuns. (Survivors of abusive clergy, outraged with complete justification, do take note!) Implicitly sensing Shibvon's danger, these nuns intercept letters from Proctor and bar his entrance
to the orphanage, becoming her first protectors. They recognize that
her father and aunt are benign and welcome their occasional visits. In relative safety and warmth, Shibvon creates a climate of healing through helpfulness: she actively seeks a role in the orphanage
nursery. Here she finds sustained, unconditional positive regard

within the naive trust of several abandoned babies. Recall that Shibvon feels that her own capacity to love was launched by her father's and aunt's high regard for her, infrequent and partial though their contact might have been. Since she finds these scanty experiences so rewarding, she artfully extends similar love by recruiting the high regard of those she cares for who care for her in return, such as the orphaned babies at Bethlehem. Thus, when I asked Shibvon, "Looking back on your life, you can certainly say it has a lot of darkness. Where are the strong points of light for you?" she quickly focused on recruited love:

> My aunt. My fifth-grade teacher. The nuns. Some of my girlfriends' parents. If somebody said something nice about me, I'd grab it and just hold onto it, even though I didn't really believe it; but I also remember thinking, "I can't be that bad, because why would someone . . . like my aunt [care for me]?" My aunt, I think, was probably the one that [carried the day]. Even though her influence was only here and there, it was somewhat steady; and she really made me feel like I mattered. . . . I also knew something was wrong with my mother. . . . I knew some of this wasn't right; I couldn't be as bad as she said. . . . And then [there was] the social worker that we had when we were at Mercy Orphanage, and the lady that came to the house the day [the police came for us]. I think I was the kind of kid [that], . . . as long as you were nice to me, I just drank it in. It didn't have to be a long thing—I don't think it had to be a twenty-four-hour-a-day thing—*but there was so much black that when the light came, when that person showed up, or that statement was made, you just drank it in, and that's what you held on to.*

Launching a Nascent Vision

Shibvon continually fights her mother's distorted perceptions about her. She also stores contradictory *positive* experiences, thus rooting a larger imagination about how she might live once she is freer to shape her own future. She locates her conscious determination to "live for more" during the nadir of her childhood: her fifth-grade year. Building on scraps and shards, she begins to fashion what a zenith might be, even though she knows she is far from *realizing* her vision during childhood:

> It was really hard to believe it, because [my mother was] always in the back of my head going, "No, you're rotten" or "You're stupid." . . . But I think when I got to the orphanage and saw that I wasn't stupid in school at all, . . . I think that's the first time I believed that I could do this, and I could sail through—not sail, but make it through school with work. . . . I wanted to be something more than what I had, and I think that [when the sexual abuse] started up—I know it sounds bizarre—but I think in fifth grade, *I was always planning my life. I was going to get out of it. . . . It was going to be better.*

When I asked Shibvon how she created a sense of "better," and what exactly she thought "better" was, she replied that she had a skeletal understanding that it revolved around *not* repeating her mother's abusiveness, although she said it never really occurred to her to act abusively. She selectively identified with the light and successfully *dis*identified with the dark. Above all, she determined to forge humane environments in which she and others were safe and well cared for. Now this is precisely how Shibvon lives:

> I knew I'd never be mean to my kids . . . and that nobody was going to hurt me. . . . Nobody's going to hurt me. . . . I pretty much thought I was going to become what the nuns at the orphanage were, and that's how I would take care of kids: come back and help these little kids who have had their bad troubles and make their lives better; so that was my first goal in life. . . . [Also,] I've always loved babies. . . . I was smart enough at that point to think that [they offered] unconditional love, and these babies didn't think I was stupid. I remember being that young and thinking, as I think now,

I don't have much to offer, but I have myself. . . . I knew I didn't have money, and I didn't have the stuff other kids had, but I could help people out. . . .

I think I wanted to stop the hurt. . . . The thought of doing [what my mother did to me or] something worse never even hit me. I didn't like it, and I didn't want to be that. . . . I remember thinking that I had no control over what happened [to me as a child] but that I certainly was going to make sure after I got out of it that I could take real good care of myself, and nobody ever was going to hurt me like that again. . . . I think . . . at times I felt defeated, but I would come out of it. . . . With enough people saying to me, "You matter"—my aunt, my father, the nuns—I think I was ahead of my time. . . . I knew by senior year in high school . . . where I was going, and I was going to get there the best I could. . . . I think something inside of me said, "I can do it. I don't know how I'm going to do it, *but I'm not going to live like this again. . . . This isn't right."* I knew from the start that, even though my mother kept trying, *she wasn't going to defeat me.*

Resilient Motifs

Many of the leitmotifs of resilient love emerge immediately in Shibvon's narrative. She recalls the critical events of her childhood with keen lucidity. She fights for her own protection and, although unsuccessful given the grave power advantage of the two vicious and remorseless abusers engineering her sexual sacrifice, she creates a sanctuary in her faith that she is shielding her brothers from similar malevolence. Thus she has the stamina to escape the pull of dark density, the light ray triumphant. At this juncture, the conscious *meanings* that she makes about her plight begin to shape her vision of a kinder life. She also soothes her own anguish by actively parenting her siblings—feeding them at times, deferring to their material needs, but feeling that love must be alive if *some* child is finding it—and develops a fierce attachment to the truth. These early prosocial inclinations at least adumbrate her well-developed empathic orientation in subsequent developmental phases.

Also, at an intuitive level, Shibvon knows as early as seven that *anywhere* is a better place to be, developing some adaptive distance from her mother's toxicity and opening her heart to other interpretations of her own worth. Thus she actively recruits surrogate love with her generous aunt, basking briefly but inspiritingly in her unconditionally high regard. Nurturing these precious early seeds of caring connection, she seeks out other caregivers while becoming a more robust giver of care herself, especially cherishing the unconditional reciprocal love that she shares with the orphaned babies at Bethlehem. Shibvon also recalls buttressing her opalescent images of sustained human concern with a wide array of extended recruited loves, revealing her unusual capacity for engaging others appropriately and experiencing gratitude:

> I was one of those "Oh, I'll push the baby carriage" kids. . . . I think I was always looking for the positive. That's why I think *some people said I was easy to fall in love with:* because I tried to please. . . . If I wasn't getting it at home, I tended to go the other way and not really act out but try to please people. . . . "Could I take your garbage out? Could I walk the cat or dog?" . . . The positive reinforcement from that made me feel good, so I think all those little interactions [were sustaining], . . . although my mother considered it negative. . . . [She would always say,] "You don't do a thing for me," but by everyone else it was viewed as positive.

Thus with gritty, stubborn determination, Shibvon devotes her soul to being all that her barbarous mother is not. And yet, to close with an emphasis on agency and accountability, Shibvon does *not* consider herself a victim as an adult. Contrasting herself to her younger siblings, she notes that they walk around thinking the world owes them for what we went through. . . . [They exploit] the welfare system; . . . and when they have failures, then that's because "we didn't have [what we needed from someone else]." . . . I feel the opposite: I really couldn't control what happened. . . . I'm realizing now more than I ever did that I was a victim as a child, realizing how bizarre it was, and the fact that I came out as well as I did is a miracle; . . . but I never realized it for a long time. . . . I figured it was accepted [practice]. . . . I think that's the part that shocks me: the times when I see people who don't fight back, who just say, "Well, what I could do?" I sit there going, "Well, do something!". . . . I guess the biggest thing is the determination that I have. Probably at times I can be short with people, because I can't believe they don't have a . . . standard that *you don't have to take it*. You *can* fight back.

Dan

Now let us consider an equally determined life—one that emerged in material prosperity but similar ethical bankruptcy. Although many of the themes in Shibvon's life echo throughout Dan's, my analysis of his narrative will focus on additional motifs in order to establish the full complement of adaptive capacities to be explored in later chapters.

Dan's family holds an impeccable social pedigree. Unfortunately, his scorching screams and frantic efforts to emerge from a wilderness of abuse went unheeded, insulated by the family's twenty acres of sedate waterfront property. He is now soft-spoken and vibrant at age fifty-eight, masterminding and directing a 520-person human service agency in Harlem. By his design, the agency tackles virtually every aspect of abuse endured by disenfranchised children and their parents. Like Shibvon, he is beloved. Family, friends, and their extended communities feel esteemed and accurately perceived—perceived often with uncanny precision—by

Dan and Shibvon. Over time they have both come—with concerted effort—to love *themselves*. Yet these are individuals whose very *existence* was unacceptable to their parents. How did they come to love so well? Let us look at the gradual emergence of Dan's resilience.

Dan's Parents

Dan's constantly enraged father stormed around and beat him ferociously from infancy onward. Dan describes virtually constant unbridled anger, especially in the evenings after his father had secretly consumed enough whiskey to release his inhibitions. When I asked Dan if he ever thought his father was attempting to murder him, he gave this response:

> The first psychiatrist I went to when I was twenty years old was convinced my father wanted to kill me and that on some level maybe both parents wanted me dead. But I can remember thinking then, and I think even now, that my father didn't really want me dead. He just wanted me seriously maimed. He got such catharsis out of hitting and abusing me: in a way it was a source of relief and pleasure to him. He wouldn't have wanted to kill me because he couldn't then have hit me anymore.

Unlike Shibvon's father, who was a benign although psychologically frail figure, Dan's abusive parental shotgun was double-barreled. His quixotic mother returned home after her many psychiatric hospitalizations either flattering her sons with nearly revivalistic joy or overseeing their routine floggings with glazed eyes. She sobbed for several hours every day. Each night she and her husband lowered their three screaming preschoolers into a scalding tub to free them of imaginary, cataclysmically invasive germs. They never considered that they as *parents* might be the plague. When Dan was six, his mother originated an elaborate, desperately painful ritual of sexual intrusion and enema cleansing, reenacting sexual encounters that she might have had with a sadomasochistic suitor. This occurred hundreds of times before Dan, at fifteen, finally awoke the protector lying dormant in his throat and shouted her to a halt.

Making Sense of the Senseless

Perhaps the most prominent aspect of Dan's inner psychology is his capacity for adaptive psychological distancing in the face of his parents' brutality. Although in his narrative Dan courses through a great range of human feeling and holds everyone—especially himself—*accountable* for individual behavior, his words distinctly lack blame. For example, Dan juxtaposes his vivid apprehension of his father's viciousness with a solid grasp of the sobering, emotionally Saharan toddlerhood this man endured:

> My father's birth mother became very sick by the time he was about one and a half years old, and she remained bedridden until she died a year later. During this time, she was increasingly unable to care for her infant; and then when she died, my grandfather, who worked as a college professor, would put my father into a playpen and leave him for five hours at a stretch, all alone in the house. He would just stay there, screaming and crying, completely alone for periods of many, many hours, and he began to lose weight and become a "failure to thrive" kind of child.
>
> Well, the woman who lived next door had been abandoned in the middle of the night, because her husband was arrested for selling spoiled meat, and so he left town in order not to be put into jail. There she was alone, and she had two children at home. She listened every day to this screaming; and finally she couldn't stand it any more, and she went over and told my grandfather, "This baby looks so sickly. Would you mind if I took care of him when you went to work?" This neighbor eventually married my grandfather, and she

told me this story when I was a teenager. She had nursed my father to the point where he gained back his physical health, but she couldn't cure the effects of his abandonment.

> I think that my father's colossal rage came from watching his mother get increasingly sick and die and then being left alone as an infant without any care. I can picture him in that playpen, screaming and shaking the bars and having a tantrum, because when my father was in his eighties, when he would be angry, he would regress to being just like a small child. I remember one time when he was eighty-eight years old and he came to my house for Thanksgiving dinner: dinner was supposed to be at one o'clock, and a half-hour later, when he realized it still wasn't ready, he began taking the fork and banging the sharp end of it into the table, yelling, "Where's my dinner?" . . . [There are] big marks on the table to this day where he did that. This was infantile stuff, but he wasn't being fed, and he was furious, and so the sense I have of him is that there was this tremendous rage when he was a very small child and no one to care for him.

Now, lest you think that all the abusive repent in the end (even if in a calculated attempt to sway divine opinion), consider the following. It clarifies Dan's parents' complete inability or refusal to relent at *any* time, which is so characteristic of extreme abusiveness:

> My father was angry all of his life. His anger ranged from situations where he would be a little bit aggressive but not mean to you to where he would be shouting and hitting you with all his might. At those times, you would be rolling over and over on the floor, trying to get under the couch while he was grabbing anything he could and hitting you with it and at the same time kicking you and screaming that you weren't good. I was always conscious of how angry he was: you could just *feel* his anger all the time. And this lasted right up until the time he died.

I could tell you a thousand stories of his anger, because there were at least a thousand incidents in which this was expressed, but there are two times I remember in particular. The first was visiting his house on a very hot day when my mother was in her later years. My mother was in shorts and a little halter top. There were black-and-blue marks all the way up and down her legs and back where he'd hit her, and I realized he was hitting her every day. At that time, both my parents were in their late eighties. She was so used to this that it didn't occur to her that it was out of line.

The second incident occurred the day before my father died. I went to visit him in the nursing home. He'd had a stroke and his left side was paralyzed, so he was cursing about not being able to move. I came close to the bed to help readjust him because he was twisted up in the bed sheets. As soon as he realized I was close enough, he hit me with all his might with his right hand. There I was—and he realized, "Ah, an opportunity to hit my son." . . . He was trying to get just one more hit in there. I thought to myself, "My God! My father is ninety-three years old; here I am trying to help him, and he's still hitting me." I had to hold his arm with both my hands to keep him from continuing to hit me, and he jerked his arm back and forth, trying to break free until he exhausted himself and slumped back down. So from the time I was an infant until the day before he died, he was still hitting. It was just his way with me.

Thus Dan's adaptive distancing does not stem from an eleventh-hour softening of parental savagery (although a few subjects reported a parental transformation reminiscent of that of Marlon Brando's elderly *Godfather* character, who tenderly cared for his tomatoes and small grandson after a lifetime of wanton slaughtering). Although his parents never relented, Dan has emphatically refused to spend his life immersed in accusing agony. Reclaiming his strip-mined emotional terrain has meant years of cathartic psychodrama as well as analytic therapy, however. Still palpably

moved when recounting the more tearing moments in his childhood, Dan describes a deliberate, ongoing choice—like that of a
devoted alchemist—to turn the vile into the whole. In the passage
that follows, Dan is taken aback by the strength of his feelings about
his abuse, although he also recognizes that his capacity to be moved
by his own past is part of his humanity and not a sign of poor resolution of the past:

> Can you imagine, at this advanced age, that I can still feel some feel-
> ings when we talk about this? [*Well, how can you not? How can you
> not? . . .*] But after all those years of therapy, you know, all the weep-
> ing and wailing I did—sometimes I can still feel it.

Dan and I agreed that his compassionate response to himself as
an infant and young child seems a reasonable reaction to savagery.
He was not unhinged by his recollections, but momentarily distressed. I also asked him whether, if he repeatedly stumbled onto
the scene of an accident in which a child had just been run over
and killed and then witnessed one more, he would fail to be moved.
Should caregivers *ever* be so practiced that they no longer respond
empathically and compassionately to human tragedy, not upset by
upsetting events? Such empathy is the very wellspring of Dan's
social activism, fueling his organization's devotion to helping lives
in perpetual, tragic turmoil. When I pointed that out to him, Dan
brightened and replied,

> That's a good point. That's a good point! Oh, but some of those
> beatings were so scary. God, they were scary! I would hide under the
> bed, curl up in a little tiny ball under the bed, and he'd be thump-
> ing the bed, but he couldn't get at me. [*Because you were a little tiny
> person.*] Little tiny person. This would be when I was four or five
> years old especially, and I'd curl right up in a corner of the bedroom
> under the bed, and he'd be hitting the bed with a stick because he
> couldn't get at me and he was in such a rage that he couldn't stop

hitting. He'd be thumping the bed, and I'd hear it above me, and shouting and yelling, so I'd be curled up absolutely terrified. Finally he'd just—he'd tire himself out and go stomping down the stairs and have another drink. I'd wait for a long time and then crawl out from underneath the bed, but it was really frightening! Especially when I was very small, because he was so much bigger than I was, and he was quite muscular, a very strong guy.

Thus Dan, like Shibvon, can recollect his past vividly yet regain his equilibrium quickly, because he has made self-growth and increasing perspective a lifelong mission. Both Dan and Shibvon certainly believe that the truth shall set you free. They hold the patina of seasoned recovery, sterling compasses for those who may not have sailed as far or as fast but deeply need to know that there *is* a better place to be.

Forging a Nonviolent Adulthood

What about the survivor's own rage? Can a person survive years of boots kicking at one's integrity without booting back? Grappling with parental violence did occasion Dan's own combativeness, although the incidents are few and transformational. While he lives a self-consciously nonviolent adulthood, devoting himself to delimiting abusiveness in the wider social arena, he and many others found that they could not survive childhood without some infrequent—but fierce and definitive—stands against the bully in their homes or on the local turf. While they are not happy that they were *ever* pressed to use physical force, they feel that they learned something critical about their own courage when they faced down their foes. Perhaps this is also the partial wellspring of their determination not to be victims. Like Dorothy in Oz, inadvertently melting the Wicked Witch of the West to stop her from immolating the wise Scarecrow—Dorothy's intelligent and humane alter ego—they learned that they could go up against great, dark forces and emerge intact, safer and more autonomous in the aftermath. Dan's initial Rubicon, which occurred in first grade, offered him an enduring image of creating a safe place through *direct* confrontation of the unbearable:

There was a bully at my school when I entered the first grade. Actually, he was a third-grader, but he was retarded and sixteen years old, and he liked to push the first-grade kids around. He could make them act as his slave. He would throw his books on the ground and make other kids pick them up. I watched this going on the first day, and I asked the other kids what it was all about. "He's much bigger and stronger than we are," they said, "but he's a dummy so you have to do what he says or he'll beat you up."

I remember feeling a kind of rage inside of me about this. I was a brand-new kid in the school [and a small six-year-old], but the third day of school I came to school with a knife in my pocket. I purposely walked right up to the bully and looked him in the eye. He grabbed me by the shirt and said, "Get out of my way." Then I pulled the knife out and stabbed him.

The interesting thing: when I had the knife, I knew I could stab him in the chest and kill him, but I was careful to stab him in the arm. I didn't want to hurt him too badly; I just wanted to give him the message, "Don't screw around with me!" One thing I had already learned before first grade was how to deal with bullies.

He was just terrified; blood was spurting out of his arm. The teacher bandaged him and then as punishment made both of us sit in the storage room where they kept paper supplies and blackboard erasers. I had expected the teachers would beat me, so this was an amazing punishment. I thought I was really going to catch hell, . . . but I didn't care. *I was going to stop this guy.* The teachers knew he was a bully, and I could see in some ways they were pleased that this

kid had finally stood up to him. I sat there in the stockroom, looking at a guy who was twice my size, . . . who could easily destroy me,
. . . and *realized there was something about me which was scaring the day-
lights out of him. This was fascinating, and it made me feel very powerful.*

I asked Dan what he learned in that moment in the stockroom
when he realized that he *did* have the power to challenge this particular bully and overcome him. I wondered if this encounter first
organized his *broader* conviction that he could confront the daunting and succeed. He readily agreed:

I think I have very much put that knowledge to good use. I can be
a good and kind person, but I'm never a patsy or a pushover. I can
be as tough as anybody needs to be, and people who have known me
well understand that. In my organization, the newer employees
sometimes will say, "Isn't Dan a nice guy? Aren't we lucky to have a
president who's such a kind and wonderful person?" But people who
have worked with me for a long time will respond, "Oh, he's a very
kind guy when you do your job. But beware of the Force" *[laugh-
ing]*— you know, from *Star Wars*. What they're saying, of course, is
that yes, I'm a nice guy, but if I need to get tough, I can push as hard
as I need to in order to accomplish my goals.

As an adolescent, Dan also faced down his father, still snarling
and smashing when Dan returned from boarding school at age sixteen. His small but triumphant match with the bully in the stockroom years earlier had spawned his confrontational courage. Now,
having encountered his first sustained months of life outside relentless abusiveness, Dan sees that perhaps savagery is *not* normative.
He suddenly realizes that he might seize this moment to change the
social order in his home:

There were so many men who were kind and good people at boarding school, and they didn't hit other people and didn't shout at you; and even if you broke a rule, they didn't beat you. It was such a revelation. I remember coming home to my parents' house, and they started shouting almost immediately, and the family situation warmed up to a good hitting fight. I remember saying to them, "Listen, you don't have to do it this way. At school, they don't do it like this."

The whole thing came to a head because they wouldn't stop. . . . At one point, . . . maybe it was [after] two or three weeks of watching all this fighting, . . . my father hit me; and I grabbed a knife and I held it to his throat, and I said, *"If you ever hit me again, I'll kill you."* I was about sixteen, and he looked in my eyes and could see that I was really furious, and he understood that sort of thing. Later on, he did hit me periodically—but quite fearfully and much less—and when he did, he was afraid that I would hit him back, so it changed that whole dimension [of our relationship]. He suddenly realized I was now big enough so that he just couldn't abuse me with me just backing off passively. This happened with my mother also. I stopped her from hitting me at the same time.

Setting Family Limits and Grappling with Forgiveness

Delimiting parental abuse is a critical aspect of adult resilience—one that survivors work on continually and determinedly. While samurai limit-setting is only half the battle, it is a half that many can never achieve. Over time, my subjects' strategies have evolved sufficiently that, by and large, they no longer feel at the mercy of their families' destructive dynamics. Yet once those dynamics are subdued or at least contained, can or should the traumatized *forgive* parents who have feral integrity? The resilient are among the pluckier of the unlucky, their actual and symbolic siblings typically crippled by the phantom-limb pain of dismembered hopes. The devastation wrought by abusers is palpable and now well docu-

ved. And there was a period of, I guess, about four years when I had
o contact with them whatsoever. Various emissaries would come
see me and they'd say, "Your parents are very upset that you won't
ee them any longer," and I'd tell them, "Well, okay, I understand
that's the case, *but . . . I'm not going to have them do to my kids what
they did to me. I've had it."*

This pivotal hiatus allows Dan to fortify his initial determina-
n to exclude all abuse from his new family life. Refusing any
going interaction on the terms that shattered his childhood and
early ruined his adulthood underscores Dan's stance to *himself* as
uch as his parents. Eventually, the parents agree to basic behav-
oral limits, to which he holds them tenaciously:

So finally my mother wrote me a letter, and she said . . . that she and
my father had been talking to the minister, and she realized that
maybe she had done things to me that weren't right, and could I possibly find it in my heart to forgive her? It was the just-right letter to
write, I think, and so I wrote back that I would have a trial meeting
but that I wanted to have certain conditions, and they had to agree
to the conditions or we would never see each other again. The conditions were that they were *not* to strike any of my children, first of
all, and second, they were not to hit each other or to fight in front
of us; they had to behave themselves. No hitting of each other or of
my kids. And no fighting. They wrote back and said they would
agree to that, so we had a tentative meeting. It went reasonably well,
and they were absolutely on their best behavior, so we agreed that
we would see each other from time to time. From that point on, I
guess, in a way things changed. *I was setting some conditions and insisting on these conditions. . . .*

I suppose in a way I was learning something that I've used very
much in my life, which is that when you're dealing with this kind

mented. So what is the cost of believing th
them? Is there another path—one that does
forgiveness but renders the horrific *intelligible*

This controversy is the topic of ample ph
cal debate, some of which will be explored in
now, Dan's clarity on this issue echoes the diffei
resolved view of most of my subjects as they ai
about the concept of forgiveness and whether the
a good life was guided by this or another compass.
vanizing moment when his parents began to abu
her first birthday. Remembering how early his own a
feeling the winds of a squaw winter beginning to bi
daughter, he bars the door and determines that his par
get an opportunity to abuse his children as they abuse
siblings:

> When my daughter Suzanne, [now in her thirties,] was one,
> ents came over to visit the house where we were living. *
> point I was having some contact with them. We would get to
> maybe six times a year. They would come visit us or I would go
> for Thanksgiving or whatever it was. It wasn't a whole lot of (
> tact. I was trying to be as—as civil as I could with them; it
> always a great stress and strain to see them. Anyway, they came
> visit us at the house, and I went upstairs to get dressed. When I cam
> downstairs, my mother and father were in the bathroom with
> Suzanne; . . . she was one year old. They were holding her on the
> toilet and hitting her because she wasn't going to the bathroom in
> the toilet. . . . They were very upset that we hadn't trained her yet,
> and so they were going to do something about it. My mother was
> holding her legs; my father was hitting her on the head and shout-
> ing at her, "Go wee-wee!" . . . whack!—like this.

> Well, I got *so* angry with them that I kicked them out of the
> house and told them I never wanted to see them again as long as I

of stuff, *you can, in fact, set conditions*. I set conditions with the patients at work. "You have to understand there's no hitting in this room. Now I know you've had a problem with that before, John, but in this program, we don't allow people to hit each other." And they agree to it, and generally they're pretty good about it, because that's the rule.

Dan also struggles significantly with ways that he might construct his own comprehension of his parents' treatment of him. He draws a firm distinction between *understanding* them and *forgiving* them. Seeking out therapies that allow him to express the full catastrophe to others, he realizes just how horrific was his childhood. Thus affirmed, he determines to tell his parents his view of it, whether or not they can grasp the gravity of his feelings. While his central aim in this is rendering their atrocities intelligible to *himself*, Dan also insists upon holding his parents fully accountable for their treatment of him. That is, although he concentrates on *making sense* out of how they came to treat their children so savagely, he does *not* forgive them, because he feels that forgiving would require his denying their complete lack of recognition, remorse, and reparation of their abusiveness. At the same time, Dan refuses to be consumed by a grinding, accusatory rage toward his parents, feeling that this would enslave his present and future to past horrors, precluding his ever having a decent life:

> In my mid thirties, I went through another whole bout of therapy. I was doing a lot of psychodrama and reliving childhood experiences and healing them in a process which was very therapeutic, very helpful for me. It could get into the kinestheses, in a way, of all the beatings and the violence. The audience shares after that, and they would say, "My God! That was violent!" and—it was good—I would think, "Huh! It *isn't* all in my head. They witnessed it, and they're telling me how ugly and violent it was. . . . Even sitting in the audi-

ence, they're saying how scared they were with all this stuff." I'm
thinking to myself, "Well, yes, I was scared, too," and I guess it's not
unreasonable to be scared under those circumstances. It was all very
therapeutic and a great healing experience.

So [since I now *really* realized how off they had been], I decided
that what I would do is confront my parents directly, face to face,
over some of the things they had done to me as a child, and I did
that. I was able to not only confront them about it but to really
express how angry I was, not by shouting at them but just by telling
them how deeply angry I felt about the things they had done. They
were mostly, I think, kind of hurt, confused over it all. My mother,
because she was so mentally ill . . . in many ways, was unable to
really grasp it in a meaningful way. But my father got it, and he said,
"Well, I just felt that you needed discipline, that I had to knock
some sense into you," and I explained to him how knocking sense
into somebody doesn't ever work, that that's not how you get somebody to be sensible [*laughter*]; that isn't the route that one takes. The
more you hit children, the less sense they have!

He was able to say that's what his rational thinking was; but of
course what really was behind it [was that] he was just full of his own
rage. . . . I spent some time writing letters that really explained my
point of view. I was never able to, on the one hand, forgive them,
because I felt, if I was going to be really fair and honest with myself,
that I clearly wasn't going to say, "Oh, it's all right you did those
awful things!" or "Sure, Mother, you forget all this sexual stuff; you
didn't mean any harm by it." I couldn't forgive them in that sense,
but what I felt I was really able to do very deeply was to *understand*
that what they did was because of what happened to them. That was
very helpful to me, and very healing to me, to get enough sense of
it for both of them, to realize that their lives were, if anything, worse
than mine. If I wasn't going to forgive them, I was going to really

understand them . . . and accept that they did what they did because they were so maimed, and that maybe their parents did the same, generation after generation after generation, so . . . in a way, it wasn't necessary to blame. It was okay just to understand that that's why it happened, and thank God it stopped.

Elaborating further, Dan emphasizes that reflexively forgiving his parents would lead him to betray himself, giving lie to his own passionate ethical convictions:

What to me seemed to be incomprehensible was to say, "Oh, it's just fine, Mother and Father, that you did all this, and now I love you." That would have been totally phony, maybe sick, to do that. But what I *could* say to them is, "I understand what it was in your lives that made you do these things, and now I understand you," you see, and I could even go so far as to say, "I'm willing to care for you in your old age, because you're my parents, if for no other reason than I wouldn't exist without you." That's reason enough to do it—and perhaps also, just in the same way that I care for chronically mentally ill people at [our organization] whom I don't know, just through my sense of wanting to be caring toward humanity.

But do I love them? No, I don't love them. Do I hate them intensely? No longer do I hate them intensely. In the end I felt sorry for my mother; I felt ashamed. I felt offended when, in her last months of life, I would come to see her and she would try to kiss me on the mouth and French-kiss me, put her tongue in my mouth. . . . It would be nauseating, . . . and I'd pull myself away when she would do that. They were true to form right to the very end. Absolutely. Both of them.

Part of the reason Dan feels unequivocally that he cannot in good conscience extend "forgiveness" to his parents is that they did not "revise" themselves at all over the years, except to be somewhat better behaved in front of him and his family as the price of admission. There was no effective change in them. For him to extend genuine forgiveness, he feels that they would have had to fulfill other basic conditions. Of this they were incapable:

> If they had, for example, both gone into extensive treatment because they wanted to, and had changed, and come to me and said, "I don't know how I could ever make this up to you; I realize some of the things I did were just so unfair," then maybe I would have found myself forgiving them and saying, "Well, I really appreciate your saying that you're sorry it happened and I can see now that you're sorry, too," and perhaps something different could have taken place. If either one of them had ever said, later in life, "I'm really interested in who you are and how you've turned out and what you think and believe," if they had had an interest in me as a human being, that would have been a great joy to me—to have a parent who cared about me. But they were always totally self-centered. They hardly knew anything about me; they were concerned only about themselves right to the very end. They were totally self-centered because they were so infantile, . . . both so primitive.

Thus for Dan, forgiveness would have required his parents' true remorse as well as a robust and sustained capacity to *apprehend* who Dan is as a human being. They would have needed to demonstrate some genuine interest in his life by decentering enough from themselves to appreciate or at least understand him in some honest form:

> Yes, to put it on another basis, to relate to me adult to adult. . . . If they had been capable of doing that, after showing remorse, to then relate to me as two adults to another adult, that would have worked; but they were infantile to the end. They were just utterly childish and outrageous to the end.

Rejecting the Role of Victim

Like Shibvon, Dan heals substantially through helping. While he recognizes that he was victimized as a child, he also refuses to see himself as a victim now; rather, he believes he is the agent of his own happiness and is determined not to be subordinated to his own suffering. Like most of those interviewed, he rejects "sadder but wiser" as a woefully inadequate ultimate outcome for such hideous early hardship. The resilient want a *good* life. For this, Dan spent years clearing his inner thickets, wrenched and anguished in therapy but progressively sunnier in his life. He believes that his suffering offers him a unique kinship with other targets of extreme violence, despite the real racial and economic differences between himself and his clients. Like the others in this study an altruistic social activist, he reclaims generous portions of the pie while serving solid pieces to as many others as he can reasonably feed:

> *I don't see myself as a victim.* I see myself as a survivor, as someone who's done more than just make the best of a difficult situation— someone who's really thrived. I see myself as a successful person, not a victim. I think of a victim as someone who's experienced great difficulty and has never been able to rise above it but has remained locked in the pain and suffering. To me, that's a victim, and I'm not a victim at all. That's not what's happened to me in my life.

When I asked Dan if there were aspects of being a victim that he had consciously chosen not to adopt—that is, if he felt that he had deliberately rejected victimization as an *identity*—he agreed emphatically:

> Yes. Choosing not to think of myself that way, not to let it get me down, drag me down. There are so many ways, all my whole life, even to this day, that if I wanted to wallow in stuff that's happened

to me, and take a certain point of view, it could get me down tremendously. It was almost like a conscious decision. I suppose it's like Nazi concentration camp survivors: some of them are for the rest of their lives going to be downtrodden and dysfunctional, and others say, "I'm going to go on and make a success out of this life. I'm going to find people I love; I'm going to be successful in my work; I'm going to have a full life, and as horrible as my past is, I'm not going to let it destroy my life." It's almost a conscious decision of some kind; that's the feeling I have about all that.

I probably could log as many beatings as most people I know. In terms of numbers, they must be in the thousands, but . . . what I want to do is use that energy in a positive way. . . . [I often feel a] really sympathetic kind of connection [with some of the toughest clients] at work. I can't know exactly what's in each of their hearts, but the basic thing we all had in common was perfectly clear. It has felt to me like, if you pulled our sleeves back, we all had numbers tattooed on our arms. Mine were old and faded; theirs were fresh and raw. I didn't even have to show them; they knew it.

Dan also feels that his life actually made him *more* than he might have been. While decrying the claim that "this will either kill you or it will make you very strong" as a paltry rationalization for allowing or encouraging suffering, he does believe that he is a far deeper person as a result of having transcended so much of his beleaguered past. Note in the next few quotes that he first describes his suffering as a source of personal strength and then shifts to why his pain can be invaluable to others as well—his ultimate redemption and reclamation:

One of the things I sometimes say to the [staff] at work is that those of us who have endured a lot of pain can be stronger in some ways than individuals who never have known suffering or difficulty; that what we can bring out of it is that we have the capacity to deal with difficulty that others don't have, so that if a tornado went through my town and destroyed my house, I wouldn't stand there devastated, saying, "This is the end of all I know; I've lost all my furniture and belongings. I can't go on," or whatever. I'd look at the house, and I'd say, "Well, let's see, this wall's still standing. I guess we can start with that. Let's rebuild the rest of it," *and we'd go on, and it would be because, having survived what I've survived, I can face almost anything.*

Dan is understandably proud of himself—a reaction that most subjects echoed (usually with mild encouragement from the interviewer, since they shy away from grandstanding). Overall, they *know* that they have struggled their way to a good life, and they realize what they have found. They feel that they have created a more precious peace, a sweeter love, because it has been so hard won. They are quietly proud of their once and future overcoming. Although I had to coax Dan out of his sense that expressing self-pride is self-congratulatory preening, he eventually elaborated on the qualities that he most values in himself:

[Are you proud of yourself?] Yes. *[Can you talk about that?]*

Hmmm *[laughter]*, . . . and not boast? *[Feel free to boast!]* Oh . . . I think I'm a genuinely good person. *[What makes you think so?]* I have the capability of loving others deeply, devoting my career life to helping others. People's work life is a big part of their existence, and for at least five days a week I spend all my time running an organization that helps other people who had childhoods like my own. That's my crusade, in a way, and I feel very good about it. I go home at night, and I can look at myself in the mirror and say, "You did a lot of good for other people today"; and that's a nice feeling to have, a genuinely nice feeling.

I think that I'm—I can't say always 100 percent of the time, but most of the time—deeply honest with other people. I'm not phony;

I don't try to manipulate others; I don't so much worry about the result as I think about my own ethics, that I be forthright and honest with other people in the way I deal with them and interact with them, and I feel very good about that. Whether I win or lose in whatever the situation is, I just feel good about the style in which I approach it. Hey, I'm not in any way perfect or remarkable in lots of ways, but I'm good. . . . I wanted to be the good witch, not the bad witch.

Resilient Motifs

To summarize, Dan's reclaimed life moves forward on the momentum of several key dynamics. He has a marked capacity for adaptive psychological distancing, but he simultaneously remains deeply open to his own and others' affective experiences. Like many resilient individuals (who often have exceptional creative capacities), he has great emotional range and sensitivity. Listening to the child that sobs within, he sustains deep empathic resonance with the plight of abused others. Yet he regulates his emotional responses well: he has achieved a highly differentiated and integrated sense of self. He also holds himself and others closely accountable for both their motives and the consequences of their actions. While Dan finds violence *intelligible*—with a subtle and complex understanding—he does not tolerate or condone it in anyone. Because he holds such a strong sense of the future, responsible action *matters*. Finally, he labors to comprehend fully the dark rivers that fed his parents' atrocious assaults, freeing himself from the life-leeching potential of his own rage. A devoted psychological Calvinist, he remains determined to work as hard as necessary on his own healing in order to set himself free.

But growth is never a smooth trajectory, and we see *seasoned* recovery here. Among his struggles, which will be explored in more depth later, Dan forcibly grappled with his own rage, taking a definitive stand against violence in his late adolescence. At the same time, he openly challenged his persecutors on a few strategic occasions, including the sad thug in the stockroom and the bullies in his bedroom. The effect was transformative. While eschewing the use of physical force as an adult, Dan still feels that these stands allowed him to seize some essential stature during childhood. They were small triumphs within defeat, tiny trumpet blasts sounding the possibility of an elevated order. They seem less a matter of vengeance and more one of faith, allowing Dan to grasp life's promise rather than to quail in the chill shadows of its cruelty.

Dan also illuminates the profound distinction between making something intelligible and rendering it forgivable. Seeing these as two separate constructs, he embarked and still remains on a path of understanding and gradual detachment rather than forgiveness. At the same time, like so many of those interviewed, he insistently refuses to be consumed by undigested, raw rage, preoccupying revenge, or hopeless attachments to impossibly unyielding parental figures—those Sirens that call to nearly every battered soul. He recognizes that hate, not love, is enslaving. Determined to be free, he wailed and sighed his way through grief—a childhood lost, a man reborn. Now Dan loves intimately only those who can love in return. While he certainly has human flaws—impatience and imperfect attunement to himself or others among them—his capacity to care is substantial (and far greater than his childhood would have predicted).

In addition, Dan feels that his intense altruistic investment in others, while not precluding solid self-care, is the anchor of his ongoing health. Since committed social activism plays such a prominent role in the lives of virtually all of my forty subjects, it will be the focus of particular consideration in this work. It seems nearly essential to these lives, serving as a poignant counterpoint to the many works now decrying pathological overgiving, or "codependence." While ill-health may certainly stem from some forms of overhelping, we hear little about health achieved *through* helping. The latter seems a better alternative to either self-absorption or self-sacrifice, since the resilient derive intense pleasure from their work (despite its codependent lacing). Thus altruism holds great transformative potency and may be essential to one's healing from horrific abuse.

Finally, Dan feels that surmounting such potentially cataclysmic cruelty has rendered him unusually strong. Although he remains intensely self-scrutinizing and shrinks from being seen in an angelic light, he is justifiably proud of himself. While not a soul in this study would wish such a fate on another, the participants feel that since childhood did not kill them—which it easily might have—it made them far, far more than they might have been in an untrammeled life. Given their measurable strengths, such as enduring and satisfying marriages and higher levels of mental health than most of us can demonstrate, we need to listen to *how* they did it and try to pass it on.

Ultimately, that a person who was literally smashed before he could sit or stand became such a decent man is astonishing. But Dan's aforementioned capacities, and certainly Shibvon's, are some of the tributaries pulsing into the larger life-stream of human resilience. To be with these people is to be in the embrace of hope.

CHAPTER THREE

The Locus of Hope: A Developmental Approach to Early Love

In the previous chapter, I introduced several of the adaptive capacities that carried Shibvon and Dan beyond their harrowing childhoods into healthy later lives. Shibvon and Dan are reminiscent of the hardy baby buried in earthquake rubble, excavated days later with a heartbeat and a future. "Hummingbird Hope" speaks to this unlikely emergence:

> In the still stark terror of the night,
> a hummingbird heart beats
> in the bedrock beneath despair.
> Smitten by empty-souled cold stone,
> yet thumping insistently,
> the faintest beat
> on the tiniest drum.
> > Love is yet alive in me.
> > Ice ashen hate
> > cannot purloin possibility.
> Hammering with small, triumphant wings
> against the stale, suffocating air,
> beckoning to tattered fellow fledglings,
> > rise above,
> > sail beyond,

Until these sturdy souls,
in collective hope,
lurch, ultimately launch
beyond the ravages of hate,
aloft in the currents formed
by the first breath
of every newborn.

—the author

I also noted in that chapter that Shibvon's and Dan's resilient capacities unfolded in connection with willing surrogates quietly digging in the wreckage, sure that they heard a muffled cry. While I am not claiming that the resilient have cornered the market on either these coping capacities or the kindness of strangers, I *am* asserting that they vigorously employ all of their inner resources in the service of determined overcoming. *How* they do it so effectively is the focal question here. As we address that question, let us consider the resilient not as a unique subspecies but as fellow travelers, amplifying qualities, dynamics, and potentials inherent in us all.

The chorus to come intones themes similar to those I introduced in Shibvon's and Dan's vignettes. I explore several lives in some detail so that you can have a comprehensive sense of just what my resilient subjects surmounted. The voices are female and male, as well as ethnically, religiously, generationally, and racially varied. Those you will hear suffered a wide range of parental abuse, from the serious to the horrific, and half encountered prolonged economic hardship as well. Several struggled with cultural hatred (such as racial, ethnic or creedal discrimination), which burdened their assaultive home lives with added challenge. They were raped, struck, ignored, or prostituted for cash. Many went hungry; a few nearly starved. Their parents drank, sank into marital deadlock, or left. Anya, a satanic cult abuse survivor, witnessed the literal sacrifice of other children, fully expecting her time to come. One of the probable casualties was her infant sister. Others were psychologically abandoned by the end of early childhood, becoming caretakers of parents hospitalized, mired in depression, or dead. I invite you to find your own predicament—or the plight of those you care for—here.

My first theme is the *locus of hope* in the early lives of the resilient, which often came from surrogate rather than direct parental care. Thirty-six out of my forty subjects identified early—although frequently fleeting—attachment figures who ignited their capacity to love. While their experiences confirm common developmental understandings about the critical role of early effective love in later healthy attachments, they do so only partially; that is, the love that the resilient encountered was often brief, circumscribed, and *not* parental. Four of the subjects recalled *no* initial attachment figure; these people, who felt that they were thrown onto themselves in large measure, found effective surrogate love later or made especially good use of the few positive caretaking shards they encountered in earliest childhood. In examining the various loci of hope in childhood, I look closely at both the resilient recruiter and the responsive recruited—those quietly concerned figures who rise up inexplicably and help endangered children with little fanfare and no finale.

The next chapter, on later loci of hope, concentrates on the expanding network of recruited others that becomes possible during adolescence. There I take into account the increasing cognitive and affective complexity of adolescents and examine how that complexity enables the resilient (or any of us) to weave a broader fabric of relationships throughout those years. Adolescent "adoptive" relationships buttress overall growth and strengthen the likelihood that the resilient will emerge from earlier turbulence with reasonable developmental integrity. I will also emphasize that, as they develop, the resilient continually internalize their positive relational experiences. They construct progressively more elaborate inner meanings, rendering themselves active inner and outer agents in finding a "better" life; for without an expanding vision of "better," we cannot seek or create "better" to make it our own.

Assumptive Lenses: Constructing New Versions of the Self

Several important theoretical constructs guide my thinking about the resilient: (1) emphasizing mental health and mental growth throughout the life span; (2) understanding the resilient—or any client, for that matter—on the basis of his or her highest level of functioning; and (3) dignifying the crucial role of Donald Winnicott's "holding environment"[1] throughout adulthood.[2]

First, I assume that *growth is an active process of constructing and organizing meaning,* thereby propelling the creation of newer versions of the self throughout the life span. This underlying assumption about the plasticity of human development is essential to *any* developmentally based therapy and is especially informative when we try to understand and help individuals whose earlier experiences predict the eclipse or foreclosure of their growth. The resilient demonstrate robustly the human capacity for stubborn, determined expansion of the self. They are proof that growth can certainly proceed even in a succession of hostile psychological climates during childhood.

I also assume that *mental health and mental growth are lifelong capacities.*[3] They certainly, and centrally, include the continuing process of psychological expansion that can occur at later moments in the life cycle, typically lumped under that clumsy global rubric "adulthood." My approach challenges the assumption that earlier developmental phases (childhood and adolescence) are typically followed by five to seven decades of either minimal change or outright developmental arrest and that trauma necessarily precludes significant growth. My hope is that you will recognize resilient capacities in yourself as well as in others and see them as reparative mechanisms that can propel you forward at *any* phase in the life cycle. You might then take a more patient, long view of yourself and others as active agents in your own growth. Although the process of change is essentially conservative and slower than any of us might wish (there is no Evelyn Wood speed recovery for severe trauma, despite what the insurance industry might want), it can indeed be substantial and enduring. The resilient seem to know this; thus they keep their sleeves rolled up over time. As the actress Mary Pickford once asserted, "There is always another chance. . . . You may have a fresh start any moment you choose, for this thing we call failure is not the falling down, but the staying down."[4]

My approach is consistent with the views of several developmentally influenced researchers, such as George Vaillant, who see adaptive mechanisms or defensive structures as phenomena that can evolve over the life span.[5] Here I challenge the validity of diagnoses as reified structures that somehow reside within the individual permanently, like a spleen or a lung, typically and rather pessimistically described as "static" personality traits. Even conditions such as bipolar disorder and schizophrenia, for which there is strong evidence of heritability, are very amenable to environmental influences, both in their emergence and in their subsequent course. Emphasizing the role of learning and development over time, many of my subjects emphatically stated that they would *not* have met the study criteria earlier in their lives, especially during late adolescence and early adulthood, although they have now met them for several years. Some were hospitalized; others received crepe-hanging diagnoses as the effects of earlier trauma erupted at childhood's end and they staggered to self-right. As I tell their stories, I will weave in their struggles, lest you think they shot seamlessly from the cellar to the celestial. Recall that Odysseus' path was certainly snarled with challenge; yet he, too, found his way home. Thus I will emphasize the path of emotional progress over the life span, to respect our human capacity for constituting and integrating fundamentally new meanings about the self and others and then operating predominantly out of these strengths rather than out of an earlier, more brittle and frightened sense of self.

Second, I assume that *we all need to be understood through our highest level of functioning*. Rather than searching reductively for a client's Achilles' heel or for regressive material simmering beneath the psychological surface, I take firm stock of the adult strengths and skills that form the overarching organization of self at any given developmental moment.[6] I also assume that earlier experiences are organized within this current level of functioning, even if those experiences (for example, inner representations of prior relationships, or what were perceived to be the relationships at that earlier time) still provoke disruptive, fragmenting, or unsettling reactions or behavior. Like an extensive set of Ukrainian nesting dolls, we are a collection of selves, simultaneously encompassing all of our previous versions yet understood by the most recent "us" through the assumptive lens of our current developmental complexity.

Whether these earlier selves are always experienced with reference to the highest organization of self or are at times so cut off from current functioning that they are immune to fresh insight is the subject of a lively and productive academic debate by scholars such as Laura Rogers and Robert Kegan, Gil Noam, and others.[7] Perhaps we can gain insight by looking at the "divorced self" experiences of people so traumatized that rudimentary or even elaborate self systems split off entirely, operating without reference to other selves, as in the experience of individuals thought to be "multiples." In any case, the relative integration of the traumatized but resilient offers a strong challenge to cherished assumptions about the preeminence of early developmental experiences—assumptions holding that our current adult selves are merely a good cover for the truer, dislocating, regressed selves that lurk within. As the later chapter on struggles suggests, the resilient see their current lives as the history of their own overcoming—the history of their learning to grapple with, befriend, and ultimately cherish the battered children that they were and are while continually respecting the evolved adult orchestrating the many prior selves.

Third, I stress that *any "holding environment," therapeutic or otherwise, that fails to dignify the "adult without"—that more competent gardener tending to the "children within"*—*ignores the great complexity of the human psyche and spirit.* But what do I mean by an effective adult "holding environment"? Winnicott observed that there is never merely an infant but that infants are psychologically intertwined with their caregivers;[8] they are thus what Kegan refers to as "embedduals" rather than individuals. Kegan then extends Winnicott's concept and characterizes growth throughout life as occurring within a succession of "holding environments" or "cultures of embeddedness" that allow us to become progressively more differentiated, sophisticated, and autonomous, although we remain dependent on the new environments fostering our growth.[9] These psychosocial climates are created by people and institutions. They may provide the concern, support, attention, information, and interventions—in short, the "holding"—necessary for us to complete developmental tasks. In Kegan's view, "good enough holding" is

> intrinsic to *evolution*. There is not one holding environment early in life, but a succession of holding environments, a life history of cultures of embeddedness. They are the psychosocial environments which hold us (with which we are fused) and which let go of us (from which we differentiate). . . . What Winnicott says is true for all of us, even for you at this moment. . . . The person is an "individual" *and* an "embeddual." There is never just a you; and at this moment your own buoyancy or lack of it, your own sense of wholeness or lack of it, is in large part a function of how your own current embeddedness culture is holding you.[10]

"Good enough holding" of adults requires clinicians' and educators' attunement to and respect for the highest levels of functioning *within* which earlier struggles, or less well integrated earlier experience, reside. In the example of the Ukrainian nesting dolls, clients need help maintaining a strong focus on the largest and most capable, healthiest and most insightful, of the selves. This robust self informs the struggles of the younger versions of the self and has the capacity, through increased perspective about the relationship between self and other,[11] to effect a greater integration of past with present experiences. For example, a client might feel overwhelmed by feelings of loss and find herself tempted to return to an abusive relationship in order to re-create the familiarity of her abusive family of origin. Yet she may recognize with insight, clarity, perspective, and humor that she is better served by talking about these feelings in therapy than enacting them or repeatedly viewing Ingrid Bergman as she struggles similarly in the 1940s film *Gaslight*. If *we* keep a clinical chair free for clients' highest functioning, then *they* are more likely to honor it, without forsaking their struggle on the floorboards.

In Chapter Seven, I focus on one particularly crucial "holding function" of the therapeutic relationship—namely, that therapy is an environment that has the potential to "hold" traumatized clients symbolically while they grapple with an especially painful ethical dilemma: whether to maintain either ties or allegiances to some or all family members during adulthood. This bind is desperately challenging when families weave a collusive fabric of denial and minimization around past assaults and assailants, insisting that it is incumbent upon the *assaulted* to paper over past hurts in the service of family unity (however thin the sheet). For the moment, I will simply note that the resilient never rest on their psychological laurels for long and that surmounting earlier abuse does not mean that the central figures from childhood evaporate during adulthood. Emerging from trauma requires a concentrated perspective on past as well as present versions of abusive others (who in turn are aspects of one's collected selves). Contact with abusive or collusive family members can be especially challenging to anyone—resilient or not. Thus clinicians can "hold" their grappling clients by bearing witness, keeping attentive company, collaboratively reworking understandings about the family, offering but not imposing new interpretations, and remaining completely open to the full catastrophe of their earlier lives. The lessons in resilient overcoming learned during childhood and adolescence need extension and elaboration well into adulthood, and therapy offers one of many environments in which the integrative work continues. The resilient seem to achieve this with singular vigor and integrity, yet many still need our help in the process.

These theoretical motifs reappear throughout this work, because my main emphasis is on *how* the resilient currently construct understandings about their past and present selves. I offer their insights in the hope that their struggles and triumphs will inform yours.

Childhood Hope and Gifted Givers

Now let us look at how effective surrogate love is recruited and sustained by the resilient and at those who provide them with surrogate love.

Recruiting Well

Let us first focus on the capacities *within* young resilient children, looking at what might reside primarily in their psyches and somas to promote growth in barren developmental soil. Their capacity to *recruit others' invested regard* is crucial here, because this is a skill

> so uniform at birth [and such a] various affair as people grow older; some people have a much greater ability to recruit people's attention to them than other people do. This obvious fact, so underinvestigated by psychologists and so commonly denied by teachers, is never forgotten by teenagers, who could have told researchers— before huge sums of money were spent to discover it—that the greatest inequalities in education were not between schools (of different economic strata, for example) but within them; that greater than the inequalities of social class or achievement test scores is the

unequal capacity of students to interest others in them—a phenomenon not reducible to social class or intelligence, and which
seems to be the more powerful determinant of future thriving.[12]

Once again, I am not ignoring the vast, fundamental cruelty of
social disadvantage, since too many get little opportunity to recruit
others who are in a position to be truly helpful to them. However,
I *am* asserting that good recruiting capacity is one of the linchpins
of resilience in my group. Remember that many of them, like Shibvon, *were* severely socially disadvantaged as children; thus we must
explore what distinguishes them from the many suffering others
whose spirits are still locked in shadowy vaults. Unlike their less
adaptive peers, the resilient use the invested regard of others effectively, buttressing a succession of inadequate and disappointing
"holding environments" by dint of their own skill, appeal, and
determination. Similar findings are reported by Emmy Werner and
Ruth Smith, who concluded their longitudinal study of resilience
by saying, "To the extent that men and women in this study were
able to elicit predominantly positive responses from their environment, they were found to be stress-resistant at each stage of their
life cycle, even under conditions of chronic poverty or in a home
with a psychotic parent. To the extent that they elicited negative
responses from their environment, they were found to be vulnerable, even in the absence of biological stress or financial con-
straints."[13] Another resilience study even concluded that more
competent high-risk children demonstrated better overall social
skills than a *low*-risk control group. Kaufmann, Grunebaum,
Cohler, and Gamer state strongly that recruiting skill is correlated
with competence. The most competent high-risk children that
they followed "reported extensive contact with an adult outside the
family, whereas none of the children in the low-competence group
had such relationships. In addition, four of the six most competent
high-risk children had at least one very close friend, and two
reported at least moderately close friends." By contrast, many more

of the low-competence children from similarly high-risk circumstances had few or no close friends, "suggesting that more competent children are better able to maintain intimate social ties with
peers."[14]

Surrogate Love

What actually takes place inside these recruited relationships? To
understand this, let us look closely at the qualities that seem to
make the resilient especially successful recruiters and look also at
those they recruited. I speculate continually about how these surrogate relationships are organized and sustained, both in actual lived
experience and in the resilients' inner representations of experience
as they form the locus of hope that lights the path of later love. I
also consider just who can be recruited into surrogacy, since all but
four out of forty subjects recalled at least one person who was a focal
and intense source of sustenance in infancy and early childhood.
These figures constitute the key "natural" support systems aug-
menting resilience during the formative years. Nonprofessional surrogates require our closest attention here, since none of those
interviewed was in therapy until midway through adolescence, only
a few found counselors in college, and most waited until at least
their mid-twenties or later to enter therapy. These voluntary, often
unofficial relationships need the dignity of our recognition, because
they seem to be very successful at keeping ice crystals from forming
on young hearts.

Sadly, although we now know a great deal about abusive parents, we understand far less about human surrogacy. We hear a great
deal about abuse in the media, but the role of spontaneous community generosity on behalf of the maltreated is often either overlooked entirely or minimized in throwaway lines. Would the current
culture seem so dangerous if the face of every potential rescuer—
the many who must be truly well intentioned and who might make
effective surrogates for these imperiled children—scrolled across our

screens on the nightly news? We might sleep better, comforted and inspired. Nobody *asks* these givers to do anything; they just appear.

Perhaps we know less about surrogates because they are a relatively silent army of foot soldiers, not seeking and not receiving particular acclaim. As I recently noted to my clinical partner, psychologist Carol Taylor, as we returned to a full afternoon of trauma work in our joint therapy practice, everyone would know us by 5 P.M. if we set ourselves on fire on the way back from lunch. "Imagine two mild-mannered psychologists doing such a thing. What got into them?" Not celebrities, but notoriously *known*. Unfortunately, being "good enough" therapists, spouses, educators, and parents would play only on the insomniacs' news channel. "They took reasonable care of their children today, paid their bills, and were generally decent to the people they met." Skip tonight's soporific.

Yet an ethically bankrupt opportunist can gain public recognition rather easily. Consider the case of a man who knowingly transmitted the AIDS virus to multiple sexual partners yet died a local hero by promoting sensitivity to AIDS victims on television. As we discussed this case, my colleague (and senior Boston psychiatrist) Russell Vasile noted that it is much harder for unassuming toilers to be seen. Although most of us, however talented, are content to be steadfast worker bees, so humbled by the severity and magnitude of human cruelty that we do not presume to be heroic figures, there is something terribly misguided about a struggling society that does not celebrate its quiet healers. While many activists of firm moral fiber *are* in the news, including those courageous enough to disclose stigmatizing conditions such as sexual abuse, AIDS, or addictions, the great majority are ignored. Thus I pay particular homage here to the gifted givers who contributed so genuinely to saving the resilient, in an effort to encourage and celebrate this capacity in all of us.

Now, what do the resilient recall about the locus of hope in their early lives? For some of those I interviewed, the initial promise was a parent, attuned and observant before the darkness fell. For others, it was an extended family member with whom they had infrequent contact (by parental standards). Many were loved well by hired help, strangers, peers, parents of friends, or even pets. Four of the individuals, as I noted earlier, had no recollection of any focal early figure. They had the astounding, rare capacity to nurture themselves in a virtual vacuum of care.

Let us look now at those who had some effective parenting from a biological parent.

Flawed but Effective Early Mothering

Mothers were occasionally mentioned as loci of hope during the earlier years. For example, Joanna, a trauma psychologist in her mid forties, echoes the thoughts of several subjects when she remembers her home as secure before serious depression, alcoholism, and unrelenting marital hostility compromised her parents' functioning:

> I think that the light is very much the first seven or eight years of my life. I don't think I'm imagining it. I think [those years] were very happy. . . . I don't think I could fool myself. . . . I think I felt like life was very, very safe and good. . . . Even now . . . there's still a lot in [my mother] that's just tremendously optimistic, has a tremendous zeal for life, and I think I'm very identified with that . . . even at my worst moments. . . . I can always remember. . . . I have a strong sense of purpose about life that really carries me over very well.

Joanna stores their light as it dims in them. At eight she experiences her parents as dead, as if the life were leeched out of them, leaving confusing corporal likenesses behind. By then her mother was severely depressed, never to recover, her father was absent, and her parents' marriage was deeply scarred by chronic discord. She and her sister were forbidden to fight, but her parents never stopped:

I remember experiencing intense loneliness when I was in the fourth grade. . . . I don't believe I was a lonely person before that. . . . I remember having . . . nightmares of my parents dying, absolutely terrible nightmares. . . . Actually, this is increasingly fascinating to me: I read a story about a girl who—in fourth grade—pretended to herself that she was orphaned . . . and wrote about all the feelings of being orphaned; and I remember thinking, "Boy, can I relate to that," and feeling, "Why? I'm not an orphan—why?" and to this day, I remember that story vividly.

Kai, another psychologist (and Joanna's husband of seventeen years), also recognizes that he made a firm early maternal attachment even though he was centrally cast in his mother's severely depressed and self-absorbed drama. Paradoxically, he believes that his subordinate role in her preoccupying tragedy also fed the wellspring of his hope:

I think that even though my mother did it for the wrong reasons, the fact that [she] needed me to be a lot of things to her, and that she sort of blindly idolized me . . . during the first five years of life (I thought I was really special to my mother and my grandparents) . . . really made a difference, no matter how I was traumatized by my father. . . . [For example,] he told me . . . at seven . . . that I could never directly disobey him, *and that if I did, he'd kill me*. . . . I sort of wrote him off then. . . . It was . . . a breakdown of any kind of sense of him protecting me or [my] trusting him. . . .

Much later I realized that . . . [my mother's idealization of me] was done in such a way that it really didn't take into account my feelings, [and that] whenever anything got tough with my father she just evaporated, . . . and that she idolized me for the wrong reasons, . . . and that [being idolized] was a way of abandonment, too. . . . [But] I was terribly *part* of her emotional life, and even though it was very depressive, . . . I was *connected* with her. . . . Even if it's all for the wrong reasons, she needed me to be there. . . . *It certainly has some kind of a price, but I think that, given the other things, that was sort of some of the glue, too, . . . some of the stuff that at least you can transform into something else.*

Both Joanna and Kai introduce the resilient leitmotif of "construing difficult events more positively," without any illusion that their childhoods were untrammeled. They hold a fierce conviction that, despite the serious "bad" they encountered, some unalterable good took place early in life that fundamentally oriented them toward the hope of love within and among people. As another woman—one whose father committed suicide when she was young—noted, the good experiences arrive at "really critical times . . . [and allow] for real hope . . . that if you sort of hang in there long enough, . . . things will get better." You sail slowly through the fog, but with a sturdy inner compass. Since early attachments play such a central role in fueling resilient optimism, the importance of this convictional hope should never be underestimated.

Flawed but Effective Early Fathering

Fathers were also the locus of hope for a few, although their time was often limited by long hours at work and their impact weakened by failure of nerve. Thus, while they were invaluable beacons of hope, many of them (like the aforementioned mothers who provided some genuine albeit fleeting love) tolerated the very circumstances that brutalized their children. They remind us that just because someone is not *intentionally* mean does not prevent that person from being *effectively* mean. Thus collusive parents present a complex challenge to the resilient: these parents often both love *and* fail their children terribly. For example, Poet, a psychologist, married at twenty. She is delighted with her husband after thirty-three years and believes that her poignant attachment to her father helped her make a beeline for a good man. While you might say,

"Well, that makes sense—a good father paves the path toward a good husband," consider Poet's personal odyssey.

Poet grew up in an extremely modest but well-maintained and safe housing project in New York City. Her parents had virtually no furniture, but they possessed the wisdom to invest in musical instruments to allow their deep love of music to inspire Poet. Her mother meets standard diagnostic criteria for multiple personality disorder; as a manifestation of that disorder, Poet was subject to vicious physical brutality at the hands of a maternal alter ego by age two (and thereafter). *Her mother completely dissociated these episodes.* Poet eerily describes seeing her mother's face change as if a hawk's shadow passed silently across it, leaving a different mother in its wake. Her father never acknowledged these radical personality shifts, although family friends corroborated Poet's perceptions in later years, finding their own Jekyll and Hyde experiences with her mother similarly baffling if not terrifying.

Intolerant of even rudimentary autonomy, Poet's mother nearly lived under the child's skin in an apartment too tiny to allow any personal retreat. Her mother also *consciously* lied, as well as shifting *unconsciously* from self to sequestered self. One of these "alter mothers" also took on lovers from time to time, including the family physician. Although we might mourn the loss of doctors who make house calls, Poet does not. She recalls that her family doctor arrived regularly in sartorial splendor, gaining her trust at an early age and then gradually abusing her sexually over the years. Her mother routinely left them alone, ostensibly to get medicine at the pharmacy. But where was her father during these years?

> Now, I'm certain that my father knew. . . . I don't think that he actually observed it, but I do know, which I can tell you if you want in detail, that *he had a lot of investment in not knowing it, and rejected what it was I told him.* [The doctor] had been my mother's doctor, and he would come to the house, and what I recalled—it took a long time to remember all of this—is that he had a sexual relationship with

my mother, with one of her alters, and with me. I don't know that I
ever said anything directly to my father about it. I said a lot of indirect things. . . . I'm fairly sure my father knew about [the affair
between the physician and] my mother. . . .

Her father's failure of nerve and sagging integrity were most
apparent to Poet at age eleven, when she was raped by her adored
sixth-grade teacher in his home. Invited for lunch, thrilled beyond
compare, Poet arrived as the teacher's impeccably groomed wife left
for the afternoon. Abruptly, her teacher became a version of himself that she had never seen before:

In sixth grade I had a teacher, a man teacher, who was greatly
beloved by all the children. . . . He loved children. He took us on
hikes every weekend. Now, in New York, this is pretty unusual. . . .
Teachers didn't invest themselves that greatly. So he took the kids
. . . to ball games, and . . . he was really involved. *And he was a
pedophile.* . . . At that time, I didn't know a thing—all I knew is he
liked children, and he liked me especially. He liked me especially
because I was very athletic and full of energy and a lot of fun. . . . He
would invite his favorite kids to his apartment, which was in
Lincoln Park, and he invited me for lunch.

I was absolutely thrilled. . . . I got to go to lunch at Mr. Thurber's
house! . . . Wonderful! I was . . . going on eleven at that point. This
was after the school term was over. . . . And I remember thinking,
"This is strange, there isn't any lunch on the table." . . . [I assumed]
that he would take it out, and we'd eat in the living room. [Suddenly]
he attacked me, and I was raped. . . . It was total shock; . . . I had no
idea. I mean, I came for lunch! So this [abuse] was really violent, and
when I left, he was very mad at me because I didn't like it. I cried
and I yelled and I was very upset; and he was very angry, and he
walked out of the room. He walked out of the living room into his
bedroom. I went home, . . . and it felt like miles. It was six blocks.

Poet staggered back home on this hot Fourth of July weekend, her face dirty and streaked from sobbing. Ordinarily no moral laggard, her father focused his entire response on helping Poet recompose her *appearance* before her mother came home. *The incident was never mentioned again.*

[After it happened,] I went home, and my father was home, and my mother wasn't home; . . . and that was a wonderful opportunity for me, . . . because I would never say anything to my mother. I would *never* broach anything with my mother, *never* rock any boats. So I started to try to tell him. I looked like hell. I was filthy, . . . I was hot and sweaty, and I was crying. . . . I looked awful, and that isn't the way I generally looked. I'm sure I went looking very neat and clean to go to lunch with this man. . . . I wanted to look my best, and [my father] could not have *not* seen . . . what I looked like [when I returned].

I started to tell him, and I said . . . that Mr. Thurber wanted me to sit on his lap and I didn't want to . . . and that he wanted to kiss me. I was sort of beginning at the beginning of the story. . . . I mean, *one can't just march in and announce that you've been abused; it wasn't exactly something I knew how to even talk about,* and I didn't know what you even called . . . some of this. That was terrible for me, because I always had to have a label for everything. I had a very big vocabulary, and I was used to being able to express myself, but I didn't know what this stuff was even called.

My father became very alarmed, and he said I should go in the bathroom and wash my face and hurry up and get cleaned up, because my mother's coming home very soon. She'll be home any minute, and then *he wouldn't talk to me about it, so it was perfectly clear to me he didn't want to hear any more.* I was very disappointed, because he didn't say *anything,* and then he never said anything to me in private either. I didn't know what it was I wanted. It was very odd, but I just felt: I want something—what is it? . . . [But he was silent.]

When Poet learned two years later that this same teacher had abused two other girls and then been banished to Harlem by cynical school administrators to inflict himself on the black community, she tore home to tell her parents the tale. This became a litmus test of their capacity to respond effectively to her abuse; she prayed that they would rally. Unfortunately, her mother suggested that events were misinterpreted unfairly by the girls and dismissed their concerns. Her father kept a locked silence.

> So with my father, [even when he knew,] he let it go on, and I never understood how he could do that. . . . He was the person who let everything happen. He never did anything wrong himself, *but he just let it . . . go on.* What he did wrong was not to listen and not to take care of me; but he never was aggressive himself in any way, . . . and he never lied. . . .[But] he could never have forgotten what I looked like coming home from that lunch. He had a mind like a steel trap in that regard. He *never* forgot anything, and even if he didn't put it 100 percent together back then, I'm sure he put it together at that point, *and it was at that point that I would date that I gave up on him.*

At this juncture Poet, like Shibvon on "the day the police took the children to jail," knew that she was abandoned in some immutable way by her otherwise lovely, artistic, musical, poetic, honest, and erudite father. She now knew definitively that he would *never* protect her from her mother's abuses, even those he must have known about; nor did he take any action on her behalf in the face of soul-tearing sexual assaults. While not abusive, he was thoroughly *collusive.* In the quote that follows, Poet gives us a flavor of her complex task of integrating the best of her father in the sad light of his severe limitations. For example, he coaches her in the most effective and fair tactics for getting whatever she wants from her work life, applauding all of her efforts. However, by completely denying her sexual abuse, he refuses to school her on the strategies that she needs as much or more—avoiding and surviving assault:

> My father was a musician, like his father before him. His father was a composer and a violin teacher, and my father was a violin soloist with the St. Louis Symphony when he was five. He was a real prodigy, and then when the Depression came, he realized he could never make a living as a musician and went into social work and psychology. . . . But he taught me the violin, and so we played duets, and that was our main way of communicating—reading books together and playing music—and into those activities my mother never intruded. So those were the areas [in which] I found both privacy and a relationship with my father, and I identified with him far more than with my mother. *I never identified with her at all.*
>
> [I particularly identified with my father's] capacity to think in a purely intellectual manner from a very distanced place. . . . That he could do magnificently, and I learned to do that. He . . . taught me how to work out problems in a linear way, how to study them, how to think them through in a way that would make you able to deal with whatever situation came up: what to do before you applied for a scholarship, what to do to prepare for an interview for a job or for a fellowship; . . . and I did it literally religiously and very successfully.
>
> I got everything I ever wanted in that regard by studying my way into it. If there was one position and 300 applicants, and I was less qualified than maybe 100 of the applicants, I would get it. And that's literally true, and I would do it aboveboard in an honest way. He didn't teach me to be competitive at all. [*He gave you a tremendous sense of agency and effectiveness?*] Absolutely. Anything I wanted to

do, he was sure I could do it. . . . And I *did* [succeed], so in that way
I got a lot . . . of survival skills.

Sadly, however, when her father failed Poet utterly in regard to
her extensive abuse, her faith in his convictional courage collapsed.
At the same time, his loving her unequivocally spawned Poet's
unshakable faith in herself. When she realized at age eleven that
she was fundamentally alone, she also determined to develop her
own ethical mettle, and she had the depth of confidence to succeed.
Exercising her convictional courage during her adulthood, she
decided to confront him about his silent complicity. She reminded
him of several of these assaultive childhood incidents, in particular
her mother's being intensely abusive to her for three months at age
seven over some slight infraction. Her father had a striking reaction: "He was just stunned." His denial was so complete that he had
no memory of *any* of the events described above. Similarly, her
father did not recall another round of abuse that was quite apparent to Poet and her suitor during her late adolescence:

My mother was . . . irrationally, hysterically, miserably unpleasant,
shall we put it, when I was nineteen and I was engaged to somebody
who, in fact, I didn't marry. She was very, very, very nasty about this
person, who was a lovely human being. You couldn't find a nicer
human being on earth. He was just a lovely person, and she hated
him! And yet she wouldn't say so; she'd always say that she thought
he was a nice young man, . . . but she reacted like a crazy person. I
never could understand it. I still haven't been able to understand it.
It must have meant something to her in her history.

And my father just sort of avoided everything, would never stand
up for my end of things. He just sort of abandoned me in the middle of it, but of course that was his pattern; and when I asked him
about that, I said, "Now, you know Mother was nuts on that subject.
You know that this man was a very lovely, fine, kind, decent, smart,

responsible human being about whom nobody could object. . . . So why didn't you at least take me aside and say to me, "Well, I know that he's really a fine person, and Mother's off the wall"? Even that much would have been helpful. And he said, "I never felt I could go against your mother." [*That makes two of you. Didn't you say that you never felt that you were able to challenge her either?*] Never on any subject of significance.

These passages have been quoted at length because they contain many of the leitmotifs of resilience introduced earlier—especially the struggle of the resilient to come to terms with the best of what they found, which so thoroughly commingles with the worst. Like many resilient adults, Poet is highly gifted, both verbally and artistically. She developed a strong identification with her father's love of the intellect and the arts—and certainly his nonabusiveness. She also possesses his clarity of perception and systematic problem-solving skills, despite the fact that he created a psychological barrier around exploring *any* feelings and recognizing abuse. Devoting her own life to crumbling these ramparts, both personally and professionally, Poet now sees many survivors of cult abuse and other severe trauma in her clinical practice. Recruiting others' invested regard is also a strong theme in her life, perhaps because she combines her considerable talent with noncompetitive tenacity, a compelling combination. Not surprisingly, she is simply easy to like.

Poet also possesses great clarity of recall, including a compelling reconstruction of her own inner thoughts from forty-two years ago. Highly observant, a trait that is invaluable to her as a clinician, she absorbs subtle, nonverbal detail to draw accurate conclusions about people's character. However, although she is highly articulate and was so as a child—she was reading an average of twelve books a week by the time she was assaulted by her sixth-grade teacher—she had *no* words or constructs with which to describe her abuse to her father; it is as if the events had been conducted in another language.

Is it any surprise, then, that disenfranchised, poorly educated, unem-powered, or terrified children cannot describe their abuse? Prosecutors, take note!

As a social activist, Poet cringes upon recalling that her second perpetrator was simply sent off to plague another community, unlikely to be challenged there. This is anathema to her. Inspired by negative example, Poet managed to seek out good love during late adolescence and found another sterling partner after her mother's success in turning her first serious suitor away. She consciously forged a path toward a fuller integrity, despite the fact that her father never found similar courage. She also chose a man who not only loves her steadfastly but loves her children and stands up for what he believes, just as she does. As we gazed at family photographs, I asked her how she explains to herself that she chose somebody who is kind, decent, and loving when so many people who have been abused choose someone who abuses in return. She replied,

> Because my father was not abusive. . . . My husband . . . is a very nice man, and I had a nice life after that, quite a nice life. I really had a model for a nice man, but I remember thinking . . . about the qualities I liked in men, . . . and I liked all those qualities that my father had of being a decent, sort of ethical person who was very thoughtful and not cruel to anybody and helpful. . . . I remember thinking, "I like all those aspects, but in addition, I want somebody who not only thinks the sun rises and sets on me *but who will always stand up for me* . . . just as I would be [steadfast] for [that person]; . . . *and I wanted somebody who would tell the truth.* I wanted a person who would *always* tell the truth. That was [all-]important to me, and I got a man who doesn't know how *not* to tell the truth. He's terrific that way.

During her interview, Poet mentioned in passing that she was one of a very few women in Matina Horner's now-famous "fear of success" research who did *not* fear success. Her comment under-scores another theme in my research: the uncommon capacity in the resilient to trust "good." I cannot be certain whether my sub-jects' ability to love originated within their earliest parental ties, through surrogate love, from a rare capacity for self-sustenance, or from a combination of all three; and it may not matter. What we *do* know is that somehow, somewhere, these people become anchored within an unshakable conviction that they deserve love. *They also trust that good love exists, and they find it.* They may self-accuse, self-reject, or even self-loathe from time to time. But at the bedrock, they still know that they are worth loving and being loved by another human being.

Evidence from my subjects' marital and relational histories points unmistakably in this direction. These people have sustained relationships for years, and they continually renegotiate when love flags or fails. In addition, it was evident to me in over 180 hours of interviews that I was in the presence of people who believed that they were worth the inquiry, giving and getting a great deal as we spoke. Jane Jacobs, a psychologist and a contemporary resilience researcher who read many of my first interviews as a reliability observer, spontaneously reported to me that my subjects were strik-ingly characterized by their deeply held conviction that they deserve love. The data suggest that this conviction was launched in the early years of their evolution; and most of the subjects are likewise convinced that it originated in the warmth before the frost.

At the same time, it is worth remembering that many abused individuals have precious little capacity to trust good in any form, and most are as cautious as field mice. Shattered by childhood hate, they often elude or repel the love they so sorely need, avoiding con-nection or even exploiting others to even the score. Yet we often assume that the trammeled will take in good automatically, some-thing that teachers, trauma therapists, adoption workers, adoptive parents of older children, and many well-intentioned lovers—among others—know to be frequently false. Your mythic ship comes in; the Hallelujah Chorus pipes in from the heavens; you leap from the dock and gaily pry open the crates. In truth, the leap is a various affair: you fear the ship will overrun you as it docks or the vessel will sink as you step on deck; the crates crack open to reveal a squirm of snakes or sacks of wheat fouled by greedy rodents, or perhaps you find nothing at all.

By contrast, the resilient acquire a fundamental faith that, despite their fears, they *will* encounter a full hold. They can allow themselves good fortune, despite cautious glances and general vigilance. And they find that their good fortune builds on itself; they come to believe, on the basis of early relational success, that even shattered shards of possibility can be shaped into a stained-glass sanctuary over time. As a somewhat tentative survivor once said to his watchful but enormously optimistic partner of twenty years, "You know what's really different about the two of us? We both came from hell, but you have an easier time trusting good fortune. Things go well for you and you say, 'Great, I'll keep it.' Things go well for me and I look for a bigger anvil to fall on my head, and I forget to pay attention to the good things."

Hired Love and Extended Family Ties

Although Joanna, Kai, and Poet found some years of devoted love from a parent, many did not. Yet all my subjects have a homing device for good relationships. Where did it originate, if not with parental love? Let us turn our attention now to hired care and extended family ties, relationships that allow a child much less time in the sun but still serve as a potent, compelling contrast to a childhood that might otherwise leave a young person with the stark-eyed stare of a skeletal steer.

Strikingly, these ties are experienced with very little ambivalence, in contrast to the preceding parental examples. Apparently, most of us expect our parents to nurture and protect us in a very comprehensive and steadfast manner. When their stamina flags, or if they nurture but fail to protect us, we feel abandoned, however subtly we understand their predicament and value their strengths. (Certainly Joanna, Kai, and Poet convey the complexity of their appreciation *and* their disappointment in their "better" parents.) By contrast, descriptions of extended family ties and nonfamilial surrogacy were more uniformly positive. Apparently we simply expect less from people who are not our parents, which renders us more at liberty to appreciate what they do. When their ministry approaches the best parental intensity and bypasses the worst, surrogates can land deeply in our psyches indeed.

Since you are acquainted with Dan's past from his vignette, we can look at his surrogate experiences with two very gifted givers, one hired and one blood-tied: Amelia, a sixteen-year-old nanny who cared for him from infancy until age three, and his grandmother, who was an infrequently seen but paramount figure throughout his formative years (and who was, you will recall, the neighbor who tried to save his father as an abandoned toddler).

Amelia arrived because Dan's mother "hated babies. . . . She detested any baby—not only her own, but just any baby; she thought they were so unclean" that the moment Dan and his twin were born, "she hired a nursemaid. . . . My mother didn't want to go near us." Fortunately, Dan gleaned an initial sense of sunrise from Amelia, which—in contrast to the subsistence emotional economy offered by his parents—taught him to gravitate to the light of his grandmother and later loves:

> There was a great deal of love in Amelia's family. . . . I visited her family only once, but it stands out to this day how much love there was when I arrived with Amelia. Everyone was laughing and singing and hugging each other and just being so warm together. I just could sense how wonderful that was, and of course I saw that manifested in her every day, in her capacity to love others, and to love us as little children. . . . *I think the most fortunate thing in my life was to have been exposed to that at such an early age.*

When Dan was just over three years old, Amelia was fired abruptly for the crime of having Dan's father sexually intrude upon her—at least that is how Dan's parents thought of it, ever externalizing all blame. But Dan recalls Amelia vividly, even though she left for good when he was extremely young:

> The very last day, since she had been fired, she did what she wasn't supposed to do, which was to take us down to the railroad tracks. We walked down the railroad tracks to her family's house because she wanted her family to see these two little boys that she'd grown so fond of. . . . [This is] something that became a problem for me for the rest of my life: they were cooking onions and garlic, and they asked me to eat some of this, and I thought, "This is really strange; I don't know if I want it." I sort of nibbled on it, and . . . it was just different and strange food. I never saw her again, and for years I would almost throw up at the smell of onions and garlic, because I ate this meal and I never saw her again.
>
> The thing that was so remarkable was that I'd *never* seen a family like that in my life. . . . In addition to my own family, I had seen my mother's twin sister's family, which, in some ways, was equally dysfunctional, except that they didn't hit each other. There was a great deal of passive anger and silence and withholding of feelings and all of that, and it was just as bad another way . . . as my own, and I'd seen just little snitches of other families. But I'd *never* seen a family like Amelia's before, and it was just so remarkable. I remember thinking at the time, "Everybody is so warm." I don't remember the words I used as a kid, but I remember the sensation of "My God, if I lived here, everybody would be hugging me all the time and laughing with me and playing games; . . . what a wonderful place." . . . And then boom! I never saw them again.
>
> *But it stood out in my life*, and I think that I had sort of a star that I could focus on in the sky, which was that *people who were deeply*

loving like Amelia were the people to latch onto and follow and to be with.
That's what I wanted to look for in life, and . . . over and over again,
when I would see someone who kind of fit that mold, I'd kind of
latch right on.

To this day, when I go to a party . . . I look around the room,
and if there's someone with a very kind face, sort of laughing and
smiling or whatever . . . I kind of sidle over and connect with that
person; and if it's who I think it is, . . . someone who is really kind
and warm, . . . I get to know that person. . . . I sort of scan . . . looking for a kind heart.

And of course I ended up marrying a woman who absolutely
embodies that in the most wonderful way, and who came from a
most loving family. . . . My wife, Janet, was as loved as Amelia was
[by her family], and so that's who I married. I've had the joy of living thirty-five years together with someone who had the deep love
that Amelia had and who has loved me and loved our children as
deeply as Amelia could have, so that's been a real joy in my life. But
it was a very intuitive thing on my part when I met her, when I saw
her family and how they treated her, and they adored her. I thought,
"Okay! That's the good thing": I just *knew* that it was good, and
that's . . . who I wanted to be the mother of my own children, this
loving and kind person. That's what I wanted our family to be like.
It was fun to be in.

Although Dan loses Amelia abruptly, he soldiers on. His grandmother becomes the second locus of hope, sought at first because
Dan recognizes in her a template of loving learned within Amelia's
care. This is a frequent theme across the interviews:

My grandmother was a lifesaving anchor for me. . . . I was her
favorite, and . . . she always wanted me to sit on her lap and . . .
[wanted to] tell me stories. The other kids could go play in different

parts of the house. . . . She was perfectly pleasant to them, *but for some reason, I'll never know why exactly, she took a real liking to me*, and I just adored her, of course. . . . And I think [from that experience] I grew up with the sense that there were good mummies and bad mummies—or good grammies and bad mummies, I guess you could say—*but that there was good.*

With great insight, Dan talks extensively about years of grappling with his tendency to dichotomize good and bad. Because he found that polarizing works against intimacy, he now views the world prismatically: "I've grown to the point where I see people in many, many shades." Since Amelia and his grandmother were literally the precious safety of the day, and his parents reminiscent of literature's black forest of the night, his struggle is understandable. Regardless, Dan feels that his relationships with Amelia and his grandmother oriented him definitively to the possibility of exceptional good between people, countering the exceptionally bad reality of his parents' relentless, at times psychotic brutality.

In this way, he is typical of most subjects. Despite infrequent or abruptly interrupted connections, surrogates serve as beacons of "goodness" in frequent tempests. Over time they become the organizing theme for human contact, so that the resilient gradually develop highly cultivated palates for constructive interaction. As Dan notes, he adeptly sidesteps the empty eyes at the party, bee-lining instead for those that seem *full*.

John Roger, a laconic forty-six-year-old machinist, captures this homing mechanism when he states tersely, "Anyone could have gone through the same things I went through, and probably taken a different road." Intriguingly, many of the subjects remarked that the contrasts that they encountered were so sharp that it was almost easy to choose a positive path, since the other one seemed *so* rutted and unpromising. Yet so many of the abused, tripped up on the starting line, continually misstep rather than self-right. *What explains this discrepancy?* Perhaps it is the unusual combination of the capacity to receive good and the rare talent in some of the most seriously maltreated for getting good emotional mileage out of what little is offered, coupled with unusual giftedness in some givers. Whatever the cause, the "good" adheres and self-replicates. Recall Shibvon's eager readiness to absorb a positive comment. Like someone who hears a few bars of a lovely melody, she hums it for weeks until it is *part* of her.

Continuing my focus on maximizing the good found within extended family surrogacy, I found similar imagery in the life of Denzel, a man in his mid thirties who married well fourteen years ago. Denzel thrives on working as a martial arts instructor in the black community and supervising the use of the athletic equipment at a large Chicago university. Like so many others, he gravitates to what is constructive in a sea of inner-city destruction. Recently, his father was gunned down in the street; that man's firstborn son—Denzel's older brother—was presumably the gunman. Denzel has serious diabetes, and his younger brother had a malignant melanoma. While Denzel is now in a prominent Chicago teaching hospital's study of well-controlled diabetics, his brother's outcome was fatal. Neither brother detected his adult medical needs until his health was seriously compromised, because seeking medical care was something they just did not do as children; there was no money to pay for it.

Denzel, like Shibvon and John Roger and many others in the study, was achingly poor growing up. His absent father's income from the army might have made a considerable difference, but his father had a secret second nuclear family in another state and never sent money to his first family. Compounding the family's difficulties, Denzel's mother soon became alcoholic. Denzel also recalls infidelity among most of his extended family and regular physical brutality among his siblings. His own work as a martial arts instructor now allows him *channeled* aggression, an art form that he teaches to willing youth while decrying violence:

Learning to deal with struggles early stands out in my life, which is why I was very independent after the age of, say, thirteen: because I've seen so many struggles in so many people's lives, and the misgivings of people toward one another, and it's not worth it. I made that correlation very early in life . . . through arguing relatives, through relationships between uncles and mothers and fathers and fathers' friends, . . . very bad relationships all around. . . . [I always saw them] dragging the kids along to get from one point to another and having the kids see all that [fighting] and then big outbursts happening and having the kids run out of the house with the adults. . . . [*So that's why you reported "chronic family discord"?*] Oh, yeah, crazy things. Definitely.

Denzel realizes that he cleaved preferentially to the mosaic of care he experienced from his mother, as well as infrequent contact with his uncle, grandmother, and great-grandmother, *although his siblings—like most in this study—did not make the same use of their care*. For Denzel, his grandmother was a quiet locus of hope, offering encouragement to advance educationally and personally without ever coercing him. His uncle was also a potent role model: he completed a doctorate in finance and now offers financial planning services to the community and his church; in addition, he has sustained a marriage to a woman he loves. Similarly, Denzel sees his great-grandmother as a guardian spirit in his life and his mother as her devoted first lieutenant.

The importance of all this extended family support evolved as Denzel's father repeatedly moved his family to strange environments and then abruptly abandoned them. The family was left to fend for themselves in Germany when Denzel was three, for example. While there, Denzel contracted several simultaneous childhood diseases, and his mother was apparently told by physicians that his prospects were hopeless. In the following recollections, Denzel recognizes his talent for absorbing solid role models and recruiting others' invested

regard, his adept skill in drawing others to him in a mutually gratifying way, and his preferential grasp of hope and possibility over
despair. He, like Dan, remarks that this way of life is simply more
pleasurable, and he will settle for no less. Here he describes the
sharply contrasting models in his life:

> [My father] moved us to Germany and left us there. He moved us to
> Virginia and he left us there. . . . Then we moved to Chicago, which
> was the last move we made. [But I had other people. My grand-
> mother] is a very strong woman, very religious, always a leader. She
> was head of the National Evangelist Organization—not overbear-
> ing, more subtle in her demands as opposed to being really overt and
> physical. . . . *There were little or no expectations*, which was kind of
> gratifying when I look back on it, because *it gave you more of a choice
> to feel out your own way*, in terms of . . . ways that you wanted to
> go. . . .
>
> [My uncle] was my dominant male role model. He got married
> when he was nineteen, and . . . all his kids are going to college now,
> which is great. He's still married to his first wife. [*How was he inspir-
> ing to you? What really stands out about him and how he was with
> you?*]. . . Oh, just the fact that *he was there when trouble happened*. I
> mean, he wasn't *always* there, but he was [there enough]. . . . When
> I was younger, he and his wife-to-be were living with us. . . . He was
> still at the University of Illinois. . . . He had a bad knee injury, and I
> remember him going through that, and seeing him sustain himself
> and trying to get himself back into shape to play football after-
> ward. . . . I always thought that that was something that could be
> appreciated. He was always in the newspaper as a high school stu-
> dent at Latin because he was a star football player or whatever and
> leading in scholastic things also, so I always held him up . . . as some-
> one to be looked at. . . . Even more so because . . . there was no
> father figure. *He was it, and he was always there, and he's . . . still
> always there.*

Denzel is also aware that his uncle, like many others, was also drawn to *him*. A steady, guileless recruiter of others' invested regard, Denzel successfully steered his way through a substantially white high school during 1960s desegregation, systematically valued for his competence, appeal, and capacity for joy:

> When I was in high school, I used to sing—I've always done something of the exceptional, whether it be football or singing. . . . I sort of excel at anything I do, . . . not because I demand it of myself, but that's just the way it happens. . . . Actually, . . . in relating to people, I'm also very inclined. . . . I've also always known how to have fun, . . . because I figure, if you're *not* going to have fun, why do something? That's always been my attitude. When I was a kid, I can remember having fun with my father. My father would ignore me, so what I would do is I'd just run, . . . and hence he gave me this name, "Speedy"—Speedy Gonzalez was that little mouse—and that's how I used to get his attention. And from that point on—that's probably one source of it, of knowing how to get attention . . . and *always* knowing how to have fun.

Denzel narrowly escaped death as a child—one of several very close passes for this inner-city black man. He was healed by the determination of the pivotal women in his life and his own capacity for regeneration. Note in what follows that he focuses *selectively* on his gratitude toward these maternal figures, toward a small girl who befriended him, and toward the literal rainbows that lit the Bavarian sky:

> When I was in Germany, I got really sick. I had scarlet fever, chicken pox, and German measles at the same time. That's why I have these scars on my face. . . . And I think that also had a great effect, because after I got out of the hospital, I was very scarred; . . . nobody would play with me. So I would have fun by myself. *[Did you almost die?]* Yes. *[What significance do you think that had to you or your mom?]* For

me, it made me realize, to this day, that you can go anytime. . . . Death, to me, isn't something to be feared. . . . It's either you're here or you're there. . . . When you're alive, do what you can do to help people and feel good about yourself; . . . but if you're dead, not much I can do for you—you're dead *[laughter]*.

Anyway, there were no other black kids in Germany; even my older brother would reject me, because I was not only sort of disfigured but also I was younger. . . . [But] there was this one young girl that was the only one that would play with me. Well, I was just so relieved that somebody would play with me. . . . I just got rid of the male dominant notion of boys only play with guns and knives and cowboy hats, because after coming out of that, I never minded playing with dolls. . . . I would play house, and even when I was a little older—nine, ten—my friend would say, "Why are you playing house?" "Because I *like* playing house."

[What was the time like that you spent alone?] Fantasy. . . . *I'd always find a rainbow.* We had rainbows . . . in Germany. . . . We lived on a mountain, so you could look from one point to another, because it would rain over here but it wouldn't rain right where you were; so it seemed like there was always a rainbow, and I was fascinated by rainbows. *[How come?]* Just the fact that they happened. The amount of colors in the rainbows. And it was a beautiful . . . scene from where we lived. It was bleak because it was an army base, but yet on the backside, there was a forest; on the front side there were hills, so . . . there was always beauty to be found, so that's what I did. *[What was powerful, in particular, do you think, about the rainbow?]* Just that it happened. Just that it *could* happen, you know? And the beauty . . . of it, I mean, from one mountain to another. From one hill to another. And . . . we're not talking small hills; we're talking . . . a mountainlike range. . . . *When you're by yourself . . . you see the rainbows.*

Thus, like so many of the resilient, Denzel organizes his faith in loving nurturance around these pivotal early incidents, and each is *inherently relational*. He goes on to say that his great-grandmother offered transatlantic folk medicine to his mother, who—ignoring the physicians tolling the knell—followed it faithfully. He thus credits their unflagging determination to keep him alive with his belief in them and in love itself. Although his alcoholic mother is terrifically disappointing to him in many ways, her mission to save him as a small child solidifies his faith:

> I knew my great-grandmother when I was one and two, and she died when we were . . . in Germany. . . . The army told my mother to get rid of me [that time I was so ill], because I was so scarred. They said, "Oh, he's going to be mentally damaged; . . . he's going to be physically handicapped. . . . Put him in a mental institution," *but my mother refused*. She brings me home and I have these big welts and scars on my body, and she talked to my great-grandmother, who said, "Put him in cornstarch for two days and just keep rubbing him," because she was Indian, and so my mother did that, and the next thing I know I'm better. All the welts went down; the scars started healing. I mean, the scabs started falling off and everything started healing. And that's all I knew of my great-grandmother.

Despite their limited interaction, so powerful is his great-grandmother's impact that Denzel conjures her image when he narrowly escapes an angry white mob as a teenager during a Chicago racial crisis. This occurs just prior to his stopping all substance use. (He feels that he abused substances to some extent as an inner-city teenager.) It is apparent in the quotes that follow that Denzel emphasizes the benevolent guardianship of his mother and great-grandmother rather than the hate of the mob. And he realizes that no racial group has a monopoly on injustice: in comments not quoted here, he remarks that one of the white mob members might easily have been beaten by a black mob later that day, with the same bat that threatened him.

The intensity of the *good* that Denzel absorbs from the nourishing figures in his life, including the love he experiences from his wife, who is white, is carved in high relief for him. Love prevails over hate in his construction of terrifying events, which is so characteristic of the resilient:

> I got out of high school. I was sixteen; I started hanging out with my boys, and we'd go buy bags of reefer and ride our bikes for miles. We got into some violent situations because of busing, almost got killed by bricks and a gun. . . . That made me realize, too, my mother was psychic. One night she begged me, . . . "Please, don't go out of the house," and I said, "Ma, I'm going out riding like I always do." She says, . . . "I'm telling you," and . . . she just started crying . . . like this wild weeping and stuff. . . . She says, "Something's going to happen," and as soon as she said it, she just ran in the house, and my friends said, "Your mother's crazy, man," and I said, "*I don't know.*" . . . Two hours later on, we ended up down by this [unfamiliar] place. . . . We go down the street, and . . . all of a sudden I hear . . . "Niggers," and I said, "*Oh, no.*" So we start riding. The next thing I know, my friend says, "This doesn't feel right," and so we're riding, and I said, "Well, let's . . . get off this street. . . . We'll hit the expressway and we'll go back up Federal Street." So we're riding, and the next thing I know, we hear . . . all these car doors. This big fat guy jumps in front of me—"I got you, nigger!" The next thing, he tries to grab me. I fall off the bike; I get ready to hit him; I look behind me. There happened to be a hundred . . . nineteen- to twenty-six-year-olds. Bricks flying by us. Guy jumps out of the car with a rifle, and we start running. I start running. My friends come zooming by me on their bikes, and I'm like, "What are you doing?" and I—the craziest thing is *the only thing I could think of was my great-grandmother*. . . . It was the wildest thing.

[What were you thinking?] Just that my great-grandmother was there, and my feet were going, and I caught up to these guys on the bikes. They were riding bikes, and I'm running in sandals, and the sandals were up around my ankles, and finally I caught up to them, and I grabbed my friend and I said, "If you leave me here, and I get out of this, I'll kill you" *[laughter]*. So he's still pedaling hard. Now I still can't picture this in my mind, and he's going down a slight hill, and I keep turning around and seeing bricks being thrown. . . . He says, "Jump on." The next thing I know I'm on the seat, pedaling the bike, and then we're out of the situation. I still can't explain it to this day. Don't know how I caught up to him. Don't know anything; and to this day, all I can think of when I think of that situation is my great-grandmother. . . . Exactly.

Thus, despite the many lacerating experiences, Denzel remains preferentially riveted upon the concerned care in his life, from which he learns how to preserve himself and others. Perhaps this focus explains why working with the resilient is so rewarding. All of us have known the frustration of pouring our considerable efforts into people who seem to make little use of anything we offer—that odd, unrequited love of Sisyphean labor. We want them to dance toward their recovery, and they cannot.

To be fair to the stumbling, it is difficult to move if you are still wearing the armor constructed to protect you from past abuse. Many long to waltz but sit out, too encumbered to hold out a hand. Others crush our toes with the weight of their cold fury. By contrast, some individuals get great emotional mileage out of very little intervention, which is gratifying to givers of all stripes. Thus I return inexorably to my focus on the *meanings that we make* about our critical experiences, the ultimate origins of which are not easily explained. *The more resilient seem to remember the good, and remember it well.* As Joanna said, "My siblings *always* thought the glass was half empty, and I *always* thought it was half full."

This reminds me of a time when I cut two pieces of pie into obviously unequal portions and gave the far larger piece to a five-year-old boy with injured self-esteem, the smaller to his envied friend. Each piece was in plain view. Half-expecting this reply but still startled, I heard the injured boy say with vehemence, "Her piece is bigger than mine." I switched the pieces immediately, and he was content. The other child surveyed the negotiations in silence, then ate her new, larger piece, baffled but greatly pleased. *Perhaps the adaptive capacity to experience deep gratitude is also unfairly distributed in the human race, although we tend to think of it as an acquired grace.*

The Reparative Kindness of Strangers

The capacity to gratefully savor the surrogate scraps life tosses— without shrinking from a keen clarity about the grievous hate encountered—is especially evident in the life of Anya, a satanic cult abuse survivor. She, too, is an unassuming psychologist with a dignified carriage, deeply respected by the seasoned clinician who referred her to this study and considered quite healthy by her therapist, a senior Boston psychologist. Anya and her colleagues work intimately with one another, having purchased a building and established a reputable psychology practice together over the course of twenty years. Now fifty and married with good satisfaction for twenty-eight years, Anya has two psychologically balanced sons in their mid twenties who enjoy her company.

Anya recalled the first of her complex, coherent cult abuse memories four years ago, when she was forty-six. Like Poet, Anya put considerable time into finding evidence to corroborate her recollections, and the material remains credible, albeit horrific. Like all the others in this study, she is a ferocious guardian of the truth. She realizes now that she dissociated from these potentially catastrophic recollections in order to *have* a life, and it worked very well. Yet she, *unlike* so many unfortunate satanic cult survivors, has never experienced significant psychopathology; nor did she marry a compromised man or reproduce anything remotely resembling catastrophic experiences in her children's lives. In fact, none of Anya's relationships outside her family of origin and the cult have ever been abusive, which her therapist and colleagues verify.

Anya's past could make you wonder why she is still ambulatory, let alone resilient. You would have expected her to shrink into a cold, tearless grief. Perhaps more than anyone else's history in this study, Anya's childhood evokes the chill sense you might have if you suddenly found yourself on an airless, extinguished planet in a remote galaxy. In stiff terror you take a step on that planet, and there, pressing its proud head through a black ash heap, is a snow crocus. Let me explain.

Unlike most others in the study, Anya found *no* sustained parental or extended family ties to light her path. Yet she had the rare capacity to build extraordinary, life-affirming meanings around slivers of care. Her most notable parental figure was, paradoxically, a sad pedophile who stumbled unwittingly into the cult and made some efforts to help Anya by inflicting less pain on her than he might have. On the surface, this might not seem to quite capture my concept of locus of hope. However, the role of context needs to be considered very carefully here. This man clearly wanted better for Anya and was severely limited in his capacity to offer her anything. *What he gave cost him his life.* While Anya recalls fierce, positive connections with peers in childhood (which is characteristic of virtually all those interviewed), this fellow offered the only semblance of effective adult surrogacy that she encountered. While I do not mean to minimize either his pedophilia or his initial participation in the cult, we *do* need to recognize that he offered Anya something life-preserving. Let us look more closely at these events from Anya's perspective:

> There was a man in the cult who befriended me, and I think that made a big difference. He protected me. He, you know, made things

less harsh for me, *and when they found out he was doing that, they killed him*. Well, it wasn't just because he was doing that, but because he was also threatening to leave, because it was much more sadistic than he wanted to be involved in, presumably. . . . I have a lot of memories about him.

[*What do you recall?*] That he would pretend to be doing those things to me that were supposed to be being done, and that he *wouldn't* be doing them, and that he liked me. There wasn't a whole lot said, but he made an attachment with me, and attachments were discouraged; they just weren't allowed at all. [*From what age do you remember him?*] Oh, early on, three or four, and he was probably in his . . . late twenties at the time. I was very on to them, and it was excruciating when I realized what was happening. Some of these things may have been staged, but that's not my memory. My memory is that they were all real, that he wanted to leave, and he felt terrible about that, because he was going to be leaving me, and I was feeling abandoned entirely, and . . . you don't leave. . . . *They hanged him. And they said it was my fault.* . . . That's how they use those kinds of things. . . . Whatever they do, they make it some way to make things worse for you. [I was] four or five, somewhere around there.

[*Did they make you bear witness to that?*] Oh, yeah [*pause*]. So . . . [*pause*] it's not so that I can tell you about what he *did* [that was positive] as much as I can tell you that it was about *feeling*, and *it was about a sense . . . of connection that he created and allowed*. . . . He probably . . . got in there by mistake because he was probably a pedophile rather than a sadist, and he didn't realize what was going on until it was too late.

Anya's description of this man is reminiscent of a portion of Nien Cheng's account of her six-year imprisonment during Mao Tse-tung's Great Proletarian Cultural Revolution.[15] Years into her solitary confinement, her captors—unable to break her spirit and gain a "confession"—wage a war of deprivation. The midday meal thins to a pile of rice at the bottom of her cup. Cut by shackles, chilled and skeletal, her fingers swollen to the size of carrots, she receives her food through a small window. As she stiffly pushes rice into her mug, she realizes that the apparently callous woman from the kitchen has buried two hard-boiled eggs at the bottom of the cup. Cheng looks up at the woman, who barks at her to avoid being thanked. Detection might end her own life.

Perhaps Anya, like Nien Cheng, invests her pedophile's minute gestures of care with a vastly different resonance than they might have in any other context. Small attempts to help are *not* small if they threaten—or cost—the giver's life. Anya's deep gratitude is apparent, even though her hero hobbles. For his help, he was hanged. Because of his help, he was a locus of hope—the only adult locus of hope that she knew. We prefer to think of hope as a soft-robed goddess, but some find it even—ironically, *chillingly*—in a pedophile.

This man's efforts need to be understood in the context of the perfunctory parental care Anya received. Although Anya's mother takes care of her competently on the surface, she is also a part of the cult. She colludes in the sexual and physical abuse of both her daughters by their father, a prominent San Francisco psychoanalyst at the time. The abuse began when Anya was three; her father was away in the service prior to that. But Anya regards her first three years alone with her mother as the absence of later horror rather than the presence of something more. Anya's reservations about her parents' capacity to offer anything substantive are based in part on her sharp recollections of her mother's third pregnancy. She recalls pride at the birth of her infant sister, who soon disappeared—presumably by sacrifice. Anya's other sister was eventually diagnosed as schizophrenic and killed herself when Anya was eighteen. Shortly afterward, Anya fell in love with her husband and left the family.

This brings us to the second major theme in Anya's overcoming: her capacity to shepherd herself effectively from an early age. This, too, is typical of the resilient. When I asked Anya how she believes she maintained psychological integrity in the face of her searing past, she replied, *"I have a calm core."* Although her circumstances seem to render her as defenseless as a penny on a railroad track, she feels that she has unusual innate ego integrity. She also believes she *recognized* her strong core early on. Self-consciously balanced on a firm emotional fulcrum, she even attempted to teach her sister survival strategies. While she now understands that such strategies may not be transferable, Anya still remains pained that she did not succeed in preserving her sister:

> How did I do it? I think I was lucky. . . . I was born with a sturdy constitution that could do what I did. I really believe that's the only answer. . . . I was born with a . . . resilient being in me . . . and . . . a *masterful* ability to dissociate, . . . in contrast to my sister. . . . She *couldn't* do it, [although] . . . I have very vivid memories of trying to teach her how to do it.
>
> *[What were you trying to teach her?]* To not pay attention, to focus on something else, to . . . *fight, to keep her fighting spirit inside and not give in*. She would get furious at me. She would say, "If you fight, it makes it worse. [Dad] gets mad or he hits you," which is true, but . . . I kept saying, *"But if you don't fight, you're going to lose yourself,"* and she did.
>
> *[How were you fighting?]* I resisted all the time. I would kick and scream and yell and run . . . at home. I'm sure I got it worse [as a result]. . . . When I just stopped fighting outwardly at one point, . . . I still felt . . . that what I was doing internally was also a total defiance of [my father] . . . and of the [cult].
>
> I *[sigh]* . . . I was trained to be a prostitute. . . . It wasn't a cult

that was focused so much on anti-Christ or evil and the devil in you. . . . [Instead,] they took a lot of the rituals as a way of torture and gaining control, but the purpose was to . . . become a prostitute. There was also pornography involved in it, and later I have one memory of being asked to carry drugs, as an older child, . . . so I had to be cooperative. . . . So . . . I don't think I've fully remembered how they managed to do this, but I remember . . . over the years just the constant torture and the constant . . . breaking me down.

Then there was this whole process of how you get signaled into becoming sexual, and it included . . . being spanked, and I don't know how that works, but it does. . . . I have a very vivid memory of the time when I could no longer stop it. I couldn't keep myself from going over into that space where they were trying to get me to go, but my memory is that I went over there and . . . I'm sexual and I'm cooperative and I'm even aroused, *but even then, I knew that I was holding onto something inside of me, and they didn't know it.* They thought they had me. *That was my victory: that they didn't know that they didn't have me.*

Thus, as my colleague Robert Kegan emphasized when he read this passage, resilience is not just about pliability—bend but do not break. It is also about *fighting:* the capacity to preserve your own soul, to preserve something that your persecutors do not get. At this juncture, I asked Anya to explain more specifically *what* she felt she was preserving, what could have kept her from splintering in the manner of other children coming of age in Satan's bedroom. She explained that she created what we might consider an inner pantheon, although she knew that these images she conjured up were of her own invention. She was able to envision, as a small child, a host of benevolent spiritual children with protective powers, charged with guarding her integrity in some inviolate manner. When I asked her what she was holding on to, she became pensive and then replied,

I want to say my heart. I have a lot of imagery around a warrior angel called Alexander. . . . I have this image of being a naked little girl and being picked up by Pegasus, . . . and then I climb up on Pegasus' back and fly up in the air. . . . Then all of a sudden, I'm turned into a grown woman and I have on this uniform that looks like a Greek army uniform from the Greek myths, so I presume that I read a book that had pictures. . . . I became this . . . woman warrior, and I was flying on Pegasus above the ground, and I looked down, and there were all these troops—troops of . . . men and women in these same outfits. . . . For miles you could see them below me. . . .

[Then] I looked down and said to them, "Who are you?" and they said, "We're here to protect you," . . . and I said to them, "Well, why didn't you do a better job?" . . . They said . . . that they couldn't cross over into my real life but that they were there to protect my spirit . . . and that I could call on them whenever I wanted to. . . . I called them my kids . . . that had different functions. . . . It feels like Alexander is one of those people, . . . but he was the one that came from this part [*gesturing toward her heart*], and *that* . . . *I hung on to.*

Anya also describes a well-internalized integrating "committee" guiding her wisely—an overarching organization of *self* highly reminiscent of my Ukrainian nesting dolls analogy:

I also have an image of this . . . conference table—it's very bizarre— up in the clouds in the sky, and there are all these wise people sitting around this table, and there's a chair for me, and I'm one of those wise people. . . . This group of people get together and make decisions about how to manage things. . . . I feel like that's more of an image about where I'm *going*, who I'm *becoming*, but somehow or another, I think they were all part of this. They were sort of . . . a governing body . . . that took care of things. I feel like I've been absent from that, and I'm about to join them. . . . I [was recently in a therapy] group that was focused on intuition [and I actually experienced, symbolically] that angel [Alexander] there with me, in all of its childlike qualities, the wings, the feathers. . . . It was really . . . quite something.

[*What was that like?*] Oh, it was overwhelming. It felt so real . . . to me; . . . it just makes me want to weep when I think about it. . . . Since then I've tried calling on him and occasionally he "comes around." But . . . not very often. . . . So sometimes it feels like it took the form of that kind of imagery that I would hold on to, and sometimes it just felt like . . . there was just a part of me, and I do associate it with my heart, but also with some sort of center that's connected to my heart, that it's just invulnerable. . . . *It was a matter of life or death to hold onto this part of myself.* . . . It's just so obvious and essential and clear to me that I don't even think about it, . . . [although] . . . it gives me great pleasure because of the way I fooled [the cult].

Altruistic Peer Relationships

Anya, as well as Dan and most of the other subjects, also spoke of fierce positive attachments to peers—either siblings or friends—as love's anchor. In a manner reminiscent of Harry Harlow's attachment deprivation experiments (always a favorite with animal rights activists), in which infant monkeys were deprived of their actual mothers and left in a cage with either wire or cloth surrogates or other young, Dan and his twin clung together for comfort.[16] They frequently hid in the bushes outside their home, shivering and hugging one another while their father literally hunted them down to beat them again. Similar peer relationships offered others solace and kind mutuality and allowed these children the opportunity to be helped themselves and to help others. Helping others allows a bit of caregiving nourishment to be felt by the young helper, albeit vicariously. It comforts some young givers simply because it feels good to them. In addition, it presumably earns them the high regard of respected adults, such as their surrogates, and gratitude from the care recipient.

Incipient peer altruism serves as a virtual developmental trigger for many, as we saw in Shibvon's case. For example, Irene, a college student who was severely battered by her mother and sexually abused by her stepbrother from age five until age eighteen, felt that her mother developed a specialized cruelty toward Irene's slightly younger brother. Once, when her grade school–age brother had a stomach flu, their mother found excrement on the toilet seat. She grabbed the brother's hair at the roots and forced him to consume the excrement in front of his friend. Galvanized by this pitiless humiliation, Irene and her brother devoted themselves to one another, both becoming older than their years. "My brother and I would really try to protect each other. I tried to stop my mother from doing something to my brother, and of course I was taking a chance, because she could turn around and lash out at me also, and she was very physical, . . . or she would ground us for months at a time." Their mutuality is reminiscent of the account given by Pulitzer Prize winner Richard Rhodes: his brother liberated them both from similarly atrocious treatment at thirteen by running away, hiding in a tunnel, seeking out the police, and insisting that the boys be placed in foster care together.[17] Many of my subjects, including Dan, ran away frequently, several as young as five or six; and they often took at least one sibling. Those who ran hit the roads. One six-year-old even took her brother, age three, on the bus to find her grandparents across town. (Consider that most children are frightened to be on their own *at home* when they are barely school-aged, let alone on a city bus.) These children were not only truly desperate; they had faith that there was a better place to be.

Anya's earlier account of attempting to help her sister indicates her deep wish to promote others' welfare even as a child. She also recalls trying to help the other captive children in the cult. When I asked her how she decided what *not* to be as a person, she focused immediately on devoting herself to the constructive treatment of her peers:

There were lots of kids in this cult, . . . and I watched them being tortured and killed. I tried every time I could to do something about it, which wasn't very often, especially with my sister. . . . Mostly in the form of bearing witness, trying to stay there so I would see it, but I often couldn't, and I had to "go away" [dissociate]; and I've always felt terrible about . . . not being able to do anything, and not being able to "stay" so that I could do something. . . .

[Remembering is an act of loyalty and an act of affiliation, isn't it?] Yes! And it feels like my connection has always been to my peers, and that's what it was then. That's where my energy was, and my focus and my guilt. . . . I did the same thing in my . . . remembered life: I put all my energy and focus there. People have said that they have other adults that were nurturing to them, and that's not my experience. . . . It was my peers and connecting to them . . . that felt like my lifeline.

[How were you trying to help the children in the cult within the very narrow confines available to you?] To talk, to reach out, to go over to comfort—none of which was allowed. . . . You'd have to sneak around to do it, if you wanted to do it: . . . eye contact, encouragement, . . . helping those look away who needed to look away [sigh], being a model. . . . And I couldn't always do it, and that always felt so crushing to me, . . . [although] I haven't thought about it in a while. . . . It just makes me feel so guilty and horrible even though my adult part said, "Well, you couldn't have done [anything more]. . . . You had to take care of yourself." . . . I would have been discouraged or killed or punished, . . . so you had to be devious in order to do it, but . . . the heart was there and that was enough.

Restorative Animal Loves

It seems that even caring for animals made a great difference to some of these children. This is not surprising, given children's fierce identification with animals: in the presence of a special animal, children often feel that they are with an alter ego, or at the very least an intimate friend. The legendary success of the Disney dynasty and most children's literature rests on this realization. Even many adults cringe when the hunters kill Bambi's mother, and this is animal *fiction*. Thus all of us seem to have some capacity to join hearts with the animal kingdom, even in industrialized America, but children are especially ripe for animal attachments. For battered children, these ties often extend the grip that keeps white-knuckled fingers from slipping off a rock ledge.

For example, after Irene spoke proudly of her jointly protective relationship with her brother, she noted how invaluable it was for her to care competently for her pets as a child. Finding virtually no warm coals and much molten lava in her mother, she savors memories of her grandparents' intense positive regard during her annual two-week visit with them in San Diego, as well as her fierce attachment to her brother and her animals. Since Irene's interview occurred in her home—in a happy, well-organized zoo of parrots, cats, and tropical fish—she demonstrated her rapport with animals throughout the four hours by managing the "crew" with insight, humor, sensitivity, and perspective. Like Rudyard Kipling's abandoned Mowgli in *The Jungle Book,* as a child she found a quality of almost parental love from her animals.[18] Now reversing roles, she gratefully continues these animal ties in preparation for creating her own *human* family with her husband.

This phenomenon is even more critical for children with thin surrogacy, no siblings, and obstructed peer relationships. For example, Eve, a social worker, is the one person in the study who had *no* significant peer relationships as a child; she sadly obeyed her mother's implicit command, "Thou shalt have no other gods before me." Captive in the family kitchen, Eve listened from earliest childhood as her mother recounted vivid, flooding memories of her own grisly childhood abuse. This unexpurgated retelling continued until recently, gloom unremitting. Eve is now forty and deals with her mother's misery with wisdom and genuinely hilarious insight. Yet she was quietly frantic and vastly helpless as a child, involuntarily witnessing uncontained maternal agony. Her mother, caught in a wrenching emotional undertow, overlooked Eve's plight.

However, Eve did have pets. She recalls seeking respite from her mother's childhood images of her flesh burning—as well as the wounds of her *own* sexual intrusion by an uncle during her toddlerhood—by settling in with her animals, calmed and calming. They quickly became her benevolent kingdom, and their accepting presence soothed her. Like Irene, Eve feels that her relationships with pets taught her something crucial about how to make viable close relationships with humans once she was beyond parental confinement. In this context Eve, Irene, and others discovered a gratifying gift for effective giving and getting. Not able to please their parents in any fundamental way, they pleased their pets. Solving the presumably simpler problems of their animals made it possible for these children to be successful "family members" *somewhere*. As one pensive, earnest six-year-old recently declared, grasping for the highest accolade she could confer upon a cherished older child who accepted and befriended her and was *never* mean, "Katie is *so* good—just *so*, so kind to me that she's *almost* good as a . . . dog."

Given my subjects' resilient creativity, we can also speculate that they brought great imaginative liveliness to their animal ties, creating rich connections reminiscent of the best animal personifications in literature. They now talk about their animal "loved ones" with an amused implicit recognition that these animals augment, rather than subordinate or replace, human love. Yet this form of natural surrogate love is gently sustaining: *it allows people to feel loved simply for being who they are*. Continuing the tradition even now, the resilient speak of their intense pleasure at awakening to patient pet faces at the bedside.

The Dynamics of Gifted Surrogate Love

From the previous accounts, we see that the resilient know all too well about attempts to purloin hope from innocents. In some respects, these attempts by their perpetrators succeeded, considering the unfettered childhoods the resilient *never* had (and the many shattered fugitives from fitful, shadowy pasts such as theirs). Yet they manage to cleave preferentially to their own humanity. Before closing the subject of surrogacy, perhaps we need to look more closely at what surrogate experiences offer to the resilient. With a richer understanding, we might encourage and amplify similar recollections in the many struggling adults we see and encourage similar relationships in the lives of children who still have a chance to find good surrogate love.

Let me first summarize the themes of effective surrogacy that have emerged in the analysis so far. First, as Romeo and Juliet knew, potent love can flourish in a short time; it can be life-giving even when the relationship spans only a few years, months, or even weeks. Unlike Shakespeare's unlucky lovers, the resilient absorbed love's light and flourished, finding similar loves later on.

Second, in all effective surrogacy—but *especially* the love that has little time—the receiver as well as the giver works to create something that is deeply life-sustaining to the resilient overcomer. The resilient certainly feel that they were given something truly extraordinary, but their many struggling siblings might not describe their time with these surrogates similarly. (Recall the esteem-injured five-year-old who saw his far larger piece of the pie as the far smaller.) Whether the resilient *found* something unique, were uniquely *responsive*, or made unique *meanings* about what they found is still a mystery. Since mine is a retrospective study, I can look only at the *ultimate* meanings that my subjects made about their experiences and conclude that the relationship itself was experienced as gifted love.

Third, the surrogates communicated—and my subjects absorbed—a sense that they were deeply special and important simply by being who they were. Unlike the conditional, manipulative, calculated, or starkly exploitative interactions that they had with their abusers, their surrogacy was founded on Carl Rogers's was very much work, and the work ethic, and *do what you have to do and don't complain*.

Joanna and Frog both recall in great detail just what was so potent about their surrogates' love. It seems to be a combination of the implicit, dignified respect that their surrogates extended and their warmth and effectiveness as human beings who had also overcome great hardship gracefully. As Joanna recalls,

My grandmother . . . was a woman of very few words. Somehow, seemingly without doing anything, I seem to have earned her respect . . . just being who I was, which helped enormously. I wasn't aware that I was doing anything special. I think she took me seriously. We didn't have that many conversations. I think, to some extent, she identified with me, and I identified with her, and that was enormously helpful, *because she was a person who had really taken charge of her life. I mean, she built a life from nothing, having been orphaned.*

[She was literally orphaned?] Yes. Her father left the family—he [was] alcoholic—when she was a little kid. There were seven kids. . . . [My] mother, my great-grandmother, was obviously very emotionally [distur]bed—I think she probably had psychotic depression or some[thing]—and just sent all the [younger] kids to orphanages and the [older on]es (my grandmother was the second-oldest) off to homes to [work]. When she was eleven or twelve, she was sent off to a home [as a m]aid. *[And she never went home again?]* No, she didn't.

[I t]hink the other thing about my grandmother that was [so h]elpful to me is that . . . *she never seemed to feel sorry for* [herself, a]nd I think that she was extremely direct. . . . People in [my family wer]en't direct. . . . If they *were* direct, it was just direct [mean]ing unconstructive. But she somehow seemed to be [saying w]hat her feelings or thoughts were in a way that [wasn't ov]erwhelming emotion but were the truth; . . . [she

celebrated "unconditional positive regard." With some sheepish apologies for sounding like the Waltons bidding one another goodnight, virtually all subjects described this extraordinary quality in their first parental or surrogate relationships. Convictional phrases such as "He loved me for who I was; I didn't need to do anything to prove myself," and "She believed I was wonderful just because I existed," and "She was strict, but she made me feel that life was worth living," and "He had a home where a kid could be a kid," and "There was never a time in all the years I knew her that she ever let me down. . . . She gave me a sense that a good person like her was *always* good. . . . There was something I could always count on" echoed through the narratives with the radiant clarity of an a cappella boys' choir.

Fourth, surrogates encouraged the resilient to let their talents unfold, whatever those strengths might be. Some of this encouragement can be characterized as survival education; it is as if the surrogates knew that they could be of limited use in stopping the actual abuse but might convey effective strategies for overcoming instead. Like the browbeaten, cowed, ineffectual, but kind father in the story of Hansel and Gretel, many collusive parents conveyed enough faith and concerned information to allow their children to find their own path out of the woods. Certainly Poet and Denzel describe this sense of potent sideline love: love that is interpreted as disappointing and life-affirming simultaneously. Such complexity places a great premium on the resilient person's capacity to integrate irony, since little that shines in their lives is undappled. As Anya demonstrates so poignantly, an occasional soul can even palm a piece of the sun within Lucifer's sepulcher.

Perhaps the most comprehensive sense of gifted surrogate giving is conveyed by Joanna and Frog, who both found it in their immigrant grandmothers. Because they capture most of the surrogacy motifs rippling through the forty interviews, I will explore their lives in some detail.

Recall that Joanna finds solid parental love in her early

formative years but necessarily augments these maternal experiences by attaching to her paternal grandmother. Although her mother obstructs this attachment, aware of her thinning connection with Joanna, Joanna's father overrides her mother's objections and takes Joanna to his mother during several of her adolescent summers.

Frog, in contrast, finds next to nothing at home. Now forty and an esteemed drama teacher in New York, he travels widely to remote cultures to study the adaptive role of theater in the struggling of the oppressed. He recently ended a five-year relationship with a woman whose career, flourishing because of her considerable talents and his sustained encouragement, took her to Kyoto. They remain fond friends.

Let me tell you more about Frog and then look at the themes that are similar in his and Joanna's lives. While growing up, Frog sees his titular parents as childish, involved in heavy gambling, and often virtually absent; thus by early adolescence, he offers the only reasonable care that his preschool siblings and their home receive. The adult Frog becomes still and sober when he recalls his brother, as a toddler, being left alone in his crib for hours by their parents, awaiting Frog's return from school. As a youngster, Frog is thus forced to navigate between the Scylla of ignoring his own teenage life and the Charybdis of abandoning his parents' children. During these early years, Frog's capacity to love was spawned by infrequent but deeply dimensional visits to his Italian grandmother, who called him *il mio piccolo professore*—"my little professor."

By age sixteen, Frog moves out to a room in his drama teacher's house, returning home to take his young sister shopping for clothes and spending the kind of time with his siblings that a concerned divorced father might. Then, in his mid twenties, he is joined by both younger siblings while he is in graduate school at Stanford; they finish high school with his sponsorship and financial support. His parents' primary struggle at that time with this process of his absorbing responsibility for their offspring is highly self-referential: ironically, they sometimes resent Frog for "taking their children

away." Revealingly, Frog's sister, Thea, recently produced and directed a widely acclaimed short film about their family, just purchased by a major educational television network. She invited various New York actors to read during casting. When her mother tried out for the role of herself, she did not get the part. Perhaps Thea was stating, in part, that more significant mothering came from her divided but highly responsive teenage brother.

Joanna and Frog, echoing the words of others about their rogates, describe them as figures with the stately grace of a ste pension bridge. They were often the only "whole" ad resilient encountered as young children, and as such immediately invoked when I asked, "Where was the life?" Here is Joanna's reply to that question:

> Concentrating on the years of nine to twenty, . .
> very good relationships. It was my paternal grandr
> subsequent best friends, . . . [and] school. .
> relationship with school, because I loved
> I *loved* it.
>
> *[What quality of light came from tho*
> *ditional love when you're a little*
> mother—*is really great*. I really
> lovable, and that certainly is
> there was the—you know—
> fourth grade. So . . . the m
> first eight years, and ju
> tragedies. . . .
>
> But the poir
> very select rel
> had come f
> people's hous
> from whom, I thn.

could] call it like it was, and that was so refreshing. . . . She really sized people up very well; . . . you got a really honest answer from her. It was enormously helpful. Even if you didn't like it, you knew she wasn't manipulating you at all.

[So she had a capacity for unconditional positive regard and simultaneously was very clearheaded and authentic about her perceptions.] Yes, yes. She also always made work seem attractive. She always made doing things seem good and useful, . . . like you were creating a life. . . . There was even something about the way she just managed a household that made me think, "Wow! You know, I could do that."

So she was certainly a very bright point, and again, it's not like I had that much access to her until I was in high school. . . . We'd spend maybe a week or two with them in the summer. . . . Never holidays, because they lived 800 miles away. . . . It wasn't quantity; it was those interactions. . . . And I had the incredible good fortune to go up there and spend summers with my grandmother; . . . that was just pivotal.

The leitmotifs that ripple through this passage are consonant with what others in the study describe: surrogates who seemed to make life full and rewarding, who did not shrink from hard work, who were not given to spells of self-pity, who shared what they had, and who told the truth. Many of them were immigrants and orphans themselves; perhaps they communicated their own resilient overcoming to receptive recipients. When my subjects tried to describe what they felt in their surrogates' presence—even those surrogates whom they did not see very often or for very long—their faces often shone with a luminous vitality. Frog elaborates on all these themes vibrantly and tenderly, capturing both his steadfast devotion to his Italian grandmother and her life-affirming love. For him she has the elegant, stoop-shouldered beauty of an aging iris. Even her simple presence was nourishing:

My grandmother would cook things for us, and she would . . . just let me play without . . . telling me to wash the dishes or . . . scrub the floor. . . . I could just actually be in her house and . . . invent these games with . . . little toy soldiers or playing cards or plastic dinosaurs and . . . go on for hours without having to feel like, "Oh, no . . . my mother's in the next room, and she's going to make me do something [like clean her home for hours]." . . . *[It was] this feeling . . . that she loved you and you just had this freedom that you didn't have to do anything, just read.* . . . She would call me her *piccolo professore*—her little professor—because I would come with my books to her house and sometimes I would just sit in her big easy chair and read; and I could do that. But in my mother's house, I couldn't do that, because she would find me and make me do something. *[Did your mother take care of the house at all, or did she expect you to do most of it?]* Either there was a maid or me, so I was . . . interchangeable with the maid.

[My grandmother] was the only person that was really our family. *She was the only person that on the holiday we would want to go and see.* . . . It wouldn't make any difference whether we saw my mother or not, but we'd go and see my grandmother.

Frog reveals his deep, lifelong attachment to his grandmother in his extraordinary sense of connection to her when he is in Bali. Although she dies in the United States while he is in Bali, he experiences her through the natural world and the rituals of a people that esteem their similarly deep, reverential attachments to their ancestors:

She died . . . just this past spring. . . . In retrospect, I would never have been so close to her [at her death] with the kind of ceremony that they had here [in the United States]. It wasn't nearly as powerful as the ceremony that I had [in Bali], and there would have been all these distractions with all those people. [But in Bali] I had a very real connection between me and her. It lasted . . . practically the whole two months that I was there.

In Bali, when somebody dies, they take that person's ashes to the sea, . . . and . . . they make offerings with flowers and rice. Then they set the person adrift in the sea . . . and burn incense, so I did that. . . . I didn't know all the exact requirements on how to arrange the flowers, but I did a makeshift offering of flowers and incense . . . with a little frog and a little flower that was like a butterfly, because she would always say that she wanted to be free like a butterfly. That's why she didn't ever live with my mother or my aunt; she always lived alone until she went to the nursing home. I always told her in Italian, *"Tu sarai sempre la mia farfalla ligero, e io saro sempre il tuo piccolo professore"*: "You will always be my free butterfly and I will always be your little professor." That was the dedication that I made to her in my book [*weeping*].

When I was in Bali, I just felt like the whole island practically was my family. I'd see people that I knew from the performances fifteen years ago; I hadn't been back for fifteen years, and they still remembered me. . . . I went to a Balinese funeral . . . where they cremated . . . a very old woman inside the body of a giant bull. . . . [The woman who died] was actually someone . . . who was from the Balinese family that I had lived with the first time I was there, so it was almost like it was a member of my family; and I went to that cremation as if it were [my grandmother's] cremation. . . . The bull burned away until it was only these four legs still standing and you could see the place where it used to be, but it wasn't there. I don't know where *she* was, but she wasn't there. I cried about that.

And I would see a lot of butterflies in Bali, and they would actually come and they would sit on my hand. It was really like *she* would come and talk to me, because I never before . . . had butterflies come and sit on me. Usually they're scared, but they would come and sit on my hand. *And I felt like she sent them.* Bali is a place where people are very close to their ancestors, even after they're dead, so I felt very close to her the whole time I was there. *And I was very connected to her in spirit through those ceremonies and through the butterflies.*

Thus Frog locates his bedrock faith in himself and the world's benevolent possibility through his kinship with this unusual woman. As an immigrant, she was a stranger in a strange land who sustained her own faith in human good. Now Frog travels widely as a scholar, making strong connections with the families that he studies, led by her convictional light. Ironically and sadly, her daughter—Frog's mother—made little use of her mother's grace:

[My grandmother] had faith . . . in me, that I would do something good, and faith in people. . . . Even when she didn't like them very much, she still . . . felt something kindly toward them, so her belief in people and her belief in the saints and the angels were all tied together. . . . So when I go to places and put myself at the mercy of the world and the people in the world, I feel like I'm putting myself at the mercy of the saints, and . . . it's partly because of her really good relationship with the saints [and with me], . . . especially in Italy. . . . When I went to Mantua I saw the church, saw the special saints of Benedict that she always had pictures of [because they were so important to her]. [*Why do you suppose you were able to make so much use of the goodness, faith, and love in her, and yet her own daughter was so very troubled?*] Mmmm . . . I don't know. I get the impression from talking to my grandmother . . . and my mother's sister that my mother was just always self-obsessed, self-involved, . . . so she didn't bother to look at any of those qualities that her mother had. . . . There also could have been qualities in my grandmother that were difficult to live with, but I didn't have to live with that . . . so they never got in the way.

On a final note, we need to credit many of the failed parents of the resilient with a hidden strength: *the capacity to let their children go*. For some, like Shibvon, this is overstating the case. Shibvon was expelled without concern for whom she might find in whatever roadside ditch she was shoved. By contrast, others felt that their parents at least tolerated or even quietly encouraged an attachment to surrogates who offered them what their parents could not give. This is well illustrated in Joanna's case. She felt that her father ignored his children entirely until they were young adolescents (whereupon he became a rather attentive and supportive parent, oddly enough); yet he challenged her mother's vehement objections to Joanna's spending her adolescent summers with her paternal grandmother, as if he knew, by then, that neither of them could offer the same sustenance to their child that she could. He was right. Similarly, Poet's father encouraged every extrafamilial relationship she formed; and Frog's mother gave him time off from cleaning the house to see her mother once a month.

Margaret, a resilient novelist, stumbled into the care of nursery teachers who annually raised the age limit at their summer preschool to allow her uninterrupted attendance. They finally hired her as a teacher's aide at their camp in her tenth summer (presumably lowering the age limit for enrollees again). Margaret's vituperative mother, while ignoring Margaret's timid reports of repeated sexual intrusion at age seven by her late-adolescent stepbrother, still drove her to these surrogates and paid the bill for a decade. Although she had been inert with terror as a child, Margaret recently found the enraged blade of her adult voice artfully expressed in several successful mystery novels, perhaps so well transformed in part because her acidic mother let her *go*, however unceremoniously, to something more.

In any case, almost all of the resilient, as children, did steal away to find another love. Whether the permission was begrudging, dutiful, or heartfelt, it was nonetheless *granted*. Some of these failed parents must have known, at some level, that their children would get from others what they themselves could not offer—a creditable form of giving in itself. Think of the many imprisoning parents who will *not* tolerate their children going to anyone else, who rip at the roots of surrogate care and salt the soil.

Similarly, the surrogates intuitively avoided pinioning the resilient in untenable loyalty conflicts. This restraint, always a relief, was experienced somewhat differently when it was found outside the family than when it was inside. When a surrogate was outside the nuclear family, the subjects felt relieved when they, as children, were spared the indignity of hearing vitriol about their parents—no matter how accurate it might have been. Yet they felt that their plight was fundamentally understood, and they were grateful for their gifted giver's concerted efforts to offer them respite. They did not expect more than that. On the other hand, if the giver was a *parent*, their gratitude was more ambivalent: while appreciating this more humane parent's circumspection—and hating the divisive malice of the abusing parent—they also felt abandoned by the one person who was in a position to make a significant difference. In neither case did they seek retaliatory retribution toward their persecutors. However, they yearned for their kinder parent—if there was one—to confront the villain and introduce accountability and thus protection into their lives. Compensatory kindness is simply not enough.

Despite these limitations, the resilient launched forth on improvised love, pushing beyond the cratered hearts that failed them. With fierce fidelity to a nascent vision, they journeyed on. Next we follow them during the strong midmorning sun of adolescence, when increasing autonomy, skill, and resolve propel them into many more occasions for surrogate care.

CHAPTER FOUR

The Later Loci of Hope: Adolescent "Adoptive" Relationships as Developmental Opportunities

I noted earlier that the resilient are characterized by a deeply held conviction that they deserve love. I also noted that my data suggest that this conviction took hold early in their evolution. Now we need to consider what organizes and sustains that convictional hope long after early positive ties have soured or meetings with extraparental surrogates have ebbed.

Assumptive Lenses: The Expansion of Self During Adolescence

I find that the concept with the best explanatory power is *internalization*. That is, these individuals not only form attachments to early parental figures, surrogates, and/or themselves, but they internalize those attachments *effectively* and *selectively* so that even when the resilient are not with these figures, their influence is profound and cumulative. This chapter focuses, then, on the ongoing process of surrogate attachments and their concurrent internalization during adolescence. My thesis is that, through profoundly important attachments outside the family of origin, the adolescents—now more cognitively and affectively complex—elaborate their vision of a better life. The visions themselves are the subject of Chapter

Five, but here you will find some foreshadowing of these inextricably interwoven phenomena. In sum, resilient relationships unfold,
become selectively internalized, and contribute to an extensive
vision of life's promise—a vision that is embellished over the life
span. Thus resilience is a cumulative process, not a product, and is
open to all in some measure.

While a comprehensive exploration of adolescence is beyond
the scope of this work, there are several capacities emerging within
this wider developmental avenue that are especially germane to the
adaptive talents of the resilient. I mention them schematically now
and elaborate further in the subsequent analysis.

First, adolescents' increasing skill in negotiating a broader environment is highly relevant to the battered and abandoned. As children, they were necessarily rather stationary, like so many evergreen
branches reaching out through accumulating snow. By adolescence,
however, they can competently walk, ride, hike, fly, and even bike
away from trouble. With increasingly complex cognitive understandings of how communities connect with one another, adolescents finally see the larger world as traversable. One enterprising
sixteen-year-old fled his explosive alcoholic Long Island home on
a Raleigh ten-speed, arriving in upstate New York five days later to
live with a farm family and their new baby. Some babysit their way
out of hell. Finally exercising substantial choice over their associates and their time, many spend days and nights at others' homes
so often that they achieve unofficial "adoptive" status. They can
now bask in a saturated exposure to love's alternatives, in contrast
to their stolen hours or occasional days with childhood surrogates.
Since teenagers are *expected* to be away from home for long hours,
social norms often mask what is tantamount to a reprieve for the
resilient. Because their travels invariably put them in contact with
greater numbers of adults, they find extensive sources of feedback
on who they are and what they can do. For many of my subjects, it
was a flooring surprise to realize how many people liked them. Such
consensual validation prompted many to revise the sorry (some-

times partially loathsome) view of themselves formed in the distorting lens of parental perception.

Teenagers can also earn significant money by midadolescence, which enables them to pay for some food and transportation as well as justifying hours away from home. Because our national Calvinism nearly deifies hard work, "getting out" through the work force renders the resilient especially valued by adults, thus buttressing their flagging self-esteem. Work may also pose a less threatening alternative to jealous abusive parents, who might obstruct their offspring's access to an actual family. For example, Stan, a highly competent community mental health organizer, virtually lived at the grocery store that employed him as a diligent teenager, attaching to an admiring adult worker in the stockroom during long business hours.

And work was not the only escape. Shibvon stayed with a skeletal crew of students in her nursing school dormitory during Thanksgiving and Christmas vacations, although the administration knew her home was a mile away. Larry camped outdoors each weekend with a vigorous Boy Scout troop throughout several New England winters, preferring the predictability of an unheated lean-to to his heated and lean home life. Rita, a sexually abused sixteen-year-old, misrepresented her age and quietly maintained a room at the YWCA, relieved that house rules precluded a romantic life. Discovering her white lie, the perceptive director let her stay, providing welcome respite from childhood sex forced upon her by her foster father. Painted into tight corners, my subjects became as ingenious as they were fearfully determined. Virtually all of them slipped away to find some sun.

This ingenuity is possible in adolescents because they finally have the mobility, skill, relative self-sufficiency, and cognitive complexity to embroider adaptive strategies that will take them into more promising niches. Although, like deer stunned by headlights, many abused teenagers stay home or suddenly bolt, terrified, toward an oncoming eighteen-wheeler, my subjects most often cited *getting out gracefully* (or gracefully enough) as their central mission during this time. Most went on to a program with formal structure, such as trade school, the armed services, or college. With good executive competence in at least *some* area, they continued recruiting supportive others who taught them adaptive occupational skills and usually far more. When we recall the many sad waifs with similar pasts who end up turning tricks in Times Square, these resilient adaptations become even more startling.

In addition, the adolescents' physical strength, blossoming sentience, and increasing autonomy lead some to definitively challenge the bullies that plague them. Thus many, like Dan and Anya, reported their first (and usually last) fisticuffs with their fathers during their teens, and most of the sexually abused found their dissenting voices at the same time. Recall that the age of sexual consent is at mid- to late adolescence in most states, providing even legal recognition that children cannot be considered willing participants until they are developmentally able to refuse sex. Although several in this study, such as Poet and Margaret, found the remarkable courage to disclose as children, most did not. Remember that their designated protectors had failed them. Perhaps the other children intuitively realized that others would dismiss them, too. However, many did take a resolute stand against their perpetrators during their teens, finding the first developmental moment that the word *no* could hold firm. Whatever the cost, repelling a persecutor often puts an empowering rein back in one's own hands.

At the same time, few of these advances are possible without the increased perspective-taking capacities for which adolescence is an essential, although not necessarily sufficient, condition. Increased abstraction allows the resilient to continually build on the selectively internalized models of self and other that allow love, rather than hate, to predominate in their relationships. In the service of love's search, the resilient continue to recruit others over time, integrating their experiences into a humane model of decency and reciprocity. Various and sometimes surprising arenas emerge, including extended families, neighbors, the Boy Scouts, ham radio contacts, friends' families, teachers, jobs, the unlikely armed services, and romantic relationships.

Romance is the high noon of recruited love, and for many it blazes over decades. But to achieve romance, adolescents must recognize that other models of interaction exist than those they grew up with and embellish these with some sophistication over time; otherwise, they risk a quick repetition of parental folly. What enables the more hardy to forge a robust *vision* of a better love?

Elaborating on the cognitive developmental theory of Jean Piaget, recent developmentalists, such as Sharon Parks, Laura Rogers and Robert Kegan, Robert Goodman, Gil Noam, Michael Basseches, Ann Fleck-Henderson, and Betsy Speicher are exploring the affective implications of formal operational thought.[1] It seems that adolescents' increasing capacity to relativize their own experiences in the wider social context—to see their own families as only one example of a larger category of "human families"—is one expression of this process. Recall your own dawning realization that your family was one of many families, with its own oddities and quirks, only part of a larger whole rather than *the* nation to which vague, shrunken foreign territories were compared. For the resilient, increased adolescent perspective deepens a crucial, early recognition that their families are indeed anomalous. Prior to this relativizing in mid- to late adolescence, the family is much like the air one breathes—implicit rather than explicit, no matter how vital. Continuing the analogy, it is as if in adolescence the resilient begin to recognize, analyze, and gradually metabolize noxious familial pollutants, eventually drafting and enforcing clean-air legislation rather than simply being choked by the acrid vapors of a withering past.

To accomplish this, adolescents must conceptually shift their families from the foreground to the less focal background, leaving room for the advance of another, more effective model of family life. For many, "better" is sustained in other families—families that become ascendant rather than subordinate to their families of origin. To do this, my resilient subjects sought—and found—active, ongoing, lively connections with others during adolescence that gave them expanding evidence about *which* "somewhere" was a better place to be.

This period of cognitive and affective growth can also usher in (without guaranteeing) adolescents' hypothetical reasoning in the interpersonal domain, thus enabling them to reflect on their own thinking and systematically take in the perspective of others. While we vary in our ability to employ these capacities, they are *possible* for many adolescents and seem to be used with particular depth and breadth by the resilient, who continue reflecting upon empty or execrable family interactions in a highly sophisticated manner. Refusing to repeat the past, they sustain outside relationships that are often enriched by their unusual, highly gratifying empathic capacity to march a mile in another's moccasins. Those who married successfully by their early twenties continued to develop empathy in this context and became more effectively attuned over time. Virtually all now occupy gratifying professional niches that place a premium on highly accurate, humane perceptions of both self and other. In addition, most now have the added abstracting capacity to step outside their interpersonal negotiations.[2] Like thoughtful drama critics, they can evaluate their interactions with others as if they were in the role of each actor while simultaneously integrating the diverse perspectives. Thus they have evolved an independent ideology of interaction that is closely responsive to others and themselves, making their empathic talents especially adaptive for them.

While I am not postulating a smooth upward developmental trajectory for the resilient (since many struggled with considerable depression and anxiety during adolescence and on into adulthood), I *am* claiming that they remained devoted to a humane model of care, determined to seize a strong future. In large measure, they now live the lives they envisioned, although they describe many detours and derailments along the road (as Chapter Seven, on struggles in love, attests). However, although most struggled significantly during adolescence, their struggles were more trouble to *themselves* than to others—a style consistent with measurably higher levels of ego development.[3] Internalizing their pain rather than inflicting it on others—and terribly *aware*—they held themselves accountable for their own recovery and eventually forged rather good mental health in the bargain.

Safe Harbors Promoting Autonomy and Competence

In the pages that follow, I will present a variety of settings in which the resilient gained respite and perspective. All these settings offered a coherent, implicit model of human decency. The specific settings mentioned in the discussion and quotes that follow—school, summer internships, and Boy Scouts—exemplify *any* setting in which adolescents can sustain ties. They provided safety and simple, visceral care, although, if you recall the glances of Anya's pedophile and the furtive but affirming eggs buried in Nien Cheng's cup, a contrasting context can make the *meaning* of the care complex and precious. The resilient continually underscore the power of simple, open, even circumscribed availability, reminding us all that we do not have to pull a dove out of our sleeve to make a difference.

I will also focus on those relationships with extended family members, college teachers, neighbors, or other attuned adults in any setting that encouraged adolescents to *reflect* on their plight, fostering critical examination and systematic insight. These settings offered them their first evaluative framework for understanding just how and why their homes were so skewed. While few found this framework in formal therapeutic relationships, many found psychologically sensitive surrogates willing to let them puzzle and grapple. Because adolescents, as opposed to children, more commonly have an independent adult friend, such reflective relationships become more sanctioned and extensive in this era. Here the resilient finally found room to explore their open disillusionment and pain. For many, this was the first time adults did not ask them to paper over their extensive hurts or attempt to silence their struggling with paltry platitudes about a parent who "means well" or "loves you beneath it all." Even when these sentiments *are* true (which is rare), they are little more than the glittering sun-sequins that brighten polluted harbors. Just below the dazzle lurks a sunken bed frame, young starfish twisted into its rusted springs. With relief, many resilient adolescents finally found surrogates willing to dredge *with* them, permitting them to honor their own naked-emperor truths about their challenging parents.

Schools

My first focus concerns those ties that soothe rather silently. Without directly acknowledging the adolescent's plight, many surrogates in schools quietly offered graceful respite and encouragement. Although daunting for so many teenagers, school can also be an especially effective setting for the intellectually competent, the socially engaging, and those who are talented in a particular domain. Although many of my subjects are all three, others found focal areas in which to shine. For some, school was the first or only order they had encountered. As Marie, a legal aid lawyer in her mid-thirties remarked, it was the first time that

> *what I did had an impact*. . . . I somehow interacted with my environment to produce results, which was a feeling I never had in my house. . . . School was fairly organized. There's somebody out there taking charge and setting some boundaries that are reasonable, identifiable, meetable. . . . Certainly the structure itself made it a lot easier. . . . *You're not busy constructing your own universe all the time*. . . . Before I was in school, . . . it was just chaos and disaster on every horizon and no predictability. I just never knew what was going to happen.

Some subjects did say that their attachments to teachers, who are also standard-setters, placed a premium on their performing perfectly: the young people were terribly eager to please and be seen. In retrospect, they believe that they had room to flounder; but at the time, their personal grading scale contained only A plus and F minus. Anything that was not the former was the latter. As Diana, a trauma psychologist, remarked, "I was horrified if I got a B." They gradually realized, however, that maintaining tyrannical standards for oneself is unkind and can even compromise one's judgment. Exhausted by this tenacious competition with their own standards, many subjects have since put strong effort, informed by insight, into relaxing these demands. I am reminded of one professional woman with a newborn who became overly discouraged when she could not effectively use a breast pump at the office, although she was nursing her baby well at home. Her sense of inadequacy continued until I pointed out to her that it was rather like worrying about being inorgasmic with an inflatable sexual surrogate. The pump was retired.

For the more depleted of my subjects, school often served as a deceptively simple safe haven. Like spring bulbs forced out of season in their childhoods, they were simply too exhausted to bloom in adolescence. Several found responsive surrogates who allowed them time to lie fallow until they could flower with fervor in their college and adult years. For example, you might recall Margaret, the successful novelist in her mid forties who found refuge in her summer nursery school and its ever-ascending age limits. She was systematically sexually abused for years by a stepbrother over a decade older. However, perhaps the crueler irony in her life was that her mother pursued a career as a respected parenting expert while remaining collusive, bilious, and cold at home. When Margaret repeatedly disclosed her ongoing abuse to her mother, she was either ignored or covertly attacked. Fleeing intolerable toxicity and hypocrisy, Margaret sought childhood solace in school and her affirming father, a man akin to Poet's loving but emotionally blind sire. She also attached deeply to her best friend's mother, whose inviting home was on an adjacent property across a field, easily crossed when streets were still off limits. Her surrogates apparently knew she was struggling with dark forces at home, although they probably did not know the fine print. They simply took her in. Finally, sustained deliverance arrived for Margaret at boarding school. Here her care was more subtle but no less effective, since she read between the lines and absorbed her respite with gratitude. At the same time, she began to see her family through other people's eyes. This permanently altered her own vision:

When I was at Bartlett Academy and I went out on a date, I got caught, and they sent me home for a week. Then my mother had to meet with the headmistress, and I did, too. . . . Mother said to me, "You know, she thinks you're really unhappy and that you're probably better off at school than at home," which was very insightful for my mother. *[Recall that she was a parenting expert.]* Mrs. Jenson [the headmistress] was . . . watching this relationship [between my mother and me], and she passed me once in the hall and said, "How are you?" . . . She was a very highly regarded headmistress. . . . She was nice, and we were all a little bit afraid of her, not in a bad sense, but . . . we were very respectful of her, though we liked her; and she said, "Did you have a nice visit with your mother?" I thought she was talking about Thanksgiving, and so I said, "Yes, we went and did this and this, . . ." and she said, "No, no—last week, when your mother was on campus." I said, "My mother was on campus?" and she said, "She came to see me, and then she came to see you, . . ." and I said, "No, she didn't. . . ."

I think that was the first moment when I realized how bad things were: [seeing the] shock in Mrs. Jenson's face that this woman would come all the way to school to see the headmistress and not bother to see her daughter. . . . It was right after I was . . . [caught dating]: she could have thrown me out of the school, and she never did. I

think she made it very clear [to the faculty], "This is a girl with problems, . . . and they're not of her own making," and she kept me in
the school. . . . I remember other girls were thrown out for doing the
same kind of thing: being caught smoking or . . . dating, or being
caught with a boy. . . . I never got into trouble after that, but I think
she understood the difference between a child who's carrying something else from home and one who's just being disobedient. . . .

[She saw with a third eye?] Yes, and she kept me in the school;
and I was grateful for that, very grateful. I didn't understand it at the
time. . . . I looked back later and thought that I was very lucky to
have stayed, because I otherwise would have gone to another prep
school or gone to high school at home, in which case I would have
been just like [my brother Art, who eventually became psychotic].
It would have been a nightmare. *Sometimes I think that's the most that
anybody can do—that they can be kind to the ones that come along—
because if she had tried to intervene, there's no telling what my mother
might have done to me. So it's . . . dangerous to intervene. [Without
authorization, you mean?]* Yes.

Note here the cognitive and deeply affective shift in Margaret's
own awareness as she registers her headmistress's shock. In a relativizing moment, she sees (or finally allows herself to see) how bad
things really are at home and realizes that she has been cast unwill-
ingly in a domestic drama. Feeling suddenly disembedded from her
prior life, she finds herself metaphorically catapulted upward, now
sitting in the lap of a spectator in the balcony, watching through
her eyes in distress as the drama unfolds on stage. This kind of relativizing and perspective-taking holds a liberating potential in that
it increases the adolescent's comprehensiveness of viewpoint,
although Margaret notes that she is simply too depleted at that time
to do much more than notice the headmistress noticing. She is
grateful simply to sit in her new safety. At the same time, she stores
this pivotal, perhaps transformative moment and mines it later,

soon separating from her family and gradually developing a highly differentiated, fierce, and autonomous construction of the interactions that she will and will not have with them. While her path has been overgrown with guilt and uncertainty, her current resolution is a joyful clearing.

Considering this historical moment, Margaret feels grateful for her headmistress's protective circumspection in the context of offering humane shelter. She was well aware even then that the cultural climate in the fifties and sixties was too anemic to encourage any serious help for the maliciously treated, a frequent theme across the interviews. She, like Shibvon, Dan, and many others, felt that a safe harbor and tacit recognition of her straits served her far better than a partial, thus ineffective, challenge to her mother under these cultural circumstances. She now believes that, unless children are going to get reasonably *competent* help, they may be helped as much or more by being in a protective setting that does not address the effects of their abuse directly. What sensible blind adult trusts a bargain-basement guide dog? Which self-preserving president wants Secret Service agents of middling talent? As Margaret notes so poignantly, "We ask courage of children that we don't ask of ourselves." Lacking competent abuse intervention, she sustained *herself* in large measure, reassured by the respectfully sheltering presence of her headmistress and the faculty:

> Most of the time when I was growing up, I was so isolated, and I thought that . . . this was just one more misery that you had to live through; and by the time I was fourteen or fifteen, I was saying to myself, "Time will carry you over. . . . The world is designed in such a way that time passes; . . . you'll survive it, just because time will pass and you won't die from it. . . ." People have to understand that children who have been abused, and who are living with abuse, . . . see themselves day to day. . . . *It's getting through the afternoon [that's focal]; . . . you don't worry about next month. . . .*

It was a very bleak time, and at prep school . . . I didn't want to compete. I just wanted to be there. . . . I just . . . wanted to be safe. [You wanted to not be at home?] Yes. I knew I was safe. . . . I didn't care about being the most popular or anything. I was just . . . recovering; . . . it was like a long rest cure for me. And Mrs. Jenson understood that and was nice to me, and I think she told the rest of the teachers, "This one has to stay. Be nice to her." [She was] being kind when kindness is . . . not forcing the child to make a courageous step. We ask courage of children that we don't ask of ourselves.

Please do not misinterpret this passage. Margaret and others resoundingly applaud the requisite, definitive interventions that benefit so many abused children *now*, when more reliable help is available. Many of us are *mandated* reporters; it is imperative that we contact protective service agencies regarding any known abuse. Although underfunded and beleaguered, these agencies often do a decent job within the limits that confine them. And if a bargain-basement guide dog walks you and your client into bushes or the Secret Service agent takes a smoke during the cavalcade, you now have far more leverage to jump-start the languid protective service system; and you *must*. Margaret also insists that, if you *are* going to address an adolescent's abuse, it is imperative to offer that person explicit guidelines about what abuse is, how to describe it, and precisely how to find the people who can help. She and others stressed that it is critical to offer children and adolescents a reality that is an alternative to the one they live in. Given that their family's reality is implicit and still largely unquestioned, they need to see that there *is* another view.

Returning to my earlier points about adolescent reasoning, this is exactly the relativizing shift that allows critical reflection in all domains during adolescence for those who have made that transition. Since school itself fosters critical evaluation (or it *should*), adolescents develop conceptual strategies that they can apply to their own personal circumstances when the time is ripe. For the mal-treated, this gives an opportunity to start calculating; they sow reflective seeds that may germinate once the adolescents acquire enough economic independence to stand on their own higher ground. As an adolescent in the early sixties, Margaret was simply not ready to move beyond her silence. This is characteristic of many maltreated people, especially the sexually abused. Thus she asks us to summon, *before* we intervene, the staples of keen judgment in any profession: careful observation, competent investigation, and that stately sequoia of all human intervention, sensitive timing:

> [Children in distress] know things are bad; [but they] don't know that they're *wrong*, and [they] don't necessarily know that adults will act on them. . . . I remember people trying to get me to talk, and I wasn't quite sure what they were up to. Was it just one more ploy the way my mother was a ploy, where she could set me up to knock me down? She was . . . always so good at it. . . . You can keep oth-ers—*strangers*—at a distance, but you still can't keep the parent at a distance, and sometimes adults [like teachers] . . . have to say, "*These* are the things in a family that are normal, and these are the things that are not normal," and just say them to a child *so that the child can start calculating*. If only somebody had told me, "If a brother or a relative does this, it's wrong; and this is what you can do about it, and this is what will happen." *[That would have helped?]* Enor-mously! . . .
>
> Practical details [are essential]. . . . It doesn't do any good to say, "Talk to the minister" . . . if the only time you see him is . . . during the sermon. . . . Are you going to go up in the sermon and say, "By the way, [I'm being sexually abused by my stepbrother]"? *[Laughter.]* Tell [abused children] how this is possible, instead of just [saying], "Talk to the minister." [Tell them,] "He has an office, and he keeps his door open, and I sort of went by one day." Work [the logistics] out [for them]. . . . Stop actually defining things in terms of

adults. . . . You're not trying to get something out of an adult; you're trying to empower a child . . . who has to take the first step, who has to say, "This has happened to me. . . . Where do I go?"

Although Margaret, like Poet in the previous chapter, is highly articulate, she had no words or images for her abuse as an adolescent. Thus she adamantly asks us to help children *find* the words that will heal them.

I don't think I would have been able to say "sexual abuse"—I didn't know there was such a word—but if you know a child is disturbed, then you have to let [that child] talk it out in whatever words [he or she] can find. . . . It's not just good enough to . . . ask leading questions. I think what adults do is ask leading questions hoping the child will by accident reveal [the abuse]. . . . I think adults really are afraid . . . of being embarrassed, making a mistake, stirring things up that won't calm down; . . . but the risk is all of this tremendous loss of . . . life for small children [and adolescents], so you have to be more practical.

. . . Mrs. Jenson asked me to see the school counselor, but I didn't understand what I was there for, because I didn't know that I was troubled, and I *wasn't*, . . . you know; *my mother* was troubled. . . . I just wanted to get on with things, just survive. . . . Children who've been through that kind of thing—they have so much static, you know; . . . we sort of develop static to screen out all the hostility that comes from the parent and so we screen out a lot of other things, too. . . . Just do your best to understand. *Sometimes all you can do is be a friend, but . . . if you can be a friend, . . . that helps enormously.*

As we leave Margaret, it is important to note that she was able to benefit from what her headmistress and faculty offered because she had an *authorized* relationship with them. Student/teacher, sitter/neighbor, niece/aunt, Scout/troop leader, and parishioner/ clergy are all potential "holding environments" or restorative relationships that allow resilience to unfold. While the trauma literature and the jarring daily news remind us of how often adults abuse the power of their relationships (and remind us they should, since even a little is too much), the majority of helpers are *not* abusive. Virtually every subject in this study had one or several adults in adolescence with whom she or he had a sanctioned tie, and the depth of their gratitude extends over several decades. Thus, through robust surrogacy, we repeatedly see the essential relational quality of resilient adaptation, as well as the importance of goodness of fit and the role of chance events in the formation of these relationships.

Summer Respite

John Roger, the taciturn forty-six-year-old machinist mentioned earlier, believes his adolescent transformation had two major sources. The first was his steadfast, self-sufficient productivity at a state agricultural high school, coupled with a good placement for the summer internship required by the school. When John Roger was fifteen, a kind crony alerted him to two openings on a Vermont farm run by a lumber magnate, risking his own chances of returning by inviting John Roger to apply with him. Essentially a failure-to-thrive adolescent until then, his growth stunted by poor nutrition and neglect, John Roger emerged from the farm five months later literally ten inches taller and sixty pounds heavier, though still slender.

The second tributary to John Roger's adolescent metamorphosis was his own underlying conviction that, despite being the fourth of eight ill-fed children whose pugnacious father repeatedly predicted worthless futures for all, *he* was going to *be* somebody. He portrays his father as a committed idler, strident bigot, and gratuitous spoiler. As if severe privation were not enough, this man—a thug carelessly tossing firecrackers into an aviary—lined his children up during childhood and predicted a bad end for all. John Roger's mother was too emotionally depleted and removed to offer any support; all she had went into surviving a husband banished from the state of Maine for years of vicious brawling and one attempted murder. Neither parent attended a single ritual event in John Roger's life—not even his graduation, his wedding, or the christenings of his children.

Recently, when his parents reached retirement age, his father made an abrupt, unilateral decision to cast his wife out of the house after calculating that this maneuver would maximize his pension benefits. Unconcerned about her plight in the face of such cost-cutting cleverness, and disregarding a half-century of marriage, he left their adult offspring scrambling to secure housing for his elderly wife. This added a telling coda to the score that left several of this man's children jailed, failed, or drunk in the street. But not his underfed middle son.

John Roger's trickling developmental course changed during adolescence. While he had difficulty comprehending what he read and usually communicated in simple, staccato sentences, his quiet competence and conviction apparently evoked a strong response in Sam, the munificent lumber magnate offering the summer internships, as well as a variety of other recruitable surrogates. In his own words, "I'm not the best talker in the world, obviously, and I'm not the best teacher, . . . but I know what I can do personally, and I know what I can't do." John Roger's ingenuous decency was (and is) deeply appealing to others. Fed literally and then emotionally by several nonexploitative males on this unusual farm, he quickly metabolized this vastly different, renewing way of life. Here he describes Sam's startling presence—a man who might seem larger than life to many of us but appeared nearly mythic to a parched street kid:

> I don't think I've ever seen a guy like Sam. [It] was like you going up and talking to the President of the United States. I had that

much respect for him. . . . He was the kindest man I ever met. . . .
He'd give you anything. First year I went, . . . he took me to the
dentist, and I got my teeth filled. I'd never been to the dentist in my
life, and that was in 1963. I never spent a dime; he paid for everything. Nobody's ever done that for me. We couldn't even go to the
dentist. My father said it was a waste of time. . . . [But Sam's
approach was] "I got the money; you need it."

 . . . And he couldn't believe I never had breakfast . . . until I
started eating [there]. I remember one time the veterinarian came
up, and he was working on one of the cows, and they were talking.
I guess everybody was in the kitchen, sitting down for breakfast, and
Sam made a bunch of little coffee cakes, and I ate all of them while
they were talking. [So he did all the cooking?] Yes. He was a good cook,
good cook. [Had you ever met a man who cooked and fed people and
took them to the dentist?] Nope. If somebody had told me there was a
person like that, I wouldn't have believed them. . . . He always had
plenty of room for [people], and when he ran [his farm], . . . he
didn't cut any corners. If you needed something . . . [for a job on the
farm], a tractor or something like that, he wouldn't spare any
expense. . . . [So it was a serious, productive farm?] Yes. They had a
hundred milking cows; his land stretched for five miles both ways.

John Roger cherished not only his relationship with Sam but
the additional surrogacy that he experienced with Sam's son, Keith,
then a college freshman. Although John Roger's entire exposure to
them lasted only two long summers—ten months in all—they
become profound lodestones of possibility, forming the models for
his kindness toward his own children. Although he still struggles
with a tendency toward social and marital withdrawal, resulting
from his relentlessly harsh childhood and the same saturated front-
line Vietnam experiences that stunned the souls of so many soldiers, he remains married to a committedly kind woman. He has
never failed to encourage his children and support them financially,

having internalized Sam's fathering and eschewed his own father's bitter miserliness. Now well connected with his fifteen-year-old son, they bowl and talk frequently in a manner reminiscent of his own relationship with Sam's son, Keith, and other male surrogates on the farm. Look carefully at the role of his own recognized competence in spurring John Roger's development:

> [*How did you gain . . . respect for yourself?*] Well, . . . I was the youngest boy on the farm, actually. . . . An older boy took me aside and let me polish his car for him, took me down to the barn and let me milk the cows, which job you rarely do. . . . He was the foreman; the only ones who milked the cows were he and Ted, [my buddy who got me the position; he] . . . was his pet. [*So that was seen as an honor?*] Yes. That was the most important job on the farm, and [the foreman] showed me how to respect myself, . . . because that's a serious job.
>
> Everybody liked me, you know; it was just one of those things like at school. . . . I was shy, quiet . . . probably a clown, too, . . . got along with everybody, maybe because of my attitude toward work. [*What about Keith? Why did he take to you?*] I was like a younger brother to him. He had a motorcycle. He took me on it to ride around, do things. I used to borrow his car from him all the time. . . . Every time he came home, he'd spend time with me. . . . He never really had a younger brother.

Reading between the lines, it seems that John Roger's native appeal, as well as Keith's yearning for a stronger sense of family in the wake of his own parents' divorce, created a well-bounded, gratifying relationship for both of them.

John Roger's respite with Sam and Keith was brief, regrettably. Although Sam offered John Roger full support for college and subsequent work in Sam's industry, he declined, afraid that his own father would poison the opportunity for him. His fear was well founded. John Roger had once been approached by an athletic scout, who offered to sponsor him as a professional bowler. His father sabotaged that offer gratuitously—a sadly aborted recruitment. John Roger declined Sam's offer for another reason, too: because he was determinedly self-sufficient—a resounding leitmotif throughout the interviews. To truly defeat his father's—or anybody's—dire predictions, he felt that he had to author his own life. Yet he solidified his faith in himself during those farm summers, finding in Sam and Keith reincarnations of the earlier, quickly extinguished love of his Polish grandmother.

When I asked John Roger why he treated his own children so differently from the way he was treated, and if there was a turning point for him in deciding who he was going to be, he immediately focused on his adolescent renaissance:

> [You've paid a lot of substantial bills for your children's care, and from what I understand, you did that very willingly.] Right. I don't work for myself. I work for . . . my family. [How do you explain that choice, given that you had a dad who was working only for himself and expected you, even as a small child, to work for him, too? It sounds as if he never questioned that assumption, but you did.] I think maybe I was on a different level than everybody else, because . . . it wouldn't worry me when he said, . . . "You're going to be a bum," or "You're going to do this [bad thing]." . . . [You didn't believe him?] No. Deep down, . . . once I went to the farm, I knew what I wanted to be. . . . I wanted to have a house; I wanted to have children, to love. . . . If I hadn't gone to the farm, maybe it would have taken longer for me to realize that.

Once again we see the themes of adolescent surrogacy and initial perspective-taking. John Roger got away. He found a "holding environment" in which men were competent and kind and in which care was simply extended. His work was seen, valued, even applauded. This led to his being given added responsibility; thus he encountered more success and a continuing rise in self-esteem. After two pivotal summers, during which he was cognitively and affectively ripe for a new view of himself, his faith in himself as a competent man was fundamentally launched.

Although John Roger struggled considerably with many symptoms of posttraumatic stress disorder after returning from heavy combat during the Vietnam War, not to mention the undeclared war of his childhood, at some crucial level his nascent faith was impregnable from adolescence onward. While he did not disclose or analyze his struggles at home with his male surrogates, they intuitively read between the lines, putting him in charge of milking 100 cows and baking him more coffee cakes. Very gradually, within a long marital relationship of sustained mutual care and some recent trauma therapy, the reparative sun has healed him. Like most of my subjects, John Roger felt that he snagged in some areas. Regardless, he knew during adolescence that he would make himself into *John Roger*, selectively integrating the images of Sam and Keith and successfully disidentifying with his father. Like almost everyone in this study, he recalls a pivotal moment, in a hopeful surround, in which he knew that home was really *off*, that he was meant for more, and that he was determined to seek it. And so he did.

Scouts

My final case of an adolescent emerging in a setting that did not foster explicit reflection but did demonstrate a powerful *implicit* model of humane interaction involves Larry, an engineer in his early forties. I introduce him because he found, in the Boy Scouts, a highly organized code to live by and a structured sequence of successful competence. *Perhaps the most intriguing aspect of the recollections quoted is the fact that Larry had forgotten them all until the interview.* As I probed about significant figures and said, "You're describing a life with a lot of darkness. Where's the light?" he suddenly recalled four years of experiences in a Scout troop. (A subsequent recollection also happened rather dramatically to another subject, Catherine, while others *always* knew that their surrogates were significant but had never systematically reflected on *why*.) Here Larry is taken aback:

> [*It's interesting: . . . your whole tone and demeanor shifted dramatically as soon as you started talking about the Boy Scouts.*] I forgot all about it. . . . I really did. *I guess I buried it.* It was a good thing. It was . . . a highlight. [*A lot of life came into the room once you started talking about them.*] I don't know how I forgot that one. . . . I used to look forward to every Wednesday night, going to the troop meeting. I was always there, never missed. . . . It made me feel good. . . .

What would make someone forget or repress such a pivotal experience? Psychological understandings and theoretical tenets have infiltrated our culture. Because the field of psychology has always overemphasized the role of parental influences on development and minimized other formative relationships and contexts (including siblings, school and the people there, race, ethnicity, socioeconomic status), perhaps our experiences are organized and thus retrieved around this bias. Even in the resilient, we may be witnessing the selective retrieval of memories that tend to underplay extrafamilial influences and contribute to even their puzzlement about why they turned out relatively well. Thus it seems crucial to dignify the best that accompanies the worst in order to amplify the former. Once I tapped the Scouting vein, Larry continued with relish and in great detail, delighted to be reunited with some unimpeachable good in his adolescence.

Like John Roger, Larry grew up in economic impoverishment. After a brief azure swell, his mother's optimism quickly clouded and the family literally ate only mashed potatoes and hamburger every night thereafter. His father cooked nothing; nor was he emotionally available. His mother went deaf as his childhood progressed, allowing her the actual sensory remove that she had achieved psychologically some years earlier. He and his three closely spaced brothers were routinely brutalized by their father. In fourth grade, Larry was accidentally hit in the eye by his brother and spent a year in a tertiary care hospital in Boston, where he was eventually diagnosed with an atypical clotting disorder. His father did not visit once during the hospitalization.

At home Larry eluded his father's furious stalking rages by playing outside with the scores of children who lived in the adjoining multifamily dwellings—a breezy pleasure. If trapped indoors, he often stowed himself skillfully in his bedroom closet for hours at a time. Larry's prowess at concealing himself is reminiscent of novelist Jerzy Kosinski's nimbly hiding as a child, escaping Polish political and personal horrors as he fled his homeland. Still agile as an adult, Kosinsky, expecting a bevy of reporters eager to interview him, once hid spontaneously under a set of cushions. The reporters came and sat patiently on the couch—and him—awaiting his arrival. Perhaps stronger surrogacy might have softened Kosinsky's understandable but continuing edge.

Larry did look for more at age eleven, slipping out of his closet into the hills near his home to camp with the Boy Scouts. Like John Roger, his surrogacy emerged in the society of men, within a Jewish troop in the fifties. He camped his way to independence and his first true collaborations, acquiring significant competence in the bargain. Once again we find a setting offering alternatives and implicit support to the beleaguered rather than fostering explicit evaluative reflection. Larry did not discuss his plight, or even recognize its gravity, during early adolescence. Yet, after initially finding in Scouting a thin link with his father and brothers (who had been Scouts before him), Larry hungrily absorbed the Boy Scouts' comprehensive view of good citizenship, gradually differentiating from his father's cruelty and his mother's emotional inaccessibility. In turn, his family manifested that hidden strength of letting go when you cannot give. While ordinarily oblivious, obtuse, or abusive, they mustered atypical support in shepherding him into the

It was something I could do. . . . We had to go out camping on our own, and if you didn't know what you were doing, you starved or you froze. . . . It was a government tract of land. There were little lean-to houses there, where one side was wide open, and you actually had bunks of wood on the inside where you could sleep all huddled together, freezing. . . . We used to make our own campfires. I used to show kids how to do that, how to split wood, how to handle an ax safely. I used to do all the training, and I was only thirteen or fourteen at the time. I remember training everybody.

Without a word of analysis at the time, Larry relativizes his own family's plight once he sees that other people do not eat the same dinner every night and that some families actually *pack* food for their sons' excursions; he marvels at the boys' ease of sharing. At the helm is a gravely ill Scoutmaster who gives well and dies young. Through the accident of an ill-fated diagnosis, he and his son became a galvanizing force, encouraging an added measure of cohesion and collaboration in the troop. Inescapably sanctified, the Scoutmaster becomes an icon of effective helping to his surviving "sons":

We'd take whatever we could. I'd come in the house and take some raw hamburger or whatever we had in the house. We'd just put it all together. We'd pool our money and we'd buy food. *And I think that's when I started to see how other families lived,* because we used to go and see how other parents would buy food for the group. And I used to show up there with nothing. But [the troop] used to have tons of food. . . . My mother didn't know how to do all these things. . . . There was always some . . . adult there. We had our Scoutmaster, . . . a big . . . guy, nice guy, like a Santa Claus– type individual. [He'd say,] "You can do it. . . . Try it." He was always the kind of positive guy that would walk around and say, "You're doing great!" . . . Mr. Shapiro, . . . he was a real strong light to the whole troop.

When he . . . got cancer in the middle of [my time as a Scout], . . . his hair fell out. . . . Evidently, he must have been undergoing chemotherapy. . . . I remember going over to his house. The whole troop used to go and have troop meetings at his house, and I remember him wearing a wig and trying to hide the fact that he lost all his hair over a period of time. . . . *We just never talked about it;* . . . he kept getting worse and worse, and he kept deteriorating in front of our eyes until he finally died. . . . After he died, we had to take over. . . . He left the troop . . . reeling for a while, and we all had to step up there and say, . . . "Well, this is going to make it." . . . And then his son took over. . . . We had about fifty or sixty kids; it was a big troop. And we went camping still; . . . we said, *"Look, we're going to survive. We're going to keep this thing going."* . . . And we did.

This communalism was in stark contrast to the family chaos that Larry experienced, which included his standing up on the backyard wall for hours to avoid having his father beat him and routinely hiding in the closet for safety. Like others in the study who often hid as children, he was desperate. But camping with the Scouts every Wednesday and most weekends, as well as summers, offered Larry extensive contact with Scout leaders and peers who were systematically positive. He selectively internalized them. He also witnessed many parents interact effectively with their sons in the sort of parent/son relationship that was otherwise foreign to him:

Some very good parents went. . . . My parents would never go, but I got a chance to see other kids, and their fathers stayed . . . with us on camping trips, and I watched the interaction between the father and the kid. It was always great. [*What did you see?*] A guy would put his arm around his kid and say, "Hey, you're doing a great job." *I never got that. I didn't dwell on that,* . . . *but I used to look at that and say, "Wow,* . . . *that's a role model.* . . . *It's wonderful."*

Maligned too often for its naive assumptive underpinnings, the Boy Scouts thus presented Larry (and presumably many struggling others) with a coherent world in which accessible heroics and cogent moral guidelines contradicted the disjointing chaos of their home lives. It would be arrogant to dismiss its potential transformative impact on the grounds that it lacks urbane sophistication. The beaten need to join the ranks of the cooperatively collected as much as or more than they need to be among the cognoscenti, at least in adolescence:

> There was a creed. We always used to start every meeting with "A Boy Scout is trustworthy, loyal, friendly, courteous, kind, obedient, cheerful, thrifty, brave, clean. . . ." You lived by that. . . . And I guess I've always been that way mentally. And whatever I do, there's a little flashing light in my head that says: "Be prepared." . . . So if I'm learning first aid or whatever, at the police station [as an auxiliary policeman], there's always something in me saying, "Are you prepared?" . . . It was so deeply ingrained in me that it carried over into life. *If I had any religious training, this was it. And we all believed in it.*

Having ignited his faith that other men can be emotionally reliable, Larry established similar interpersonal connections after the Scouting years as an amateur radio operator. On the airwaves, a haven not only for the incipient psychotic, this more resilient adolescent found that older males, perhaps hundreds of miles away, were readily available to help him work with a radio that his father denigrated or ignored. He forged a variety of satisfying emotional ties through the airwaves, based on the exchange of technical information—a precursor to his later job competence as an engineering project manager. Thus increasing his technical and social competence (and thereby thwarting his father's dire predictions that he would never amount to anything) was the sweet reward of Larry's largely self-sustaining late-adolescent years:

There were good things. I had . . . really super friends. When . . . I was in high school and got into electronics, . . . it opened up a whole new world, and I remember from that point on, I became a more outside person. All of a sudden, I started . . . talking to people on the ham radio, and . . . I had never talked to people before; . . . people didn't know I was in the room. If you asked people who hung around with me as a kid [what I was like, they would say] that Larry Bloom never said more than two words. . . . They didn't know I existed, but once I got into radio, . . . you could talk into a microphone and nobody had to look at you. . . . I always considered myself not a very good-looking person, so when I could . . . talk into a microphone and *nobody had to see you, and you were your voice* . . .

[*So there was some power in finding a voice, allowing your voice to be powerful?*] Yes. And I'd have long conversations with adults at night on the radio. It really got me out of my shell, . . . because we'd all get on frequency and we'd have a nice little roundtable discussion. . . . I always related better to adults than I did to other kids, so I really enjoyed talking . . . about electronics. We talked for hours. I remember that very clearly. It was a lot of fun.

In closing Larry's narrative, it is worth noting that his developmental trajectory soon included the formation of what became a twenty-three-year marriage to Eve, who was mentioned in the previous chapter as someone for whom pets were the locus of hope. They raised their neurologically impaired son at home, despite many professional recommendations to institutionalize him. Recall that Shibvon's adolescent sons are also thriving in the midst of frequent surgeries, leg braces, and casts, and that most of my other subjects also have offspring who are highly competent and emotionally healthy. When I talked to Eve about her mission to shepherd her behaviorally imposing child into a strong adulthood, I asked where she learned to have faith that this was in fact possible. She said that, while she had little belief in herself during childhood, at sixteen she encountered someone who believed in her completely: Larry. Listen to the canyon echo of Larry's Scoutmaster and Scouting's collective faith in agency, which eventually led to their son's relative success as a mainstreamed high school sophomore and Eve's recent acceptance to social work school:

> [Larry] never once ridiculed any of my ideas. . . . At one point, I thought I wanted to be an interior decorator. My mother had all sorts of . . . reasons why I shouldn't. He thought it was great. "Great. Just do it; go ahead." There was never any . . . "Go ahead, *but.*" For him, everything that I wanted to do was attainable. There were no major obstacles. . . . "You have the capacity to do it." And he *continued* to do that with *anything* that I wanted to do. . . . *He would give me the courage to do it.*

Thus what might at first seem a naive faith in surmounting such obstacles as wooden bridges and winter marches led Larry and Eve to create a sound environment for a boy who might otherwise have been interred in the mental health system. Refusing to see him as a visitation or a forced march, this pair mobilized their own resilience on his behalf and thus spawned significant resilience in their son. Their achievements move well beyond the more limited notions of skill acquisition that are associated with a competent middle childhood (the ceiling of Robert White's celebrated competence motivation[5]). Larry's promoting competence in others, against sobering odds and at great personal cost, demonstrates an important aspect of his ability to "love well." Organizational surrogacy within the Scouts anchored his capacity to love, just as farms, boarding schools, YWCAs, and similar settings promoted humanity in receptive others.

In sum, the adolescent experiences of Margaret, John Roger, and Larry capture several themes of adolescent resilience mentioned in the opening pages of this chapter. They were chosen as the focus here because they are emblematic of the experiences of the many who found a surrogacy of silent respite. These resilient adolescents felt an underlying conviction that they deserved better than their scabrous plights, and all quickly plunged themselves into the "better" that they found. They sought geographical distance by midadolescence, quickly recognizing that a hundred road miles could become the welcome psychological equivalent of a continent. When they found an authorized setting that was at least tolerable to their parents, they stayed in that setting with grace. As the rim of the sun pressed upward, they found their first sustained sense that there was another way to lead their lives. Teeth were fixed, breakfast was served, and their bodies were newly inviolate. In this first prolonged safety, their hypervigilance was able to stretch and relax, quieting from a roar into a watchful purr. As their executive competence escalated, others began to take notice. Through sharp implicit contrast and some startled silences, they began to see what they came from. Their eyes would never again adjust to such dim light. Several bold new brushstrokes fell onto their sketch of another future, and most found enduring love soon after. Finally safe in their respite settings, they prolonged their stay, despite accommodations that would have seemed harsh or bare to those who had known an easier way. They began to know what better *is*, and they resolved to keep it.

Yet unless young people employ *critical reflection*, the other avenues that potentially widen during adolescence remain underutilized. Although all of those interviewed *eventually* recognized just how defeating their families were, many found evaluative conversational partners *during* mid- to late adolescence and became highly articulate about what was wrong at home. As they declared the emperor ever more starkly bare, they tailored a more extensive wardrobe of adaptive alternatives for themselves. Here are some of the surrogacies that helped them weave the fabric.

Havens Promoting Evaluative Reflection

Resilience is fostered by a probing cognitive and affective approach to one's life circumstances. As an admiring acquaintance of Shibvon's remarked to her solemnly at their twentieth high school reunion, "Geez, now I remember. You were *always* deep." The following section explores a variety of reflective relationships marked not only by their surprising depth of affection and sustained regard—the linchpins of effective surrogacy—but also by a *mutual awareness* of how childhood, for some, can fan out in unbroken rows of disappointment.

Perceptive Adults

Many of the resilient, including those quoted in the previous section, felt that they had only a modest exposure to critical awareness during adolescence. However, just as many felt that they found the first few bricks of the yellow road when an adult noticed that they had an inner life and confirmed some of its contents. This process can happen in virtually any setting; but whatever the setting, once resilient adolescents find a reflective path, they do not stop. Here Diana, a psychologist in her early forties, conveys the relieved gratitude of a child famished for this kind of recognition:

> I remember an event once where a ninth-grade high school English teacher, whom I respected a lot, asked us to do . . . an assignment where we had to write ten of our favorite poems. I used to read a lot of poetry, and so I felt very proud that I had ten favorite poems. I chose . . . either lengthy or verbose or kind of superficially obscure poems that I liked, but I chose them *very* carefully, and I remember writing them in painstakingly careful handwriting. . . . I clearly did it for her, not for the assignment, and she wrote back to me on the paper, "Thank you for sharing these. Now I have a much better idea of who you are and what's important to you," and I remember

bursting into tears. It was a pretty middle-of-the-road comment, but yet . . . it just seemed so surprising that *anybody would know*. . . . *[It was] just that she "saw" me*. . . .

I also had an aunt and uncle who clearly "saw" very early in life, [although I didn't connect with them until I went to college]. . . . Actually, my uncle died . . . about a year and a half ago, and I remember talking to my aunt at his funeral about how, when I went to college, I had a very hard time. . . . I got really depressed and fell apart, and they took care of me a lot. They gave me the key to their house . . . in Westchester and I was in Manhattan, and I used to go out there on the train and hang around with them. They would say, "Why don't you come out Saturday afternoon?" Now, what college-age person wouldn't have dates, events, studying to do? But I would go out and spend Saturday night at their house.

Through her extended family's competent surrogacy, Diana realized that many parents *do* listen to children and that people *can* resolve psychological problems through active reflection and critical self-examination. That reflective surrogacy also helped her to see that her own mother was so psychologically compromised that she was shunned by her immediate and extended families as well as her Jewish community in a small southern town. (Diana recalls that her mother never seemed to think about anything that she could not literally see.) Diana learned, too, from her comparison of her uncle and her father: she saw her depressed uncle recover and make coherent life choices rather than sit inert on the couch for years at a time like her chronically suicidal, manic-depressive father—a former judge. And she was shocked to discover that some people actually have friends who visit regularly. Perhaps most life-preserving of all, she discovered the sweet embrace of laughter in a home:

They were a very lively, politically oriented family. . . . [My uncle was my] father's younger brother, who had been very depressed when he was in his thirties; this is a really interesting guy who got himself some therapy and decided he was having a hard time making a go of the profession he had chosen. He decided to opt out of professional life, . . . which was a difficult decision, but—and this is very inspiring to me—he's a very talented artist, and I have some sketches that he did of me when I was in my teens that I really treasure, and a painting that he did for me when I got married, which . . . is a small segment of a Goya. It's very dramatic looking, and . . . I cherish having it.

I used to go out to their house and then all their friends would come over, and they'd sit around usually and have dinner, and their kids, who were slightly younger than I was, would come and go. . . . [My aunt and uncle] would always be telling jokes and laughing and telling stories, and their kids would tell a joke and everybody would laugh. . . . *I thought this was unbelievable. I'd never been listened to long enough to have a joke.* . . . So I really got a lot from that family, and in retrospect spoke with my aunt about what it was like for her during those days. She said they were really scared for me, and they didn't know if they were helping, and they didn't know what to do, but they felt that I was a responsibility that they couldn't . . . refuse.

Diana believes that the reflective orientation of her extended family also helped her aim a miner's hat into her own inner life. Prowling around this terrain for the first time, she discovered she was rather good at it. The probing yet enlivening climate of the respite weekends with her extended family complemented the vibrant intellectual climate she encountered at Columbia University in the late sixties. For Diana, the combination was nearly combustible. Newly immersed in psychology, art, and delectable philosophical conversations, she gradually cast her previous family experiences in high relief and then relativized them. Like a Renaissance artist discovering perspective, Diana created a new portrait of her nuclear family, more homunculus than human. She studied it continually, aggrieved but relieved. Her pain began to make sense.

Others found mentors who helped them map the chaos even more explicitly. Olivia, also now a psychologist, emerged into a turbulent adolescence out of a turbulent childhood. Her father attempted to kill himself on the day of her birth and again—successfully this time—on her first birthday. Her self-esteem was punctured during childhood by her angry and understandably bereft mother, who was highly abusive to Olivia's brother. Then Olivia found Jason, a minister and psychologist with whom she has sustained a close tie over decades. He, like many other surrogates, was disarmed by the gravitational pull of their relationship. With the chaste warmth of a good father, he began to sponsor Olivia at school and within his own family. She also sculpted a program for other floundering youth with him. Note the reciprocal intensity of their tie, bounded well enough so that it continues safely over time:

> I think he thinks that I credit him too much with what my . . . growth and development were about. . . . He feels as though he really loved me. I remember his saying, kind of early on—and I think it was quite genuine—that *he was kind of astonished by his own response to me* and his own involvement and love and that he saw me as being [not only] withdrawn and depressed but this really special kid and precocious in some ways. . . . I think that he felt like there was a lot of depth and thoughtfulness and sensitivity and compassion in me, and I think he was touched . . . by who he came to know in me. . . . He's a real psychological midwife. . . . Somehow he stayed with me [while I struggled]. . . . It was a real time of blossoming.

Surrogates who were therapists or sought therapy themselves were especially compelling to several subjects. Because they used psychology in their daily lives, its benefits became more obvious to their struggling recruits. For example, Ariana, a psychiatric social worker, was the oldest of nine children. In response to Ariana's childhood disclosure of her father's prolonged sexual abuse, she was ostracized by the phalanx of twenty immediate and extended family members living under one Dorchester roof. While her father was banished corporally after she divulged his abuse, *she* became invisible psychologically. At eleven she was virtually mute. But Ariana moved to a suburb during her midadolescence. She found a second chance in her psychologically astute neighbor, Caitlin, who hired Ariana to babysit while she went to therapy. Her interactional pump primed by an unexpectedly warm reception at school, Ariana still had enough faith at that time to connect well with Caitlin, whose similar Irish Catholic background undoubtedly drew *her* to Ariana.

> We moved. . . . Somehow it helped. . . . First of all, I . . . went to school and I found that a lot of people seemed to be interested in me. . . . *It was a constant shock to me that people would be interested in me.* It was just such a surprise—everyone from the art teacher to the students, . . . [even] kids that seemed to come from extremely different backgrounds than what I was coming from. It was overwhelming and intimidating, and I didn't deal with it very well. But at the same time, it was . . . a little edge. . . . Something [was] changing.
>
> . . . And then I met Caitlin, who was also from an Irish Catholic background, so she had that cultural history [and] could relate to me. . . . She was my neighbor, and . . . she often asked me if I'd babysit for them. We became friends, and *I saw a person who treated children as people,* and it was another surprise, a shock to my system. Oh, my God!
>
> [*Do you feel that a lot of who you have become is modeled on Caitlin?*] Yes. . . . Caitlin always looked beautiful, and [although] she had very little money, . . . she created the space around her. Her environment was lovely. It was just very pleasing visually. She had a lot of pain and struggles in her family, and yet she had a wonderful sense of humor and she laughed a lot, and she had fun! *So she was*

a model for someone who had great difficulties in her life—and she could talk about them. She was also very open about talking about all of this stuff, or at least she was open with me. And she used her pain and her struggle in her humor. It was also—she had a biting humor, but very, very funny, and so it didn't have to be hidden. It was another way of . . . being able to express a little bit more. . . . I admired that tremendously. . . . I was able to open up and to talk for the first time in my life.

Ariana realizes that Caitlin's capacity to reflect on her own circumstances is closely linked to Caitlin's forging a better life for herself. Safe and encouraged within this receptive emotional climate, she discloses her own sexual abuse. Once again, note that even under *optimal* circumstances, it takes this bright, reflective adolescent *three years* to find the words to say it:

It was 1960. . . . I don't think I told her anything about the abuse probably until I was about seventeen, so I had known her for about three years. . . . Something . . . that allowed me to tell her was that she was in therapy. . . . I always babysat for her when she went to therapy, and she told me that she had had a very difficult childhood and . . . that's why *she went to therapy; and I think that that gave me permission to tell her.* . . . *I just remember she took action.* That's what sticks out in my mind. It's not even so much how she responded personally, in terms of nurturing and loving; it was that she took action, and she said, . . . "I want you to see a therapist. . . . This is something that you really need to work on, and I think that there could be help for you."

That felt like a change; it felt like a great sense of relief. . . . *[Before that, I saw that] the world I was living in was not right. . . . I felt as if I had to . . . create a world that would be right . . . so that my brothers and sisters could survive.* . . . I'm sure it was probably a projection [so that the] part of me that was a child could survive. . . . I did a lot of compartmentalizing, and I sort of faked it until I made it; I just chose ways of being until I could get there.

> [When did the "getting there" start to set in?] . . . If I could think of the moment: . . . I remember having been to therapy; . . . it was after then, and I remember walking down the street [long pause—sobbing]. . . . It was spring, and I saw a dogwood tree, and . . . I felt an affinity. Up until then it was dark, really dark. . . . I was about eighteen. . . . I don't mean that there wasn't any light up until then, [but] it was pretty dark. [Then] . . . I saw the colors.

Here Ariana reclaimed a lost light through her relationship to her receptive surrogate, her subsequent disclosure of her abuse, and the beginning of her therapy. While the therapeutic community was not prepared to deal well with sexual abuse in 1960, enough came of the process for her to regain hope. Most potently, in Caitlin she located a competent role model who was psychologically articulate, hardworking, hilarious, self-sustaining, and well able to create beauty out of very little. She sounds rather resilient herself.

Perhaps Caitlin and other surrogates located some earlier version of themselves in their young recruits, offering them accurate insights that might have benefited themselves at an earlier developmental moment. In any case, these attuned surrogates were conversant with and employed psychological constructs and meanings that eased their recruits' passage substantially. By spring Ariana was able to see the dogwood flowering.

Finally, to illustrate that no human group has cornered the market on either critical thinking or sensitivity, I want to describe the reflective surrogacy that Stan, a community mental health organizer, encountered in the navy at nineteen. As a new navy recruit, Stan was randomly assigned to room with two men on their second hitch. In the quoted passages that follow, Stan underscores the transformative effect of his association with those men as well as with a group of college-educated draftees who continually reflected about their inner experiences and political beliefs. Now, although the armed services have long been a route for the more disenfranchised to acquire skills, discipline, and higher education, they are not ordinarily thought of as a way to sample the buffet of the human potential movement. But Stan, away from his small Vermont hometown for the first time, suddenly stationed in Manila without any accountability to his old crowd or his family, sat up with interest when he realized that these men really *talked* to one another about their inner lives:

> [My two roommates] were . . . unusually sensitive men who cared about people, . . . both very interesting guys. . . . They were the type of people you meet very seldom, who, when you meet, . . . don't just say, "How are you?" and you say, "Fine." They said, *"How are you?"* and they *meant* it. *I never met anyone like that before*, certainly not in my family, because you kept feelings [entirely to yourself]; . . . you did the cursory . . . and stayed away from issues. . . . My group [at home] was blue-collar, out every Saturday night and drinking and trying to [find women]. . . . I was struck by the fact that I liked [these roommates], . . . that I respected them. . . . I was also struck by the fact that these are people I might have laughed at [at home]. . . . It was a real revelation for me to say, "Well, wait a minute. Some of your thinking here, Stan, distanced by 8,000 miles from Thetford, Vermont, [needs to change]. . . . It's hard to hold on to those old belief systems when you're that drastically distanced. . . . You couldn't call home for fifteen months.
>
> I roomed with them for a very long time, seven or eight months, [by choice]. . . . I also had another unique experience. . . . Ten of us became close. [I still see these people annually,] . . . all really bright guys. . . . We were always challenging authority; . . . we were distributing antiwar leaflets on the base. . . . We got close enough so that we could really share and began to share some of the more deep things. . . . There were a lot of tremendous, deep, long rap sessions

about what's right and what's wrong, . . . real soul-searching. . . . I was comfortable with the group; but at the same time, [it was] a challenging group. . . . *I knew I was choosing to find out something about myself.*

I could have gone in any direction [after high school; I was with a rowdy group]. . . . I was going with a nice girl, very Irish Catholic girl, and we were talking about getting married. I was nineteen years old, . . . riding in my car, and I thought, "Oh, man, . . . I can see where I was born to be: . . . lots of kids, cheating on my wife—really nowhere. Working at the Food Mart for the rest of my life. . . . I didn't know *what* I wanted, . . . [but] I knew . . . I wanted to have an opportunity to do *something* different, . . . so I joined the service. . . . Getting there was my decision, and I'm really proud about that. . . . I lost complete touch with the old peer group and just never really reconnected.

Again, the [initial] source of the transition for me from those two men was very important. Seeing them and realizing that educated, sensitive men . . . weren't weird people, and weren't intimidating, and they didn't put me down. . . . I could've very easily changed rooms, . . . but I said, "This feels pretty good. What's this all about?" and *I really spent some time working with those feelings in myself.*

Thus in adolescence Stan, Ariana, Olivia, and Diana (and many others) found explicit recognition that they *possessed* an inner life. Interested companionship lent dignity to their experiences. As their more reflective surrogates encouraged them to think and speak psychologically, these young people discovered the language of insight. Not only did they finally announce the headline that their families of origin were anomalous, but they got a chance to *converse* their way through some of the fine print with psychologically attuned adults. Now, most abused children keep the contained silence of the tundra during childhood. But some, during the emergence of adolescent autonomy, erupt with insight.

While all of my subjects achieved some necessary geographical distance from their families during adolescence, increasing critical reflection accelerated their *emotional* differentiation. And that differentiation was sorely needed. Evidently, their surrogate relationships "held" them and soothed some of their sense of abandonment as they began to mourn what they never had—that most tenacious of griefs. It should not surprise you that subjects who developed these more reflective relationships were more frequently among those who became therapists. I do not think this is causal in any simple sense. Rather, I assume that these adolescents had a higher receptivity to adults who could be more reflective *with* them. They then chose the helping professions because those encourage the same modus vivendi. The evolution of the resilient adolescent's outlook and his or her choice of profession are inextricably mutually influenced, with the added spin of chance circumstances. I once remarked to my own shepherding figure, Anne Carpenter, that I was lucky to find her at fourteen. I still attribute much of my reasonable developmental trajectory to her reflective availability during my adolescence. She quickly replied, "Yes, but remember that you were in decent shape when you arrived, and you *kept* coming around when the others stopped." Not belittling her own contribution, she reminded me that motivation and goodness of fit reign supreme in any human relationship—particularly ties born of a certain amount of desperation. Recruiting is *always* a two-way street.

Peer Relationships and Romantic Love

I have not yet spoken of peer relationships or romantic love—perhaps the greatest preoccupations of adolescents (besides making sense of themselves). They are often one and the same. Several subjects specifically mentioned that their peer relationships, especially with romantic partners who were also good friends, were utterly invaluable to them. Many achieved their unofficial adoption status through these ties. Subjects often spoke of eating most meals or even having a room at a friend's home. Men in particular spoke of nearly joining a girlfriend's family and being shocked that they were accepted on their own terms there. Grady, a former state prosecutor in his late thirties who remains happily married to a woman he met in high school, captures this well:

> You can look at things that you consider to be tough times in life, and you can realize you also have some great luck. . . . That's what it came down to for me. . . . [During my adolescence, my father was severely alcoholic and having affairs, my mother was hospitalized for months on end for depression,] and it was really bad stuff, toxic stuff. . . . I got so upset about things . . . [that] I used to get nosebleeds, . . . sometimes twice a week. . . . I didn't want my mother to see I was getting nosebleeds, [so] I'd be running into the bathroom. . . . *I was hiding my face.* . . .

> So I . . . put a terrible burden on the girl that I met, that I ended up marrying, in the sense that not only were we going through a normal teenage relationship, but I was kind of clingy toward her because there was some stability. She was a normal kid [from a] normal family. Boy, that was nice. The parents seemed very nice. I didn't want them to know what was going on in my family, . . . because I was paranoid about it, but I wanted them to accept me. . . . *I threw the anchor out, and it hooked onto that island.*

> It was a very ethnic family, second generation: . . . a father with a very responsible position, a mother who had parents who had come over from the old country. . . . What I really liked was that the parents respected each other, and they were nice to each other [and the family]. . . . I needed something that was stoic, . . . but there was love; there was warmth. . . . I'd *never* seen that sort of respect that they had for each other. . . . That's so important to somebody . . .

who's going through . . . what I . . . was going through at the
time. . . . Perhaps it would have been normal to want to be in [a
troubled] situation [like my own], . . . if, [for example,] I had met a
girl whose father or mother was an alcoholic . . . or [had] a family
that was all messed up, because it's comfortable to some people. *But
no, I didn't want that. I wanted something that was stable.*

Grady and many others also noted gratefully that their surrogates never assumed that they were "bad seeds" because they came
from trouble. Startled by this acceptance, it in turn allowed them
to see themselves as independent operators—an exhilarating new
reconstruction and relativizing of their shameful predicaments:

They didn't intrude, I remember that very well. . . . *I really believe
that they didn't make judgments about me, based on anything other than
what I was about.* I'm pretty sure that they knew that my father had
a drinking problem, but that never seemed to be of concern to
them. . . . My wife said one time [twenty years later] that her father
had once said, "Well, does this affect him? I mean, is he going to
turn out like this?" and she said no and that was it, end of story; it
didn't go any further. No judgments made; no questions asked. . . .
All they cared about was that I was nice to their daughter and that
she enjoyed my company.

Many subjects also said that these peer and romantic ties were
normalizing for them, reducing their exaggerated sense that they
were somehow morbidly different from everybody else. Since they
knew by adolescence that their families were deeply off base, they
obviously feared that they had been smeared with the devil's paintbrush. By discovering some success in more mainstream families,
disembedding themselves from home, they began to revise their *self-*
definition to include more normalcy. Comparing notes endlessly
with friends or romantic partners was highly emotionally corrective, giving sorrow wings and uncertainty a compass. A few men

also noted, trying to be circumspect, that being sexual was very sta-
bilizing for them. Within the context of a committed relationship,
they often felt anchored and authentic, and human touch became
reunited with care. After some initial hesitation, Kai discusses this
poignantly:

> It's sort of embarrassing to tell a woman this, but the thing that saved
> me in young adolescence and young adulthood [and kept me] hang-
> ing in there was that sexuality . . . really tied me to earth at a time
> when I was probably . . . acting up. I was angry about my child-
> hood. . . . But sexuality was an incredible way to still be a part of
> earth and alive, . . . with all the mistakes that go with it; but it was
> really an important sustaining aspect, . . . especially for men, who
> have unverbalized dependency needs.
>
> I think that had I not been able to either find girlfriends or be
> attractive in that arena, I would have been *really* one angry or one
> unhappy dude; and I think that really carried through a lot until I
> could . . . average out the limbic stuff . . . and start paying attention
> to the cortical stuff more. If I'd been isolated, . . . I would have been
> really unhappy in one way or another. . . . It sounds so crass in a cer-
> tain sort of way, but . . . it was really important to me. . . . [Other-
> wise,] the outcome psychologically could have been *drastically*
> different. . . . [Also,] I was always interested in longer-term rela-
> tionships. . . . That was part of being alive, and it really . . . tied
> together a lot of the other [pain and confusion] that I couldn't fig-
> ure out. . . . *That was one thing that never changed.* I was always inter-
> ested in dating women, and I found friendships, companionship . . .
> very important; . . . it was really a sustaining part.

Thus the advent of romantic love offers a chance for a deeper
and more extensive level of repair, regardless of its hazards. It is the
most complex instance of recruiting and being recruited by others
outside the family. Sooner or later, my subjects became competent

in this domain as they had in their previous relationships. (Recall, though, that my definition of "loving well" includes active negotiation of differences and a capacity to integrate the darker side of love in a manner that does not eclipse the light [see the Preface]). My findings corroborate those of George Vaillant, who concludes his analysis of the Grant Study at Harvard—a longitudinal study of adult male development—by saying that later love can be emotionally corrective. His findings contradict the Antigone chorus that warns, "When a house has once been shaken from heaven, there the curse falls evermore, passing from life to life of the race." Rather, Vaillant found that "successful careers and satisfying marriages were relatively independent of unhappy childhoods. An unusually close marriage . . . or a dazzling business success often seemed to be a way of compensating for relatively loveless childhoods" for some. "More important still, ingenious adaptive mechanisms often intervened to comfort the poorly parented and to foil the 'Gods infernal' of Sophocles. . . . My guess—and it is not more than a guess—is that we stop growing when our human losses are no longer replaced; . . . the seeds of love must be eternally resown."[6] For those who are adept at sowing their seeds outside the gardens into which they were born, recruited love certainly seems to have the capacity to flourish and thereby restore.

CHAPTER FIVE

Faith and Vision

[And] the greatest of these is love. . . .

—*1 Corinthians 13:13*[1]

How does faith fuel the resilient spirit? How does one sustain the glow of an ember in an icy, moonless night? In the preceding few chapters, I have pressed the significance of our *interpretations* of our experiences. I have said that the resilient forge their bedrock faith in a benevolent kingdom despite childhood experiences that would predict the repetition of a dark life. Actively recruiting surrogates, sustaining recruited love, and selectively internalizing relationships are some of the resilient processes that solidify this hopeful foundation. During adolescence, continued recruiting and robust use of emerging reflective capacities intensify the earlier resolve of the resilient to find a better path. However, we still need something with stronger explanatory power to grasp the depth and strength of their attachment to "better," since their capacity to keep those embers alive strengthens over time, despite some dark developmental moments. Thus it is essential to look closely at what may be a uniquely human capacity to locate and create images and symbols in the service of sustaining our faith in a larger future.

Among the resilient in this study, there were two overarching themes: *faith in surmounting* and *faith in human relationships* as the wellspring of overcoming. This chapter will explicate these themes in some detail while simultaneously exploring the *sources* of my subjects' sustaining imagery. But first, since my own understanding has been enriched by the thinking of faith developmentalists such as Sharon Parks and James Fowler, I briefly review here their understandings of faith and offer illustrative examples that inform the rest of the discussion. Those of their ideas discussed below include faith as "convictional knowing," faith as distinguished from belief, faith as an inherently relational enterprise, and the role of the imagination in creating the master narratives that sustain faith. I am especially indebted to Sharon Parks for her lucid and inspiring thinking on this subject, as well her steady example of a faithful life lived well.

My own observation and conviction is that it is possible to build on our relational experiences, generating and adhering to images of an elevated order. Just as we can *devolve* over time, we can encourage the self-replication of resilience so that an upward spiral of personal evolution can emerge despite some of the sorriest childhoods. We are not like the sailor shaken from his crow's nest watch and snagged by rigging, flapping limp and mute in the gale, lodged in a limbo of inaction. Bruised and sobered though we may be, many of us are up and about. Disentangling those still caught in the snarl, we are faithfully under sail in a steadier sea.

A Brief Tour of Faith Development Theory

Faith development theory arises from the dialogue between developmental psychology and the study of religion. From this perspective, whether it is found in religious or secular forms, faith development theory invites us to recognize that faith is the activity of meaning-making in its most ultimate and intimate dimensions—finding pattern, order, and significance to our lives.[2] There are several themes in the faith literature that illuminate the ways in which my subjects overcome hardship. First, the resilient develop a core convictional foundation about the importance of loving well that withstands their harsh treatment as children. Second, their faith undergirds whatever specific religious or secular beliefs they might hold. Third, their faith is anchored in their relationships with others—originally in their loci of hope and ultimately in the network of relational ties that propels their adult mental health. Finally, the resilient have an unusually strong capacity to imagine and elaborate symbols. They effectively integrate these into coherent "master narratives," buttressing their faith and thus sustaining themselves. Let me explain each in turn.

Faith as "Convictional Knowing"

As is discussed in the recent works of Sharon Parks, faith can be conceived as a unifying pattern that organizes a person's deepest convictions about him- or herself and others—an individual's firmest core understanding of what is true.[3] "Convictional knowing," notes Parks, is that in which we invest our hearts, the anchor "which is adequate to ground, unify, and order" our lives. It is "an activity in which the whole of being has been affected and is engaged. The 'connections' which are achieved in this meaning-making process, whether profound or superficial, strong or fragile, are the 'knowledge' one has woven or patterned. The connections one has patterned are one's 'truth.' This is the only canvas certain enough to receive the commitment of one's being in trust and loyalty. This is one's faith—it is the unseen order one 'sees.'"[4] James Fowler refers to this inclusively as "the logic of conviction."[5] We are always involved in an underlying, ongoing process of making coherent sense of our lives through our deeper convictions, whether or not these are articulated or conscious.

Because the convictional lives of my resilient subjects were so desperately challenged by their earlier experiences, these people are unusual examples of both the force and depth of *humane* convictional logic, now as strongly riveted as it was once severely tested.

They demonstrate that, as Parks asserts, faith can persist "in spite of the massive evidence of the finite, the mundane, and the ugly in human experience," since human beings "still harbor a perennial conviction that 'we were made for more.' Something more was promised; . . . time, the world-as-it-is, the world of sight is to be transcended. . . . It is therefore important to discern something of how transcendence . . . occurs in the human soul."[6] When we observe the dynamics of transcendence among those who have endured much of what is ugly in human experience—the resilient—it is important and useful to examine the role of faith quite closely.

Illustratively, some of the most moving examples of this convictional faith can be found among those who endured one of the more horrifying challenges to their "centers of value": survivors of the Nazi concentration camps. When Bruno Bettelheim spoke of his own experiences and subsequent Holocaust studies, he stressed that "it is a well-known fact of the concentration camps that those who had strong religious and moral convictions managed life there much better than the rest. Their beliefs, including belief in an afterlife, gave them a strength to endure which was far above that of most others. Deeply religious persons often helped others, and some voluntarily sacrificed themselves—more than the average prisoners."[7] Like my subjects, these resilient souls seem to meet Reinhold Niebuhr's criteria for "faith-full" human beings: "giving themselves for that which is greater than themselves."[8]

Distinguishing Faith from Belief

To understand the resilient, it is also important to know that faith is not dependent upon a formal religious tie, a set of specific propositions, or a system of articulated convictions. Denying "the reality of a supernatural being called God is one thing," notes Neibuhr; but living without "confidence in some center of value and without loyalty to a cause is another. . . . So wherever and whenever we see [persons] giving themselves for that which is greater than themselves and greater than all the particular forces impinging upon them, there we meet the faithful [faith-full] human being."[9] Hence we need not look necessarily for a formal religious affiliation in the resilient, but we should find fierce fidelity to an anchored and elaborate vision of a more humane life. Germanely, most of my subjects found and still sustain their faith *outside* formal religious communities, although they are no less devout for their secularity. More on this in a moment, but as Sharon Parks once said to me in conversation, "Faith isn't something that only religious folks have; it's something that all human beings *do.*"

Faith as an Inherently Relational Enterprise

Fowler and Parks also assert that faith is *inherently relational.*[10] Conveying the fact that faith is a process rather than a trait or a state—a word that can be considered a verb as well as a noun—Parks asserts that "faithing" is a relational activity. From its inception at a persons's birth, when the most fundamental meanings about life are shaped within early caretaking relationships, convictional faith is forged *with* others. These meanings are both vivid and dynamic.[11] Thus Parks links both faith and intimacy, which I see as linchpins of resilience. This point is poignantly illustrated in Alice Walker's novel *The Color Purple,* in which the protagonist is a profoundly impoverished black woman named Celie.[12] Although Celie is sexually abused and impregnated twice by her father, then deprived of letters sent to her over the years by the sister that she was torn from during adolescence, Celie maintains a rich and intense inner life through her internal correspondence with God. She and her sister also carry on daily internal conversations with one another, remaining in touch in this way although they do not receive one another's letters until late in their lives. Her sister articulates the profound strength of these internalized relationships quite clearly when she writes to Celie and declares that even if Celie never actually reads her words, writing them keeps her soul from choking on its own shame. The *imagined* connection is vivid and healing. It gives her grace. In turn, Celie's ties to both God and her sister, elaborated and sustained only in her imagination, serve as the only blueprints from which she develops a few highly nourishing relationships in actuality. Her enduring capacity to love may be Celie's greatest triumph over the bleak outer landscape that repeatedly assaults her faith. Ultimately, loving these others so well allows her to love *herself*.[13]

Similarly moving references to faith as a central and inherently relational aspect of resilience can also be found if we look at survivors of the Nazi Holocaust. For example, Victor Frankl's timeless account of his experiences at Auschwitz and other Nazi prisons is anchored in his conviction that caring with and about others both sustains us and infuses our lives with meaning. Well into his internment, he had the following realization:

My mind clung to my wife's image, imagining it with uncanny acuteness. I heard her answering me, saw her smile, her frank and encouraging look. Real or not, her look was then more luminous than the sun which was beginning to rise. A thought transfixed me: for the first time in my life I saw the truth as it is set into song by so many poets, proclaimed as the final wisdom by so many thinkers. . . . *The salvation of man is through love and in love*. I understood how a man who has nothing left in this world still may know bliss, be it only for a brief moment, in the contemplation of his beloved. In a position of utter desolation, when man cannot express himself in positive action, when his only achievement may consist in enduring his sufferings in the right way—an honorable way—in such a position a man can, through loving contemplation of the image he carries of his beloved, achieve fulfillment. For the first time in my life I was able to understand the meaning of the words, "The angels are lost in perpetual contemplation of an infinite glory." . . . A thought crossed my mind: I didn't even know if she were still alive. I knew only one thing—which I have learned well by now: Love goes very far beyond the physical person of the beloved. It finds its deepest meaning in his spiritual being, his inner self. Whether or not he is actually present, whether or not he is still alive at all, ceases somehow to be of importance. "Set me like a seal upon thy heart, love is as strong as death."[14]

Imagination and Faith

As Joanna, who was introduced in an earlier chapter, noted, "When a father is so uninvolved with you for the first ten or twelve years of your life, you do leave a lot to the imagination. There's no doubt about that." Like Joanna and most of my subjects, both Parks and Fowler make a strong case for the activity of the *imagination* in the process of "faithing." Parks stresses that "to adequately understand and sponsor the journey toward mature adult faith, we are compelled by the reflections of . . . [Samuel Taylor] Coleridge and his inheritors to attend to the significance of the process of imagination in the composing that is faith. For collectively these persons teach us that . . . existence is transcended by means of the *imagination*. We reach for 'the gates of heaven'—the 'ideal'—by means of images, which infused with spirit have the power to give unifying form to the disparate elements of existence. By means of imagination, human beings grasp a transcendent wholeness that was the Promise."[15] Fowler extends this idea by asserting that we actively use our imaginations to create coherent *"master narratives"*; through these we "discern the patterns of power and value in action which give character to the conditions" of our lives. As Parks elaborates, "Our 'master stories' are the interpretive paradigms, conscious or unconscious, by which we make order or coherence of the force fields of our life. They help us discern the . . . overarching meanings unto which we seek to fit—or oppose—our lives."[16] In a moment, I will offer evidence that the resilient have especially coherent "master narratives." Their narrative visions require deeply imaginative, integrative processes that remain integrally linked to our relationships with others. While recruiting capacity may turn out to be the keystone of earlier resilience, these processes of "faithing"—using the imagination to develop a coherent system of beliefs and ideals, then weaving these into inherently relational "master narratives" (which in turn become the center of a person's "convictional knowing")—may easily turn out to be the sources that sustain later love and even resilience itself. Listen for these motifs in the following discussion.

Faith Among the Resilient

I will not explicate linearly the aforementioned ideas about faith here; nor will I offer an encyclopedic exploration of all that the resilient value. Rather, I invite you to stroll on some of the common ground that characterizes their faith. You will see some overlap in their understanding of their own "faithing" and the previous concepts from faith development theory. Whenever the tenets from faith development theory help us understand *how* the resilient flourish, then I will offer a reprise. However, you will see that resilient faith has its own song to sing as well. Note, too, that as we shift to the light in the lives of the resilient, I will no longer make a pointed effort to convince you of their earlier miseries. Some troubles will be cited in context, but now it seems most fruitful to focus on what the resilient seek, not what they flee.

The warp and weft of this faithful fabric is complex. First, the resilient are largely convinced that they can *choose* their own path. They share Victor Frankl's and Nien Cheng's realization that perhaps the greatest freedom in any human circumstance is our capacity to forge our own view of ourselves and our plight, particularly in such extreme situations as death camps, political prisons, and hellish childhoods.[17] There is ample evidence that they choose how to *see*, how to *be*, and how *not* to be. Second, my subjects' faith is largely sustained outside formal religious communities, although, as I said earlier, these people are no less devout for their secularity.

Third, they prize human relationships and see them as integral to their own overcoming. Thus not only do they experience faith as inherently relational, but, in many respects, humane relationships *are* their faith.

Fourth, when the resilient are far from earlier surrogate light, their faith is imaginatively sustained through *symbols* that buttress their vision of caring concern and ethical interactions with others. Aside from human relationships, sources of potent symbolic imagery include literature, films, art, and even—do not be appalled—*television*. Books, the most accessible source of imagery during my subjects' childhoods in the forties and fifties, were especially pivotal to virtually all of them. Hungry readers from early on, they found in literature an omnipresent, movable feast. Authors often write to communicate their own vision, and many children feel that an author is writing to them personally. Thus many subjects said that literature provided deeply influential and satisfying company. One woman even declared, "Books were my *friends*." (I still comfort my own fears of mortality by thinking that I might be buried in a library, surrounded and soothed by an accumulation of human wisdom with no further threat of overdue notices.) In sum, surrogate care through literature is a prominent theme for the resilient. Just as actual surrogates become internalized symbolically, so do literary characters become highly personal, immediate, and sustaining symbols for the resilient.

Fifth and last, the resilient feel a peculiar pride in being chosen to beat the odds, because their suffering, since it did not crush them, *made them more*. Once chosen, many feel an ethical responsibility to help others surmount the odds. This brings us to their strong social activism, the subject of my next chapter—but first, the fabric of their faith.

Faithfully Choosing How to See

Many subjects said that they worked actively with imagery about their lives in a manner that allowed them to both master anxiety

going to be annihilated," and that's pretty funny. . . . So that's . . . what I did, way back then. *I just made the connection now*. . . . You're in the middle of this horrible moment and you say, "Okay, I've got a perspective." . . . So I found a way to control my terror even then . . . as a young girl.

Molly resurrected this strategy during adulthood after she married a man who actually threatened her life. As if rediscovering an amulet, she found that her strategy worked once again:

I went through a period of horrendous nightmares [after I divorced my first husband]. . . . These were awful nightmares with excretions; . . . [they were] grotesque, . . . obsessing about these horrible things. . . . I really had an intense feeling that [my exhusband] was going to murder me. . . . That [time that he actually held a knife to my throat] was still with me; . . . it came back and just hit me. . . . And [now] that's gone; . . . I don't have those nightmares . . . at all. . . . But it takes a while.

Ultimately, Molly links her mastery of her dreams to her faith in *herself*. She believed in her own capacity to script alternative outcomes for her dreams because renewed vision worked so successfully in her *waking* life:

Actually, you asked me about faith, and something occurs to me. . . . *It's faith in myself*, because when . . . I'm having a bad time or a bad moment or feeling just really depressed or . . . just sort of slipping back into something where I don't feel I'm worth very much, . . . I've learned to look at it and say, "I'm feeling really awful now, but I do have faith; . . . I've been through this before, [and I know] that if I just hang on and wait until tomorrow or the next day, then I won't feel this way anymore, and this isn't the real picture." So that's faith, too. . . . It's a way of taking that perspective and using it.

Like a person frightened by shutters smashing in a storm, Molly secures her nightmares with a deceptively mundane hammer and nail. Faithful that her life will not remain this bad, she uses her own symbolic strategies to alter terror's trajectory. Thus she infuses even her *sleeping* thoughts with self-authored meanings. Notice that she calls up a time in her mother's life that is reassuringly ordinary yet filled with that delicious sense of promise that we all feel as children—cruising through a catalog of crackling possibilities, embracing them as our own for an imaginative moment. Molly believes that this fundamental sense of promise and determination also led her to separate from her threatening first husband through the realization that she essentially remarried her childhood nightmares. She now sustains a long relationship with an utterly decent, lively man who is as reassuring as the Sears catalog (and well able to appreciate the quiet comedy of this comparison).

Faithfully Choosing How to Be

The resilient did not stop at adeptly managing their annihilating anxiety through the use of imagery. Rather, they soared past *coping* on to *thriving* through their imaginatively inspired spirituality. Many said that declaring their faith in a better future became the mainspring of their motivation not just to overcome their literal nightmares or future adult challenges (as just discussed) but to surmount their actual childhood circumstances. And the data hold ample evidence of long-standing human "faithing" amidst ice, stone, and darkness.

Brenda, a psychologist in her forties, captures some of the intensity with which many subjects forged their original conviction that life and love are worth the struggle, despite the ugliness encountered. Although she launches her nascent faith through her initial surrogate relationship, she sees it transcending this precious tie:

> I think you have to believe in something. . . . The person who was most instrumental [to this] in my life was my grandmother, who was really a very uneducated peasant woman, but she had this real love

of life. . . . She said there was always something good; there's something you always can live for. I remember just loving to be around her, because she was the only really happy person I knew, and sort of modeling myself after her in that way. . . . I got from her something I never got from either of my parents, which is there *is* something out there. If you work hard and you try, *there is something out there that makes it all worthwhile*. . . . You did what you had to do, . . . but you didn't let that stop you; you didn't let that go away from you. . . .

Although her grandmother dies just when Brenda's family life hits its worst downward spiral, she does not see herself as bereft and empty. She is not content to simply land her hijacked past and have a sadder but wiser future. She starts actively choosing *how to be:*

She died the same year my parents were divorced, [my brother was diagnosed schizophrenic, and I began raising my sister because my parents became so depressed]. . . . But in a funny way, it didn't matter. . . . It's sort of like she kept on going. She didn't really die; . . . the part of her I needed didn't die. . . . Probably *because* she wasn't there, I could turn to some kind of internal resource. . . . I could find something else [inside myself].

Brenda attributes her expansive vision to internalizing this tie and then imaginatively embellishing it with her own inner resources:

I came to believe there was sort of this *spirit:* there was something that maintains you; . . . there's some reason for all of this. . . . I suppose I do look back and I'm really angry lots of times about the earlier years—that *wasn't* fair—but at the same time, I also have to believe I am who I am because of it. . . . I could have been a very different person and maybe a better person, but I don't believe that. I believe it gave me a kind of strength that I wouldn't have [had otherwise]. . . . *You either bounce back or you die,* . . . and life is more precious than just giving up; . . . *there has to be more.*

Here Brenda, like most others in the study, makes it clear that her faith is inherently relational and embedded in a conviction of being "made for more," as Parks and Fowler suggest. However, her statements also suggest that, while her faith was inspired within the context of her relationship with her grandmother, it soars past that specific tie and becomes an ongoing, integrative conviction in resilience itself. Thus she is able to elaborate and sustain her faith well beyond its initial roots. She does this by imaginatively composing a "master narrative" that gives her Neibuhr's "confidence in some center of value and . . . loyalty to a cause."[18] Adumbrating a theme to be explored more later, this woman also believes that her trying past made her more than she would have been otherwise, since she chose a path contrary to it.

Faithfully Choosing What Not to Be

Herman Melville can set the stage for us here with a passage from *Moby Dick:* "As the silent harpoon burned there like a serpent's tongue, Starbuck grasped Ahab by the arm—'God, God is against thee, old man; forbear! 'tis an ill voyage! ill begun, ill continued; let me square the yards, while we may, old man, and make a fair wind of it homewards, to go on a better voyage than this.'"[19] Like Starbuck, most subjects were adamant about what they refused to become. For them, "to be" was spawned by "what *not* to be." Recall that two-thirds of those abused in childhood do *not* abuse their own children. I do not believe this is a random statistical outcome. Rather, it bespeaks an active, even impassioned daily choice not to fall prey to the sins of the House of Atreus. Thus "what *not* to be" may be the substantial spiritual fuel propelling many of them. Virtually every subject in this study reported making ongoing decisions to live in contradiction to what they endured as children. Unlike those who vow, "I'll never treat my children or anyone else that way," yet succumb and repeat past horrors, the resilient hold steadfastly to their ethical resolve. They consider it almost a form of religious practice. Perhaps you recall Anya, the ritual cult abuse survivor. When I asked her what guides her faith, she replied firmly,

> You have to do everything you can to be as good to people and as kind and thoughtful as possible, because . . . *the only way to counter evil . . . is to practice not being evil.* It's the only way, and it's very hard, because, boy!—there are plenty of times I feel like being nasty [when someone is being nasty to me] and probably times when I *am,* but . . . it's so important [*not* to be]. . . . I think it's a life's task.

Several people also spoke fervently about re-creating neither their parents' abusive and/or abandoning parenting nor their hostile marriages. Many spontaneously elaborated on this particular ethical resolve when I asked them, "How did you decide what *not* to be?" For example, Dan—the subject of one of my clinical portraits in Chapter Two—replied that his resolve to foil the family curse was galvanized whenever he reflexively lunged toward his first daughter. He recalls almost literally holding his own arm back from smacking her. Thus Dan quickly made that crucial distinction typical of most honest parents: while it may be normal to have destructive or even murderous *impulses* toward your children, it is certainly not normal to *act* on them. Despite what organized Catholicism might say, there is a grave difference between *thinking* something and *doing* something. Nearly attacking a psychological mirror, Dan saw his own terrified young face in his daughter's and froze abruptly. Dan also assumed responsibility for constantly reeducating himself about managing his anger and hurt rather than inflicting it on his children, revealing an internal locus of responsibility characteristic of the resilient:

> I had so many years of therapy that I had to relearn how to deal with anger and hurt. It was one of the major issues I had to learn; and

because it was *so* important, . . . I eventually learned so well that I even became rather good at it. . . . It's so [crucial] that I overcompensated in a way. . . . I had vowed to myself, by the time I was ten or eleven, that when I grew up I would *not* be like my parents. I knew *that* was no good, and I absolutely vowed to myself that . . . I would not be brutal and abusive. I would hold in angry feelings, because God knows I didn't want to be like them. . . . I'd hold it in until finally I couldn't stand it any longer, and even then I wouldn't vent it in the same way they did; I'd vent it with a lot of crying and frustration. . . . *I wasn't dealing with it very well, but at least I wasn't hitting anybody.* . . .

I even knew [when my first child was a toddler] that I was at such risk for [abusing her], and there were a couple of times when . . . she would do something I didn't like, and I'd hold my hand up like this and realize, "My God! I'm about to whack her!" [I'd] stop right there and say, "My God! Am I going to turn into a monster like my father? . . . My instinct was, when your child doesn't obey, you strike her as hard as you can strike her; . . . it must have been a dozen times that I would almost stop my hand. I *did* spank the children occasionally when they did particularly naughty acts like biting one of their brothers, but the spankings were very infrequent and not particularly harsh. I tried to strike a healthy balance between being too lenient and too punitive.

I then asked Dan why he stopped himself from striking out when so many people, abused or not, condone hitting children. Moreover, why did he hold back when many like him, so *desperately* brutalized since infancy, understandably—although never acceptably—savage their children? He replied resolutely,

That's a good question. *I just remembered how awful it was, as a kid myself,* and I was young enough, in my twenties when my children were young, to remember . . . it was no fun. . . . [Earlier, at seventeen,] I just decided that you can be a good person or a rotten person, and I wanted to be good. *It was a decision.* I was seeing everything in black-and-white terms in those days, as very much good versus evil, and . . . I wanted to do all the good things that I admired in other people, so I sort of chose that.

One morning not long ago I went to the mailbox and found a video from Dan, sent at my request. A few days before the scene pictured, his middle daughter had given birth to *her* first daughter. Mother and child were getting to know one another, unobtrusively filmed by the father. At one moment in the film, Dan's daughter looked unpretentiously into her baby's eyes and suddenly, in a low murmur, began to sing "Amazing Grace." I immediately recalled what Dan had said to me about this birth—that here was the first mother in many generations in his family who had *not* been so brutalized as a child that she had to struggle constantly against herself and her past in order to give her infant competent care. At ease with her mother's love, the baby gazed calmly (and I wept).

Similarly determined not to repeat the curse, Joanna refused to re-create her parents' rabid marital hostility. In explaining the deep regard and dignified respect that characterize her marriage to Kai, she noted that the bold contrast is a deliberate, ongoing choice:

> The only thing that I can conclude about [the sharp departure] is that parents can either be models for how you *do* want to live in a relationship or they can be very strong models for how you *don't* want to lead a relationship. *My parents were so off together you couldn't miss it.* . . . You said to yourself, "Good God, who in their right minds would *do* that to themselves?" You couldn't miss the obvious in our family. There was no saying, "Well, it's kind of a bad relationship, but I'm not exactly sure what's going on." I can remember one time after a fight between my parents, . . . [when] I had gotten a little braver, at thirteen or fourteen, . . . and I turned on them contemptuously, and I said, "I just want you two to know I'm *never* getting married!" . . . I know at some level I said to myself, "I

either will not be married or I will not be in a marriage like that."
. . . Why put up with it? . . . I don't think it's all murky and dark and
confusing to me. I think at a very conscious level I said, "Screw
that—life is too short."

Joanna's fierce vision reminds me that once, when I was in a
small Harvard history of psychology seminar with developmentalist Shep White, he said, "If there is no model of fixing in the mind
of the fixer, how can you know what to fix?" His insight is highly
relevant to the history of personal evolution, since my subjects
found no mystery about what needed fixing and drafted elaborate
blueprints for "better." Their marital and parental models were *so*
extreme and dark that they saw little ambiguity of choice. Decision
making seemed to bifurcate sharply for them, and they consciously
chose a more humane path. As Frog, the drama professor, noted,

> You had this negative role model in my mother that was really
> strong. You knew what you *didn't* want to do and how you *didn't*
> want to live your life, so you could set up values in opposition to
> that. . . . And in school there were these teachers who supported
> efforts to be human. . . . [Their modeling] was pretty crucial. . . .
> And then [taking calculated risks to put myself on a better track]
> worked out well.

Many of the subjects said that they feel that people make *systematically* good or bad choices for themselves over time and that
decency evolves through an *accumulation* of relatively good decisions. After they had taken a few risks whose outcome was resoundingly positive, their loyalty to the calculated leap of faith was
launched. In any case, their major personal choices did *not* feel
ambiguous. With no limp determination, Joanna decided, "I'm not
going to spend a lifetime doing what they did. I may stupidly
imbibe another poison, but not that one."

Joanna's husband, Kai, also said that aside from the pain that his family members inflicted on him, their lives seemed terribly *empty*. In what quickly became a humorous exchange, we looked at the absurd contrast between his father's beating and threatening to kill him, on the one hand, and both parents' anxious and preoccupied efforts to prevent him from having home accidents. As one earnest teenager once sighed to me, "No matter what I wanted to do as a child, my father knew someone who died of it." Thus Kai's parents' confining caution made life into flat seltzer:

> What really motivated me [to seek a different path] wasn't the harshness of my parents' discipline; . . . it was the *void* of what looked to be their lives. . . . I didn't know how they enjoyed being alive if they didn't do things or take risks. They were so safety-conscious, to me it appeared that they were planning their death from the time they were twenty. . . . My father used to give me accident reports of how people died in their homes. . . . So I learned to define myself through negation first.

Many subjects also said that their adult choices have been inspired by their deep *contempt* for the way their own parents acted in the past. They feel that they would rather not be parents—in fact, would rather not be *alive*—than have their own children or partners ever view them similarly. Although their adult views of their parents have become complex, differentiated, philosophical, and often tolerant, their childhood memories are like the scent of great hazard to any self-preserving animal. Speaking for many others, Grady declared that, while he finds it *intelligible* that someone from his circumstances would choose a similar path, he will *not* tolerate that in himself:

> My past was unfortunate. It hurt. It caused embarrassment. It caused pain. [But] . . . my life also helped create a mold of what I would *not* be. . . . I truly believe there are people who have had alcoholic, abusive parents, and who've become that way [themselves] . . . because

in a genuine sense, that's the only way they knew. *But I would never, ever let myself do that. I'd blow my head off before I'd do that to my kids,* [to re-create] what happened to me or let my kids have the lack of respect [I had for my father]. . . . It would truly mortify me to have my children not respect me. . . . I'm not trying to be melodramatic, but I'd end my own life before I'd let my kids have such low regard and disdain for me, because it wouldn't be worth my going on. They'd be better off without a father than with a father that they truly hated and didn't respect. *So I'm not going to let it happen.*

It seems that these resilient people selectively internalized more humane ways of being so that they deeply identified with the better models that they encountered and ferociously *disidentified* with the worst. They developed an *alternative imagination* to hold their hope.[20] Why and how they hoarded "better," coaxing these coals until their lives were aflame with humane choices, is ultimately an unsolved mystery. But they knew, with faithful certainty, that they were made for more, and they began by repudiating the worst. As Shibvon concluded plainly, "This ain't me. I don't want any part of it."

Sustaining the Faith

Although for some of my subjects, faith in something "better" and religious faith are synonymous, most sustain their vision outside organized religion. Some are grounded in the ultimacy of human relationship, for example; others sustain their faith through literature and other art forms. Let us look first at those whose faith lies outside the church.

Faith Outside Formal Religious Affiliations. As I have noted, a striking theme of this study is the considerable extent to which my subjects sustain fierce fidelity to their visions *outside* organized religion. With so much richness to be found within the world's religions, why would this be so? Let me speculate about this trend before letting some of my subjects speak for themselves.

First, my subjects' high levels of ego development and personal evolution as adults may render them less comfortable in more conventional faith communities, which tend to impose or to assume an uncritical acceptance of ideologies. Most prefer a spiritual home encouraging probing, pondering, and continually renegotiating strictures, rituals, and beliefs. Second, half the subjects are therapists, and the profession itself tends to be comparatively secular. Perhaps psychology is essentially an implicit faith system that embraces debate and a multiplicity of perspectives, allowing its participants to find deeper meanings and human connections in a manner that can be considered spiritual. This may be especially true among clinicians—those who seek sustained, reparative relationships with the struggling. Whether their work is focal to their spirituality or augments it, many clinicians feel that it has invaluable transcendent aspects. Third, many subjects did not participate strongly in organized religious activity as children and thus gradually found other settings, such as intellectual communities and their own evolving faithfulness, in which to invest their hearts.

Fourth, many of those who *did* participate in specific religious communities during a particular historical moment (such as 1950s Catholicism) feel that their religious communities hurt them through harsh treatment in parochial school or through nearly unattainable, thus unreasonable, behavioral expectations. Particular thorns include the virtues of infinite self-sacrifice and unreflective compliance, unfounded accusations and guilt-engendering admonitions, the tenet of original sin, and the perception of sex as sin. Burdened and battered at home, they did not need more ways to feel bad about themselves or more reasons to remain shrunken and silent. Although some, like Shibvon, were quietly sheltered by compassionate clergy, many others felt betrayed by particular church officials. This occurred when clergy who knew the gravity of their troubles failed to challenge—some even *condoned*—their abusive home lives or preached general beliefs that amplified their parents' harshness. Finally, several subjects said that organized religious teachings simply did not help enough with their unlivable home lives. They needed a more adequate spiritual tool kit to solve the problems they faced as children, so they began to fashion their own.

Most who had childhood religious exposure did feel that, despite its shortcomings, it gave them some grounding in human decency, integrity, and character. Although they may be under sail toward more self-authored shores, they continually integrate what seems most accurate and inspiring to them from their religious understandings. In addition, while most are ultimately faithful to their *own* vision, they maintain a firm reference to "something larger" and more inclusive. In our interviews together, they often wept as they pressed the pulse of that which they hold most precious—the anchor of their souls' investment. But for most, "larger" seems to be founded in the primacy of sound human relationships and a sense of mission about making the world more humane, specific religious tenets aside.

When I asked Joanna if religion or any broad spiritual influence was important to her while she was growing up, she replied in a manner characteristic of many others. In this passage, she describes her feeling that her own immense spirituality was born of a hidden parental gift: the right to choose her own faith *outside* a formal religious practice.

> . . . I have come to realize how valuable were some of the things that my parents inadvertently gave us. . . . I don't think they had any idea that they were doing it right, but . . . they didn't inflict religion or any sort of "ism" on us. . . . Although your behavior had to be impeccable, the implication was always *"Think whatever you want. Your mind belongs to you;* . . . don't let anybody constrain it. . . . As long as you're impeccable in your behavior, use it in any way you want to—nothing's taboo. Be really careful what you show or what you say, but you do get to *have* it. It's *your* brain. It's *your* mind. Those

are *your* feelings." There was never any sense of . . . "If you're thinking this, it's wrong," or "If you're questioning that, you're wrong." It
was a . . . personal decision. In fact, it's so amazing to me that they
were somewhat apologetic that they couldn't give us a religion. It
was "Gee, . . . we don't do this ourselves, so we encourage you to go
out and find what you can find, but we can't give you much guidance." It was enormously helpful. I think it's so ironic that, to some
extent, they felt they were *not* giving us something. That really
turned out to be quite a gift.

Similarly, Kai asserts, "Faith has been important to me, but not
religion." When I asked him how he made this distinction, he
focused on his need to have his faith remain magical and mysteri-
ous, although his own research niche within psychology is relatively
scientific. While his upbringing was not religious, and he dislikes
most formal religious strictures (such as those within the ideological
rigidity of Catholicism), he says, "As much as I don't like the
Catholic Church, the one thing I *love* about the Catholic Church is
its icons, because I can interpret them any way I want"—especially
imagery about his own relationship to the universe. Although Kai
resists the idea of anyone interpreting this imagery for him and certainly would not impose *his* interpretations on anyone else, he prizes
the richness of church architecture and symbolism. (Remember,
although most of these subjects are technically areligious, they are
faithful to their *own* humane visions and to integrating what they
believe is the best of what organized religions offer.)

As a child, Dan also adored religious icons and for a time put
great stock in their ability to deliver him from his plight. While his
nuclear family was areligious, his grandmother—his adored surrogate—was Episcopalian. From age eight to ten, Dan sought solace
spontaneously in what seemed to him the monolithic redemptive
strength of religion. By ten he was beginning to make a normal
developmental shift from concrete religious beliefs to a more reflective, abstract faith:

My grandmother was Episcopalian and believed very sincerely in the whole doctrine: that Jesus Christ was the son of God and that if you prayed to Jesus that thing that you asked for would come true and that if you were a good person you died and went to heaven, . . . all the standard type of Episcopalian ritual. She wanted somebody to go to church with her, because other people in the family didn't believe in it. . . . Since I thought she was just wonderful, I was her church companion, and I'd sit beside her snuggling into her fur coat. . . . I remember singing all the hymns and praying all the prayers. . . . I used to pray over and over and over again as a kid that God would save me. . . . I'd say the Lord's Prayer over and over and over again—like fifty times—in the morning. . . . I'd be there praying and I could hear my father shouting and [hitting], and I was praying to God to save me. . . . It felt as if there was somebody more powerful than my father. . . . If he only could hear, he would make things all right, . . . and this was really very important to me.

However, the complete protective failure of both icon and belief drove Dan from the fold:

I believed up until the time I was eight or ten years old and I sent away in the mail for this crucifix that glowed in the dark. . . . I thought that would be pretty terrific. . . . I put it on my wall, and my mother came in and said, "What's this?" I said, "It's a cross; I sent away for it," and she said, "You can't have that; that's Catholic!" She was, among other things, also very prejudiced. So she grabbed the cross and she threw it in the wastebasket, and I thought to myself, "Now you're going to get it!" My own twisted sense of religion was that having thrown the cross in the wastebasket, [she would be] struck dead by lightning or something. I sat there for three days waiting for something awful to happen and nothing happened! And then I lost my faith. . . . I ended up, very shortly afterward, deciding that reality didn't test out with all the things that I had believed up until then. At least *from my own perspective* [these beliefs] weren't so.

While Dan abandons his concrete faith abruptly and never returns, he refashions the best of what he absorbed from his few years of fervent adherence. Without skipping a beat, his conversation shifts from his failed faith in specific religious tenets and icons to a deeper faith in humane comportment and social justice:

> There's been a by-product of all this which is a very good thing, which is what I believe in now, very much. [It's] what is sometimes referred to as karma. *I believe that you really do get back from life what you give.* . . . I don't care whether it's for any religious purposes, or just somehow the law of nature, but I really do believe that's the case; and I tried *that* and it *worked.* I find myself very often getting a bit preachy with people who work for me about [this. I tell them that] . . . if you do something just because it's right, . . . in doing it you're giving to the world something that's making it a better place. . . . Somehow in the end that's going to help, and I really do believe that; it's a very big part of my life. . . . That's the theme in all religions: "Do unto others as you would have them do unto you," . . . and that's my religion.

Marie, a legal aid lawyer in her mid thirties, has also transformed her disappointing, even assaultive childhood experiences with 1950s clerical interpretation of Catholic doctrine into a sophisticated, autonomous adult faith. Her experiences in parochial school—combined with her desperately poor, rejecting, and humiliating slum childhood—turned her toward these firmly self-authored convictions. When I asked her if religion or any broad spiritual influence had shaped her life in any way, she replied that religion per se had had an extremely negative impact:

> My mother is Catholic, and she's very devout. I was sent to Catholic school for the first eight years, until I felt I couldn't deal with another nun, and went to public schools for the last four years but went to these religious classes on Monday night for continued indoctrina-

tion. . . . I say *negative* because I felt that the most that could be said is that this very dogmatic [teaching]—well, I don't want to engage in too much labeling—but the antifemale, antisexual, antifeeling theology that was taught, at least when I was being indoctrinated, provided another focus to push against, if nothing else. It was another source of rebellion. . . . When I think about those years, I can feel resentment start to build . . . [about] the tyranny of religious orders that have God on their side. . . . It makes for a really uneven encounter.

Marie's encounters created almost a photo negative of faith for her. Since Catholicism seemed to team up with her family in an attempt to hijack her childhood, she rejected it as a formal organization. Yet she is a woman piloted by deeply held convictions. Here you see that what she holds precious commingles intimately with what she abhors:

I suppose to the extent that the [Catholic] Church seemed to me [to be a] very unforgiving, judgmental, damning institution, somehow I sort of inverted a lot of what I took to be the teaching and just fought against that feeling of doom and evil and the ugliness of humanity and tried to counter it with ideas about people who may be forgiving and warm. . . . *Given a choice between good and evil, they would pick good, maybe.* . . . [Fifties' Catholicism painted] just such an onerous picture of life, and so hideous—suffering and pain and torture. . . . Forget it, I just didn't see how this could be a source of comfort to people that you have the next life. . . .

I definitely felt that this life was worth more of a shot and that I couldn't accept pain and failure and agony as my lot in life. . . . *I wasn't going to take that, absolutely not.* . . . Life looked like it could be *long*, and I just didn't make the assumption that you should sit miserably and hope for martyrdom. . . . It seems like a lot of rationalizations for people living in misery. Instead of taking an active role and trying to make things better, this whole thing is geared to making you rationalize why you feel so bad, explaining why life is hell.

There's just so much lack of vitality—it's like being dead the whole time you're alive. . . . That was just impossible. . . . I just couldn't see it. I couldn't see living by that philosophy or trying to gain any comfort from it at all. *I kept seeing that there's a lot more worth and a lot more action and a lot more vitality out there* if you just let go of this morbid fascination with death, dying, and pain; . . . it just seemed so morbid and so grotesque, so antilife. . . . It was just very dark and gloomy and moody. . . . *I was driven in the opposite direction, just as hard as I could run.* I suppose to that extent the negative resulted in what I consider to be a more positive set of values.

I was once presenting Marie's photo-negative faith to a group of clinicians interested in faith and resilience when a storm swelled outside. Just as I was about to stress that Marie remains no less impassioned or enlightened for her self-authored convictions, lightning literally struck the building. I stopped making my point to the astounded group and began exclaiming toward the roiling heavens, "You're not listening! I didn't say that the resilient were unfaithful, but that *human interpretations* of faith failed or even persecuted them. They're deeply faithful, but largely *outside* organized religious affiliations. *You* above all should know that nobody has cornered the market on spiritual truth!" Perhaps I'm indulging the pathetic fallacy, but I do want to close this section with an example of the subjects who *did* find remarkable comfort within their religious lives (although they, too, found inspiration rather than complete direction there). This will help me bridge to my discussion of faith as an inherently relational phenomenon.

Faith Within Formal Religious Affiliations.   When I asked Robert, a fifth-grade teacher in his mid forties, if religion or faith was a strong part of his life, he declared that his sense of Christ, although always evolving, was paramount to him even as a young child. In a manner reminiscent of Celie in *The Color Purple*, Robert found surrogacy in Christ, including that lodestone of resilient love, unconditional acceptance. From the time Robert was five, his father tried repeatedly to slash his own wrists. Both parents tried to hang themselves, and by Robert's late adolescence, they had succeeded. Yet the surrogate relationship that he forged with Christ was literally and spiritually life-preserving, a startling example of Robert's imaginative mastery of his condition:

> Born-again Christians . . . talk about Christ coming into their lives. [Actually,] . . . a lot of people talk about that. . . . I don't really relate very well to that because Christ has *always* been in my life. I can't think back to a time when I didn't know that Christ was there with me, so there was that tremendous strength. . . . No matter how bad things got, . . . no matter whether I was going to lose my father or not, [no matter] what happened to him, there was that assurance. . . . I'm describing to you a feeling that Christ was closer than you and I are sitting now. I could have touched him if I wanted to. He was that real—not that I *saw* him, . . . but he was that real to me.

When I asked Robert what Christ held for him, since his image of Christ seemed comforting, reassuring, and powerful, he replied,

> Probably that he loved me. . . . I know that my parents loved me. I'm not sure I knew that all along in the midst of the turmoil, [though]. . . . I don't think that came in until later. . . . *[You realized it in adulthood?]* Right, . . . [but] as a child, I don't think I felt awfully loved. I was there; they . . . fed me, and I had a place to sleep and all, but do you really love somebody if you create chaos? I don't know what I was thinking as a child, but it didn't *feel* like love. But the relationship I had with Christ did, and I went to church, and I enjoyed reading the Bible and studying.

Unfortunately, like Dan, Robert found the natural transition from his concrete childhood beliefs to a more reflective, abstract faith particularly wrenching. Perhaps this is because *his* Christ was serving as a virtual foster father for him while his deeply struggling parents tried, unsuccessfully, to pull their own lives out of a tailspin. Unlike Dan, however, Robert revised his faith to include a more abstract but no less powerful Christ. Yet both men feel that their *own* interpretations of basic spiritual tenets guide their lives:

> When I reached about the age of twelve, something very traumatic happened. I lost that concrete feeling, and God turned into an abstraction, which totally, totally just really shook me. It was terrible. It was almost like abandonment in a way. . . . But the abstract faith that I have now . . . is so much better, so much richer, than what I had . . . in that concrete mode. . . . The possibilities are just infinite, but I didn't know that at the time.

Thus, whether the faith of the resilient is spawned and propelled *within* or *outside* the world's religions, it is deeply held and fiercely reparative.

In closing this section, let me make it clear that I have no wish to start a building fund for the First Resilience Church, order sunny vestments, and search for a pulpit. However, I do think that faith systems, broadly but passionately conceived, that operate outside formal religious organizations are no less powerful than formal organizations for those who live by them. This section has reviewed a variety of faithful symbols, images, and convictions that are the fingerprints of the resilient, and they are undoubtedly dear to many others as well. These spiritual tools for overcoming are germane and inspiring to all of us and are especially precious to those who use them to illuminate the darkest nights. But we must also recognize that, whether the resilient are within a formal religious organization or not, a hallmark of their faith is that it is located within *relationships* of merit, dimension, and promise with actual human beings as well as larger, more inclusive spiritual forces. Now let us take a brief look at relationships *as* faith and explore the faith-related imagery that emerges in literature, films, art, and even television.

Faith in the Ultimacy of Human Relationships. Grady has made a commitment to himself: "Every single day I tell my kids individually that I love them *[weeping]*. . . . As long as they live under my roof, every day of my life, I will tell my kids that I love them." In preceding pages, you have heard the resilient make many such statements about the primacy of love in their lives. This is such an overarching, highly textured theme that it is difficult to find a few voices to capture the sound of the symphony. Let me offer the most explicit statements they made about dignified, committed loving as a passion unto itself. The leitmotifs that emerged include a dedication to creating depth of contact in all important relationships; the restorative power of their human bonds; the value of relating to others in a manner that includes each person in the relationship while embracing the broader human context that includes us all; their determination to "make the world a home" for themselves and others; and the recognition that creating irreplaceable attachments is fundamentally humanizing to them, capturing the depth of their investment in life itself.

Perhaps you recall the horrors that befell Anya, the ritual abuse survivor. Bearing witness to infant sacrifices as a child might certainly have left a small human heart blackened and cold. But when I asked her where her light comes from, Anya said she clears a path through her rage and seizes upon

> knowing *how important it is to be loving and to love* and to . . . work on maintaining those relationships and having compassion for people: . . . it feels like *it's all the little moments.* All the little moments when you feel like you made contact with somebody in a real way. . . . Each one of those just feels like a jewel to me, . . . and it's hard *[sigh].* . . . I don't do it all the time. . . . And I get furious and all the

rest of it, but . . . when it happens, [it's a jewel]. . . . I think it's one
of the things I like about being a therapist: . . . that there's a space
where . . . everybody's saying, "Okay, now, we're going to [con-
nect]. . . . We can do this; . . . we're not going to get all the rest of
muddled life involved in this," so you can have those moments, . . .
those points of light.

Alison, a children's art teacher, extends this motif when she
declares that, like many abandoned children, she has *always* had a
homing device for the caring connection and a deep faith that it
will be generative for her and others:

> I think I've always had tremendous faith in relationships with peo-
> ple, even if the central parental ones haven't been that constant or
> that easy. . . . It's always been important to me to find other [rela-
> tionships] that could fill those holes, and . . . I've chosen well. I really
> do feel like I've been very, very fortunate that there have been peo-
> ple there. . . . [It's given me] a tremendous sense, in retrospect, of the
> wisdom of children—that they make wonderful decisions for them-
> selves more often than not.

Yet these people do not simply attach indiscriminately. Speaking for the group, Joanna preferentially seeks fellow travelers who
avoid either a self-sacrificial or self-referential imbalance in their
ties. Rather, they seek bonds with overall reciprocity and a more
inclusive embrace of broader human concerns:

> I've noticed among people who care a lot about their lives that it
> often means that they're not quite so wrapped up in themselves and
> therefore they also have a lot more to give to a relationship. They're
> just readier to see a lot of value in every kind of connectedness, so
> they're not afraid to connect to ideas, and they're not afraid to con-
> nect to having strong feelings about what's going on in the
> world. . . . I must see it as a sign of openness and an ability to get out
> of themselves.

Nearly echoing her words, Frog underscores that these overarching connections are his form of spirituality, an ethic of

> doing things for people [simply] because it's important to be morally
> good to people. . . . When I studied theater in Bali, it was very much
> connected to the religion and the spiritual beliefs of the people, and
> there was a sense of giving up yourself for the spirit of what was being
> communicated through the performance and for the people you
> were performing it for. It was a gift to them, that you were serving
> something higher than yourself and, without becoming Hindu in
> the Balinese sense, that made a lot of sense to me.

Thus, like ribbons of water cutting through ice floes in the Arctic summer, the convictions of the resilient proclaim their investment in finding connections that allow them to be an integral part of others' lives as well as their own and at the same time part of something more comprehensive, including but not quite reducible to the individuals in the relationship. Their faithful devotion to participation in the human community is deeply enlivening to them.

Frog and Diana amplify these voices when they speak of their determination "to make the world home." Constructing an elaborate inner fabric of relatedness to themselves, past ties, present family and friends, and future love, they feel that they have woven themselves into a sense of stability and promise that goes well beyond their immediate circumstances. Early on, they found that human beings at large, and many individuals in particular, offered silken threads of connection to them when their original families held out only nettles and straw. Now their fabric of connection is intricate and strong. Thus, while they would be staggered by losing those they love, they would rise again, because they have created a new life before. They remain convinced that they could—*and would have to*—do it again. Living sparingly within good connections as children, they would *never* live far outside them again.

Frog's experiences with the calculated leap of faith into the

world at large have worked so well for him that he has repeatedly
left this country to find a home in remote cultures while maintaining strong ties over decades in the States. He became a sojourner
at sixteen, finishing high school from a rented room, yet quickly
forged a supportive community among teachers and friends. This
initial success in "making the world home" was infectious. While
he now seeks the deeper roots of a more traditional home in New
England, he has spent the past two decades creating a sense of connection in foreign communities by being genuinely interested in
them and writing two books about them:

> I have often had the experience—as recently as last summer when
> I went to Africa—of kind of throwing myself at the mercy of the
> world and seeing if it will take care of me. . . . Somehow I have this
> faith that people will take care of me, and they always do. It always
> amazes me. . . . When I was in jail in South Africa [with 800 black
> men, for protesting apartheid], these people took care of me and
> invited me to their homes. So I got out of jail into this community of
> people, and I ran into other people that I lived with in the villages;
> . . . and [I found a home] with Michael Firenze in Italy, when I trav-
> eled with his theater company. In each one of these adventures that
> I've had in these other cultures, I'm always looking for a family; *I'm
> always kind of throwing myself on the mercy of the world* and then hop-
> ing that I'll find a family there, that I can be a friend. . . .

> It makes them feel important to know that somebody thinks
> they're interesting and cares about them and really wants to find out
> about them. Lately, it's been these kind of theatrical families that I
> write about, and they're so happy. They're usually people that
> nobody has ever heard of or written about, so it makes them feel
> honored that some professor wants to write about them; but that's
> only now that I'm more established. . . . Before, I just think that for
> them it was this feeling of being happy to have somebody care
> enough to be interested. . . . I feel like that's what I give in

exchange. . . . I find a way to give something back, however it's possible. After Michael Firenze and his theater company took me in for a year, then I brought him to this country, on his tour. . . . [In other cases,] I write about some people who are happy to be written about.

Similarly, Diana spent the first half of her life, before she married and had a family, "making the world home." Outside rewarding family ties for so long in her early years, but always deeply connected to a strong network of friends and community, she realizes that if she lost her husband and small sons now, the scars would always ache but she would go on. This faithful stamina stems from

that sense of always feeling relief when you walked out the front door. *[There] was a challenge to make the world home.* I don't feel like families are the only thing, just the way I don't feel like my current nuclear family is the only thing right now. I don't feel like a marriage can fulfill everything, and I think in some ways [my family of origin] taught me a form of resourcefulness—[something] that, had they been just a little less abusive, I might not have learned. You know, they were so infantilizing; and . . . once you're [living among the] completely regressed, there's nothing as good as [taking to the highway]. . . . My always wanting to get away and travel was certainly a result of knowing that it wasn't safe to stay where I was. . . . Absolutely. . . . [My family] didn't give me the part about connections with other people. They sent me places that allowed me to find . . . friends that I've had for twenty years or more. That's a real accomplishment. . . .

A kind of a hidden asset of all of that misery was that I don't feel afraid of very much. . . . I have the sense . . . [that] if some terrible disaster came and beclouded my whole life and I lost my family or I got terminally ill or something, I really feel like I could take on whatever I needed to take on. . . . When I would see all those little kids who had been sexually abused, it didn't scare me particularly or

. . . make me want to back up. Not that I would wish to have horrible things happen to me. But I don't feel [I would ever give up].

A number of other people spoke of literally creating life and then recognizing the impact of death as a testament to the grave importance of their human bonds. They often groped for words to convey the depth of their sustaining, even overwhelming experience of connection to those they love. Many wept, not out of sadness but because they were terribly moved by what they beheld. I conclude this section with Rita's recognition that her salvation came through bearing her first child and Kai's recognition that he has let his loved ones matter so much that he would never really recover from losing them.

Rita is a clinician in a well-respected family therapy institute, especially esteemed for her work with incestuous families. Her childhood was essentially her first clinical internship. In a Dickensian swirl, she survived her sexually abusive foster father, briefly escaped to some adolescent peace at the YWCA, then slipped back into turbulent waters at twenty through her brief affiliation with a reeling alcoholic. Transported from a home for unwed mothers to a maternity hospital, facing last rites, she waged a fundamental battle with life itself:

A priest came in and said I was dying and that I needed to go to confession. . . . I remember looking at myself bleeding to death. . . . The people at the hospital called the woman who had brought me and asked her to find a relative because I was alone at five o'clock in the morning; and she told them that I didn't have any family and I didn't have any relatives. They said, "Well, find somebody, because she's not going to live." I asked them what I had and they said, "You had a baby girl, . . . and you have this packing inside of you. We're going to take it out, and you might die." . . . I can't believe they said that, but they did. . . .

And I remember—it's all very real to me—I thought, *"I'm not going to die, and I'm not going to confession"* . . . and I *wouldn't* go to confession. . . . I don't know if I saw God, but I knew there was somebody else watching over me, and that . . . I was meant to live to take care of this little girl. . . . It was like the testing ground to see if that's what I really wanted. . . . I had to give her away at three months and put her in a home [for a short time], and I went to work immediately, . . . so full of milk. . . . My girlfriend and I had her baptized, and I was all alone.

There was just nobody around, *but I knew there was somebody. I just knew. . . . There was an inconceivable strength that I began to develop,* and it got me through. . . . I got this sense of calling on something when I needed it.

Thus, in a sudden, transforming moment, Rita forcibly decides that she is good, not bad, deserving of a future because *she* created a supreme and unassailable good—her child:

All of a sudden I realized, "This shouldn't happen to me": . . . Something made me feel . . . that this was *good*; it wasn't bad. How can you make the birth of a baby that was born healthy bad? How do you blame yourself for something like that? Because it was too beautiful to make ugly, and I had given something beautiful [to the world]. . . . It was too good to say that I had done something bad. I couldn't have. . . . You can't pin this one on me. *I did this one just perfect.* At least, that's how I felt. . . .

There were some horrible times after that—some despair and some craziness and some times that I thought it was just never going to get any better. . . . I was very angry. I was very, very angry, . . . and at times I gave up on the strength that I thought I needed and had; but somehow or other I always knew that if I really did call on it, [that strength] was going to get me out. . . . It wasn't going to come easy; I was going to have to work for it. . . . But it has gotten me through a lot of things.

On the threshold, Rita experiences her first child as her raison d'être and her occasion for grace. She decides that conceiving such beauty, despite her ecclesiastically unsanctioned circumstances, reigns above church law and speaks to a more elevated order. So she bypasses the priest and experiences an *immediate* connection with God. Creating such good through her baby, she finds faith that she *herself* is good—perhaps the greatest triumph of the maltreated.

Just as Rita renews her fundamental faith in carrying on with the birth of her child, Kai recognizes that his ties to loved ones are so deep that their loss would be devastating. His is a voice of mature love, candid here about the sense of endless opportunity for affection that colored his youth. While he does not feel that his life would end or that he would never love again if he lost his wife or children or his dearest friends, he soberly sees that losing them would be a permanent impoverishment:

> I must admit this embarrassment of my youth: when I was younger, I thought women were replaceable. It was certainly a more two-dimensional cardboard quality. . . . "A relationship's a relationship, and it's all for fun"—that sort of adolescent narcissism that you're both just sort of playing. And if that doesn't work out—well, there are a lot of great people in the world. . . . But [now, in imagining] any of those awful scenarios you can think of, like what it would be like if Joanna died for some reason, . . . *for the first time in my life, I don't know what I would do.* . . . I can think about it and get sad, . . . but I can't think about it and know what it would do to my life. It's really that scary. That's what those relationships in adult life open up, just how important they are, and *how they're totally irreplaceable.* . . . I know that I usually land on my feet, and I think I would;

but that really scares me about those kinds of relationships. . . .
There's no replacement for them.

And so the resilient find much of their faith in love, which is
sustaining and terrifying all at once. Love anchors them. It gives
their lives texture and contour. It propels them toward "something
larger." It allows them resonance with the human race. Treated terribly as children, they should be among the least faithful of the loving, yet they are among the most. Having lacked or lost, then
found, such devotion, they know that they will never quite get over
losing anyone they have ever loved. Yet they are prepared to pay
the price. Like Wilbur, the endlessly endearing pig of E. B. White's
Charlotte's Web, Kai can now tolerate loving Joanna so deeply that
losing her would leave him intact but forever changed: Wilbur
never relinquishes Charlotte. Long after she dies, he realizes that,
while he loves her spider children and grandchildren with the most
tender regard, none could dislodge Charlotte from the center of his
heart. Without peer, Charlotte was not only a good writer, but a
rare friend. Joanna is Charlotte for Kai.[21]

Faith Through Literature, Film, and the Arts.   I noted earlier
that when the resilient are far from earlier surrogate light, their faith
is imaginatively sustained through *symbols* that buttress their vision
of caring concern and ethical interaction with others. Elaborated
symbols can become a mature form of self-sustaining surrogacy. Listen to Nien Cheng:

How could I have thought for one moment that they would loosen
the handcuffs? Now that I had shown them my weakness, they
would be glad and think I might indeed succumb to their pressure
out of concern for my hands. I said to myself, "I'll forget about my
hands. If I have to be crippled, then I'll accept being crippled. In this
world there are many worthy people with crippled hands or no

hands at all." I remembered that when my late husband and I were in Holland in 1957, we had bought a painting by a veteran of the Second World War who had lost both his hands. He used his toes to hold the paintbrush, I was told. I used to treasure this painting as a symbol of human courage and resourcefulness. It was slashed by the Red Guards when they looted my home. But the thought of this artist whom I had never met inspired me with courage and helped me to become reconciled to the possibility of losing the use of my hands after this ordeal.[22]

Literature, films, and other art forms offer the resilient the accessibility, respite, companionship, comprehension, enlightenment, modeling, witnessing, and unconditional acceptance that are so characteristic of sponsoring love. You can never get to the end of the feast, and you never have to leave the banquet. My subjects readily described artistic images that were deeply comforting to them, sheltering and fueling their faith like old friends who stood by them in hard times. Beloved images are company you can trust. Remember that many artists create to communicate what *they* experience most powerfully, and the resilient keep a hungry eye out for *anything* that will help them prevail.

Surrogacy through literature is a particularly prominent theme in the interviews, since books in particular are highly accessible. Several subjects said that they had adult library cards as children, skipped school to go to the library, or regularly took out a stack of books and read them all in a week. And, since many of the resilient had very vivid imaginative capacities, their cherished images were especially potent and enduring for them. They were happy to be reunited with their "old friends" in the course of the interviews, reminiscing in thick, animated detail. Together we probed just why their images were so important to them. As Joanna exclaimed,

I get a nearly dizzy feeling of giddiness when I go into libraries. I mean, I literally like the smell of books; I like the feel of books. I like the idea that somebody wrote something five hundred years ago, and I can read it if I want to so the author can talk to me out of the past, or I can talk to somebody from five hundred years ago. That has always just been exhilarating. . . . Books were absolutely like company to me. It was a very isolated family, and in some ways I felt closer to many of the characters I would read about in the novels or short stories [than to my family]. . . . I would read volume after volume after volume of short stories, or novels, and I forever felt to some extent that I was having relationships with the characters in the book.

Although many people casually mentioned that they would "escape" into reading and films as children, I think that their retreat was far more adaptive than avoidant. While they were fleeing chaos and often hate, it is very different to seek out enlightenment than to seek out oblivion. "There he goes now; to [Ahab] nothing's happened; but to me, the skewer seems loosening out of the middle of the world."[23] They sought insight, wisdom, and sheer information that might relieve their pain. (And that search for relief through literature can start early: my then-four-year-old daughter Taryn, deeply distraught but determined, said upon shattering one high heel of her most cherished shoes in the dress-up box, "Well, I can be Cinderella today. She had only one shoe.") With adaptive elegance, they also encountered great pleasure in the bargain.

The resilient did not systematically resort to brittle defenses that delimit or distort awareness, nor did they clutch anesthetizing modes such as alcohol that only remove us from other people through psychological distance. Because of that, even their more painful awarenesses are easily accessible, like features of an inner landscape that are visible under a light dusting of snow, the underlying structure of important matters readily apparent. By contrast, people with similar pasts often deny in more glacial proportions, so that half-lives are lived around crucial issues rendered perpetually invisible.

Actively embracing *images* that acknowledge and explain their pain is a way for the resilient to engage, rather than avoid, their difficulties. Their adaptive refueling through art is reminiscent of Melville's speculations about the restorative retreat of the great whales:

> These Leviathans . . . have [a] firm fortress, which, in all human probability, will for ever remain impregnable. And as upon the invasion of their valleys, the frosty Swiss have retreated to their mountains; so, hunted from the savannas and glades of the middle seas, the whale-bone whales can at last resort to their Polar citadels, and diving under the ultimate glassy barriers and walls there, come up among icy fields and floes; and in all charmed circle of everlasting December, bid defiance to all pursuit from man.[24]

Spiritually harpooned, finding little inspiration or guidance in their outer circumstances, the resilient periodically withdrew into vision's wellspring in a move that seems strategically self-preserving. Given that they took definitive action to improve their circumstances and sought healthier ties when they could, their retreat follows the wisdom of the whales, not the ostrich.

Although there are abundant literary and artistic sources that fueled their resilient faith, the oft-mentioned works were typically tales of resourceful overcoming. Now, a great deal of human experience involves struggling, and the resilient cited classics beloved by many dealing with that subject. They often reread such novels as Charlotte Brontë's *Jane Eyre* and Frances Hodgson Burnett's *Secret Garden*, as well as J. M. Barrie's *Peter Pan*. And they kept returning to the movie version of Frank Baum's *Wizard of Oz* and the films of Charlie Chaplin.

When I questioned them carefully about why they resonated so strongly with these artists' intentions, their reasons were specific. They explained that they were desperately relieved to know that they were not alone in their struggles. They were also captivated by orphaned protagonists who, although plain and unexceptional in many ways, find a path out of the most daunting circumstances by dint of special talent and/or steady persistence. Their favorite characters seem to have no doubt about their ultimate destination. In addition, they typically create simple, profound ties with wise creatures and other lost children; these friends then help them summon their inner resources and rise with great dignity. Thus the heroic figures of the resilient are integrally related to others, and their struggling usually includes learning how to love well as they overcome their dislocating plight.

In one poignant example, Dan speaks of his attachment to the imagery in *The Wizard of Oz*, although, at least superficially, it seems to fail him—a sharp reminder that the resilient make meanings of their plight that might be atypically optimistic for others. Dan's abuse was so serious he and his twin came home from seeing that movie at age seven and threw a bucket of water on their mother. "She was standing there dripping wet, furious! And we were watching to see if she would shrivel right down and disappear." When I asked him why he thought he didn't lose faith at this juncture, he said that he made a choice to "fall back and regroup," searching the story for another metaphor:

> That same week I also tried running away from home, to my grandmother's; . . . but [in thinking about *The Wizard of Oz*, I realized that] the really powerful thing was [that] . . . good triumphed over evil, which was wonderful to see, . . . and that Dorothy had on the ruby slippers all along. She just didn't *know* that was the case, and I can remember saying to myself, . . . "It's the same with me. . . . I have on [something] like the ruby slippers. If I want to make things right in my life, *I can do it*. . . . It was a very clear sense: . . . the power was always there, you just had to know it was there.

Dan's reworking of the Oz imagery includes some of the fundamentals of faith mentioned in the beginning of this chapter. His

faith is inherently relational, he has a robust capacity for imaginatively recomposing (thus extending and elaborating) his "master
narrative," and he believes that he is "becoming more" in the
process.

Alison, an elementary school art teacher, finds that similar
themes compel her attachment to Paul Gallico's *Snow Goose;*[25] they
are prominent aspects of the way she summarizes, then analyzes the
tale:

> It's the story of an artist. . . . One of his hands is crippled, . . . and he
> lives out by himself in . . . these marshes in England. He paints and
> has built this world for himself that's very separate from other
> humans but is very rich in some ways—rich in the sense that he's
> learned how to live with solitude and he paints and he's befriended
> animals and it really gives him an opportunity to sort of express a lot
> of things within himself without being, without *feeling,* . . . under
> the scrutiny of society and a lot of convention. Into this picture this
> young girl—probably thirteen or something—befriends him and gets
> to know him. . . . She brings him this wounded goose, a snow goose,
> which is . . . unlike a Canada goose—it's pure white—and she's very
> frightened of [the man] at first, but the relationship builds and builds
> and builds and builds. . . .
>
> The message in it for me was this: . . . First, it was very appealing
> to me that this guy had learned how to live on his own in a way that
> was very special and very rich, that *aloneness didn't mean loneliness.*
> Second, the child having something that was so important to her
> that she would risk being afraid of this man and overcome her own
> set of fears for something else. It was very, very important to her. . . .
> Then the whole process of building their relationship touched me a
> lot, . . . to see how they respected one another and how they gave
> each other distance when they had to and how they were able to
> make connections. . . .

The end of the story comes [when this artist helps England during the invasion of France by sailing his little boat across the English Channel] and he's shot. . . . The goose doesn't know what's happened to him, [but] she's mended and healed and fixed by this time and has gone with him as he's sailing back and forth with all these soldiers; and when he's killed, the goose circles the boat two or three times and then rises up and instead of just going off, comes back, . . . then circles around once over his house where the girl is, which is to let her know that this has happened. . . .

So in this tale I found all the threads of loss, but [also] connection and ongoingness. . . . You knew that it was devastating for [the girl] in one way, but she was strong, and she was going to survive. . . . [She] could come up against a lot and get through. . . . I've always had tremendous faith in relationships with people, and I've been very, very fortunate that there have people out there.

In fertile retreat, Alison associates nourishing solitude ("aloneness didn't mean loneliness") with creating and embellishing aspects of her "master narrative." At the same time, she identifies with a relationship that "builds and builds and builds and builds." She notes that caring for one another enhances both the artist and the girl who comes to him for repair and inspiration ("She brings him this wounded goose, a snow goose; . . . it's pure white"). That relationship *anchors* her narrative. It becomes the locus for Alison's convictions about the profound value of hurt and reparation, steadfastness, personal risk, and overcoming itself. While separation is inevitable, our ties to others become part of us—igniting life, inspiring us to be more. Thus, in one integrative sweep, Alison's narrative provides for her essential autonomy and connection as she, like the snow goose, transcends adversity.

Note, too, that while Alison's heroic figure integrates his vision both alone and within pivotal relationships, he remains largely outside "the scrutiny of society and a lot of convention" in some essential, symbolic way. Once again we see her, like most others in the study, maintaining a coherent perspective independent of the negative influence of others, and the seeds of this level of independence seem to have been sown early on. It may be quite a lonely path at times, but perhaps the strength and integrity of the resilient vision are based on this autonomy and on the *selective* positive connections made by the resilient.

Negotiating a desert of parental unavailability, Dan and Alison, like so many others, drank from the oasis of guiding metaphors. Most read omnivorously, turning to the accumulated wisdom of other adults just as they turned to their actual surrogates. These stories became beacons of possibility, offering the resilient an opportunity to model other modes of behavior and address life's innumerable challenges. Tired of trying to master trouble on their own, they found company in written accounts, where they were relieved to find that stamina and independent vision were typically rewarded. It was also thrilling for them to see so many *young* protagonists who were the authors and agents of their own lives—kids such as Nancy Drew, Peter Pan, Anne of Green Gables, and Tom Sawyer.

Greek mythology was also inspiring, since the figures were flamboyant and full of foibles but ultimately triumphant. Irene, an English student, waxed rhapsodic about the myths: "Wow, Jason, that guy! He's going to get the fleece! That's what I felt like. And Perseus and the sea monster and Medusa. [They were all] conquering a problem, something that had bothered people for thousands of years. I probably wanted to exorcise my own demons and fix what was wrong in my family."

Even the inane situation comedies of the 1950s were a source of illumination to the resilient, who had little sense that families ever ate congenial meals together or that parents spoke to children rather than hitting and shouting at them. Kai's family began dinner at 5:45 and finished at 5:49. Shibvon's family never ate together at all. So through television they found a welcome point of reference for another way to be, although they hold no simplistic, naive notion that the TV scenarios were prototypical. Unlike Grady, Ricky Nelson never had to drop his face in his plate like a dog to screen out chaos. Others with fitfully impulsive parents noticed that Donna Reed dumped Campbell's cream of mushroom soup *into* casseroles, not *onto* the kids. As Shibvon noted, "On those shows, the father would come home and the mother was nice all the time. . . . No one divorced; . . . nobody had a mother that screamed the way mine did." This was news to her.

Now, nobody tried jamming these imaginative visions into everyday life—a ridiculous Procrustean bed. Nor would they have placed Ozzie and Harriet on a par with Odysseus and Penelope. Yet each possibility for a life better lived became welcome grist for the mill.

Artistic works, especially literature, also offered the resilient detailed knowledge about how others felt and thought, opening a window into the soul of another's struggle. Since so many of the subjects were relatively isolated, locked in by unspoken codes of silence about their family's pain, literature and film gave them an uncommon opportunity to be included in others' inner lives. Suddenly, these children gained access to a repertoire of *emotional* strategies for tackling trouble. I vividly recall viewing and then reading *A Tree Grows in Brooklyn* at age twelve and being stunned. "There's one other girl in life whose father is about to die of the drink. She loves him, and she'll lose him. And she wants to read her way through the public library, word by word. She's going to figure this out." Many mentioned similar revelatory experiences. As children's librarians will attest, fan letters to authors reveal that younger readers feel that the author is writing to them personally and knows their circumstances. This conviction of intimacy and immediacy has particular reparative power for the oppressed.

Finally, since the arts are all a part of *recorded* history, they are a testament to the sheer strength of *voice* in steering one's way through a swamp. Ariana said she held on to Edna St. Vincent Millay's poem "Renaissance" as if it were a talisman: "In that poem she dies and comes back to life. She resurrected herself." Riveting first-person accounts such as *Anne Frank: The Diary of a Young Girl* made these youngsters see that a young adolescent like themselves could maintain her humanity even in the shadow of organized evil. Perhaps if her faith could survive, they could survive. In the darkest of circumstances, Anne Frank wrote these words:

> It's really a wonder that I haven't dropped all my ideals, because they seem so absurd and impossible to carry out. Yet I keep them, because, in spite of everything, I still believe that people are good at heart. I simply can't build up my hopes on a foundation consisting of confusion, misery, and death. I see the world gradually being turned into a wilderness. I hear the ever approaching thunder, which will destroy us too. I can feel the suffering of millions and yet, if I look up in to the heavens, I think that it will come right, that this cruelty too will end, and that peace and tranquility will return again.[26]

Anne Frank, creating a great something out of virtually nothing, convinces us that there is fertile possibility in the most parched, barren soil. Her singular young voice becomes a part of the human chorus, singing a paean in the gathering gloom. Like so many authors, filmmakers, and other artists, Anne offers spiritual surrogacy to the resilient. She makes us realize that even those who have very little, if they listen intently, can hear the wings of a hummingbird on the rise.

The Obligations of the Chosen

I said earlier that the resilient feel an odd pride in being chosen for survival—no, transcendence—because their suffering, since it did not crush them, *made them more*. Because this passionate certitude

of chosenness cannot be reduced to minimization or mere disso-
nance reduction, it deserves some respectful discussion. The
resilient have a genuine sense that their suffering has put a rich
patina on their souls—an assurance that goes well beyond platitude
or the plastering over of their pain. As Grady notes, "People who
. . . go through what I went through . . . will honestly tell you that
they're also fortunate. . . . You appreciate the right things so much
more when you've been through the wrong things." Similarly, Nien
Cheng recognizes after her six years of imprisonment during the
Chinese Cultural Revolution that her suffering has fortified her
faith rather than corroding it:

> Throughout the years of my imprisonment I had turned to God
> often and felt His presence. In the drab surroundings of the gray cell,
> *I had known magic moments of transcendence that I had not experienced*
> *in the ease and comfort of my normal life.* My belief in the ultimate tri-
> umph and goodness had been restored, and I had renewed courage
> to fight on. My faith had sustained me in these darkest hours of my
> life and brought me safely through privation, sickness, and tor-
> ture. . . . My suffering had strengthened my faith [italics added].[27]

Although many of my subjects feel that they were somehow
chosen to conquer near impossibility, they certainly do not condone, in *any* measure, treatment such as that which they received.
They would rather have their own children—or *anyone*—be shal-
low rather than have to face even remotely similar abuse. We all
need enough callus to walk barefoot on the beach or trek through
some trouble, but *nobody* should have to develop enough to cross
hot coals. In fact, many have devoted their lives to preventing others from being hurt. Having been chosen, they feel an ethical
responsibility to help others surmount the odds.

Let us look more closely now at the common perception of the
resilient that "this made me more." When I asked Seagull, an inner-

city first-grade teacher, where she finds the strongest light in her life, she paused for some time, wept, and then offered this paradoxical reply:

> It's hard to answer in some ways, and I think sometimes only people that have been abused can understand, but I feel . . . the sexual abuse affected me in a positive way, because it's allowed me to tap into a reservoir of strength and, more important, compassion . . . that I might not have had had it not occurred. . . . I feel that everybody has had something in . . . life to contend with, and for me, it's sexual abuse; and I think it's made me, in the long run, a much better person. I especially see that in my family of origin. . . . I have a sensitivity and a kindness that some of my siblings lack, and in some ways, I'm very grateful that I was able to get beyond the lack of feeling and empathy that I experienced as a kid, and I've been able to reach a different depth of understanding and compassion.

Ariana also captures this conviction: "I feel as if, because of the chaos, because of the confusion, I had to find very creative ways of surviving, and it brought in a lot of [dimension] to play in my life and in my feelings and in my way of coping, and I feel like I've done that very well."

It is critical to realize that their sense of being chosen is not meant to exclude others from some essential humanity or to create elitism based on suffering. Perish the thought! Surmounting well is not a closed membership. Yet the resilient recognize that, while we are not able to choose our childhoods, we can at least *influence,* if not direct, what we do with childhood pain in our adult lives. For those with the fewest degrees of freedom, this may mean simply improving on the past in the smallest measure by making their children's lives somewhat less destructive than their own. For those with greater degrees of freedom, or perhaps more conviction, it means turning the past on its head and loving as fiercely as they were harmed. As one resilient fugitive from a punishing past recently declared to his devoted surrogate, "The good that you do is so much larger than the bad that they did—and that, as you know, means you had a *lot* of competition." Perhaps this is why the heroic figures of the resilient are all protagonists who negotiate hardship with grace and why they expect no less of themselves. Certainly Brenda, a psychologist, alludes to this when she says, "You either bounce back or you die, . . . and life is more precious than just giving up." Olivia, another psychologist, is even more emphatic; she says that her respect for others rests on "what you *do* with what you get hit with." Joanna echoes their conviction: "We damn well ought to do what we can with this life." All of them imply that they were in a sense chosen to surmount the odds.

The most elaborate mythological aspects of this conviction of "specialness" through overcoming are best captured by David, a businessman. His older brother, Isaac, locus of David's determination and sage surrogate, helps David identify himself as "special but human" in order to combat frequent anti-Semitism in a small provincial town. By protecting David and their younger sisters from some of the worst abuses in their family, Isaac becomes nearly mythic in David's young eyes. Isaac also forages for a more potent way to help his siblings. Finding some guiding imagery, he embroiders a myth for them: Alla Nuvi. Soothing his hurtful childhood, this myth also helps David carry into adulthood an active promise to repair a damaged world. His brother's sponsorship, embodied in the Alla Nuvi myth, solidifies David's conviction that no one has cornered the market on grace and inspires his extensive civil rights work during the Kennedy era, as well as subsequent political activities on behalf of the disenfranchised. Thus, while fiercely determined to "be more," David eschews elitism and recognizes a moral imperative to (in the words of Philip Berrigan) "avoid like the plague the plague we promised to heal."[28]

> [My brother Isaac] was really a rabbi. He was everything. He was a human being. . . . When I get in touch with those feelings from

when I was a kid, he was absolutely everything. I remember one thing [about being] surrounded by swamp Yankees and Irish Catholics. Christmas time. I remember saying, "How come we don't have Santa Claus?" He said to me, "Do you want Santa Claus?" and I said to him, "I don't know. I don't think so." You know, Santa Claus wasn't such a big thing; I didn't believe in him. "You really believe it?" [I asked him.] "No." Then he said, "Well, there's an ancient story in Judaism that during Hanukkah, there's this guy called Alla Nuvi. He flies through the night on a white horse, and he leaves the Hanukkah gelt on the ledge, on your windowsill." And I said, "Really?" And he said, "You like that idea?" and I said, "Yeah," and he said, "Take it, take it." So we started this thing call Alla Nuvi, and my sisters . . . did it, too, but I had an inside little track, because my brother [first gave it to me]. . . .

Although his faith originates in his brother's love, David carries it forward once his brother leaves, an indistinguishable convictional lamplight:

It stayed that core story over time. . . . The powerful part was a white horse, a lone ranger, flying through the night. I could see horses fly-ing, but I couldn't see this jolly guy and the reindeer. . . . I could see something about horses in mythology. I felt it. It could fly. And the guy—I think he was my brother on the horse at the beginning—that's the image I had, and I loved it.

We used to tell our neighborhood friends, Jewish kids, [about Alla Nuvi], and when the others said, "You must feel awful. You don't have Santa Claus," [we would say,] "Hey, *you're talking to me? We got Alla Nuvi.*" "What?" . . . I loved telling these kids the story. Every year they would ask the same question, from which I learned something. . . . I had to know about their religion, and had to know it on an ongoing basis, and they never knew anything about me, but every year they got reminded about it. Because of their religion, they

would ask me, "Aren't you having your Easter now?" "No, you're
having your Passover now."

> I really felt I had this special thing that the other kids didn't
> have. At times it was a burden; it really was. But most of the time it
> was really uplifting.

Just as David takes this root metaphor and goes forth to help
heal a hurt world (as his brother had helped heal him), Robert feels
he was chosen to live altruistically because he was in some inex-
plicable way saved by the spiritual fostering of his Christ. Once
again, the resilient feel *included* in the deeply felt concerns of the
struggling many, honor-bound to return a gift that enabled their
thriving:

> I've felt from very early on that God did have a calling for me. [I've
> sensed that] he did have a plan for me in my life, that I might not
> know what it is, but that he . . . has a real purpose for me. *It might be
> a minor deed in a whole life span.* . . . And I think maybe [I've always
> had] that kind of assurance that no matter what life has to offer, no
> matter what direction this life takes for me, ultimately I don't have
> to worry about it. That's my own faith, and it's actually become even
> more reinforced as I grow older; it's become even stronger. . . . I'm
> human, and I sin, and I have doubts like everyone. . . . Many times
> I've probably *really* doubted. . . . [But] suppose God really changed
> his mind at the end? It doesn't matter to me. Even if I knew he was
> going to change his mind, I would still strive to live my life the way
> I think he intended.

Robert and David also hint at another prominent theme in the
data, which is the firm belief that, now chosen, they have an ethical responsibility to live for better. By "better" they do not mean
improved social stature, financial fortune, or endless acquisition.
Rather, they feel compelled to sustain a life of contribution, actively

choosing a morally informed vision and then pursuing it in contradiction to what is narrowly self-interested, grim, or despairing. As
Olivia characterizes it, we must continuously exercise our capacity
to make a

> sudden leap of faith for a worthy cause. . . . I respect [that]. . . . I
> guess I feel like lots of people have to go through all kinds of aches
> and pains and sufferings. The question isn't so much, "Do you have
> to endure that?" but "What are you able to do with it and make of
> what you endure?" . . . In some ways, I can think . . . [that on] Judg-
> ment Day when people face St. Peter, . . . who they are is in part a
> product of what they've been hit with. . . . But the meaning of
> respect for me has to do with a sense of there [being] some real *choice*
> about what you *do* with what you get hit with.

Joanna has a similar conviction that she must "live for better,"
basing the bare bones of her faith on the utter improbability that
any one of us is here in the first place. While this perspective might
dwarf or eclipse another person, Joanna's gratitude sings and com-
mands her to make her life into a great deal:

> If I were to pick one fact that just intrigues me about people, it's the
> fact that it seems to me that individually we're all statistically impos-
> sible. . . . [The genetic odds] are eighty zillion to one that any *one* of
> us managed to be here. . . . It makes me realize not how irrelevant
> we are but what products of chance we are, and therefore how . . .
> remarkable it is, . . . and that we damn well ought to do the best we
> can with [this life]. . . . The continuity of human life on this earth
> is . . . absolutely incredible. . . . This gives me very strong faith, just
> the fact that *we're all here*. . . . I'm glad I have this belief; I really do
> think we just have one chance.

Either one of these "ultimate environments" (the inevitability
of judgment, the improbability of our beginning at all) could easily

become an occasion for defeat—especially among the maltreated. However, their statements imply that the resilient rise to what they perceive to be a spiritual challenge. They locate themselves within a faith that requires them, as Fowler says, to "search for an overarching, integrating and grounding trust in a center of value and power sufficiently worthy to give our lives unity and meaning."[29] The daily enactment of their faith is woven into their strong, sustained family lives and their social and political activism, the subject of my next chapter.

The Pursuit of Resilient Faith

The resilient are the last people to boast about their accomplishments or proselytize about their faith. However, they did not come this far this firmly to have their overcoming characterized as merely an "adequate adaptive repertoire," or a "collection of effective coping strategies." While these descriptors are accurate, they seem awkward and pale, and they certainly do not embrace the symphony of brave lives lived so well. Furthermore, the pathologically tinged language of clinical intervention seems nearly offensive beside the elegance of their ethos. Thus to understand the majesty of their ascent, it is essential to understand *resilient faith*.

Within the fold and without, the resilient pursue their convictions with heart. Their faith seems to go well beyond what they might have learned within any single religious community, and many even forged their faith in opposition to formal doctrine. Connecting with others as closely and accurately as they can, fighting both fairly and frequently against the abundant social ills that surround us, their sanctuaries are the *lives* that they lead and the faithful *choices* that they make, rather than some secluded edifice. As Alan indicates in the passage that follows, not a soul in this study preferred to live an early life of hardship. Each has felt exhausted by surmounting the odds along the way. On occasion, a great, billowing sadness stretches across all that was lost:

I feel teary. I feel like it's been a very hard road, and I feel, like my [novel's] protagonist, that I missed a lot. . . . The light comes from me. . . . I can shine a light for myself to see where I want to go, and I can do things that bring me joy; and by being myself, I can help other people do that, too. . . . I see it in my work. I'm amazed, . . . and people are amazed at some of the things that [we've] created together. But there's got to have been an easier way.

While honoring the rutted road the resilient have traveled, I do not want to lose sight of the fact that they have repeatedly declared, through their faithful visions of a better life and their determination to live out those visions, that "the challenge with this kind of past is to take it all and *do* something with it—to use it as a catalyst to solidify your life into something strong and peaceful" (André).

And so I came first to see how they recover balance, then to hear the hymn of the upright stance. I discovered what they became faithful to and how they step to that faith day by day. I came, most of all, to celebrate their courage and their strength. Interspersing my words with those of journalist John Leonard, I recognize that "it takes a long time and a lot of practice to become a human being. . . . All our lives, . . . especially if we almost deserve it, we want and need," for a day or a month or even "a single act of the intelligence and imagination," to be judged for what went right. "Just once." Remember that love that did *not* go sour? The moment that sang? "It would make dying less of a cold surprise."[30]

CHAPTER SIX

Social and Political Activism:
Healing Pathways

> If you view the world or your community as a
> collective pot of food, and if you're more capable of
> giving, then your job is to make sure that you give
> more than you take, . . . because there are always
> going to be people who will *need* to take more than
> they give. . . . If you've got it to give, be sure you
> give it.
>
> —*Joanna, trauma psychologist*

In discussing resilient motifs in Chapter Two, I said that altruism holds great transformative potency among the resilient—that it may even be *essential* to healing from horrific abuse. Shibvon and Dan, exemplars of altruistic investment, feel that their intense altruism, while not precluding solid self-care, is the *anchor* of their ongoing health. As Shibvon declares,

> I didn't want to be mean. I just knew it wasn't right. . . . I wanted
> to be good to people. . . . I wanted to stop the hurt. It's my chance
> to make the bad better. I remember being young and thinking, "I
> don't have much to offer, but I have myself."

In fact, committed social activism plays such a prominent role in the lives of so many of my forty subjects that it warrants careful consideration here. Serving as a poignant counterpoint to the many works now decrying either self-indulgent narcissism or pathological overgiving—also known as "codependence"—their lives compel us to consider the reparative potential of "giving well." They remind us that, while ill-health certainly stems from some forms of overhelping, we hear little about health *through* helping. The latter seems a better alternative to either self-absorption or self-sacrifice. Since the resilient derive intense pleasure and a sense of spiritual expansion from their altruism, they offer us insights into how a more balanced capacity to give well to the self *and* others both demonstrates and potentiates human overcoming. Dan's passion about this process is evident when he says,

> At least five days a week I spend all my time helping other people who had childhoods like my own. . . . That's my whole life, not only my work. . . . I go home at night, and I can look at myself in the mirror and say, "You did a lot of good for other people today." It's become a crusade of joy.

Convictional Mettle and Activist Vision

In the previous chapter, I noted that the resilient are characterized by their depth of vision: they actively compose their ideals and feel compelled to pursue them, spurred by rich imaginative processes, a conviction that they were "made for more," and a sense of being inescapably "chosen." Virtually all of the resilient in this sample expanded their vision of a better world through self-conscious, inclusive humanitarianism, and 85 percent make social and political activism a near mission. The contrast between the darkness of their lives as children and the quiet light of their covenant to help heal a hurt world might have inspired Søren Kierkegaard to proclaim, "There is nothing so conducive to sound sleep as admiration of another person's ethical reality. . . . If there is anything that can stir and rouse [us], it is possibility ideally requiring itself of a human being."[1] Kai, capturing the "ethical reality" characteristic of this resilient group, declares,

> I like to see bravery that isn't macho, . . . people acting on strong feelings when they're scared or when they don't know what to do. To me, that's bravery: . . . *being* afraid, but doing what you think is the right thing despite the personal consequences to yourself or the appropriateness that seems to be defined by other people. . . . I guess it touches on all those other things I said about . . . religion and spiritualism. I just love it when [people have] the bravery to follow their inner convictions, if they really think it's right, even if it flies in the face of authority or conventions. I think that there's a price that goes with it—a loneliness, reprisals from other people for breaking some world taboo or something else—but if a person does it with integrity and conviction, not just to act out and put on a show, I find it extremely moving even if I don't agree with it. I [certainly don't] believe that there's one moral order in the world. . . . But I just love to see that [courage] in people and actually can't stand for anything else anymore.

Thus the most dramatic evidence to support my speculations about my subjects' depth of vision as well as the role of altruism in healing is the data that suggest that they actually *live* by their humanitarian convictions. The majority of them are professionally involved in the human services, and most are active community change-agents. Since the process by which subjects were selected for this study does not obviously suggest that they should be any more involved in the helping professions than anyone else, this is a significant finding. Examining their activism offers us a more complete sense of the content of their vision, since in the interviews they frequently clarified their convictions by describing what they are fighting to change.

Over half the subjects are therapists, and virtually all in the therapist group are working substantially with the disenfranchised. Those from the business sector, however, also talked spontaneously and passionately about establishing more egalitarian policies within their organizations, and they frequently described conflicts that they deliberately stirred up in order to work toward their vision of a more just workplace. Several even gave specific evidence that they were astute about pseudo-egalitarianism and challenged it regularly, suggesting that they hold a fiercely honest determination to practice what they preach. Here David is particularly impassioned:

> Most employers don't get down dirty and make the bridges for people that need to be connected. . . . They purport to be community-oriented and interested in the people who are making the business happen—the people in the boiler room, if you will—and they're just not there at all. I find that really offensive. . . . You can't just give lip service to respecting their work; . . . you put your money where your mouth is and you empower people.

Many also said that they were carefully self-scrutinizing about their own motives, well aware of their own potential for self-righteous indignation and for misusing the often considerable power that they have amassed within their occupational niches. As Kai described his own mission as the head of a large psychology department at a Yale teaching hospital, he concluded, that

> it comes down to two things: . . . [people] either get on the track of being more human all their life and helping other people do that or they're off the track, and it's that simple about work. My work really involves me trying to be as human as I can be with all the forces that I [encounter] . . . and helping other people do that. If I don't either become more human or face up to the things that make you more human, I'm on the wrong track. And if I don't help other people do that, again, I'm on the wrong track. And I'm lucky that I get [the opportunity to do] both, helping other people—whether it's

trainees or staff members or patients—or having many challenges thrown in front of *me*. I get to . . . confront myself all the time about whether I'm doing something right, whether I'm misusing power, whether I'm being fair. . . . It's an unending challenge, and I love it. . . . It's the quest to be human.

This group has sought social change through a variety of different avenues—some professional, some avocational: running a fuel assistance program; directing theater productions designed to provide alternative perspectives on classic social problems; offering foster care for struggling teenagers within a strong church community; campaigning for candidates who are trying to increase the effectiveness of social welfare programs; coordinating services for a spinal cord–injury unit; directing a pivotal OXFAM program; volunteering for the Peace Corps; providing medical care to welfare recipients and disenfranchised AIDS patients; instructing in educational programs for working-class and low-income students; welfare rights work; directing a 520–staff member inner-city mental health agency; systematically undercharging for professional services; and frequently providing pro bono legal services. A few subjects who are not activists in the broader community have children with consuming special needs; these parents advocate for their children with competence and devotion. This partial roster conveys the direct, deliberate involvement in social change sought by the resilient. Although there may be some cohort effect here, since many of the subjects are in their forties, this does not explain why they *remained* so committed when much of the reformist fervor of the late sixties waned. Perhaps a few additional ideas from the literature on faith development will offer a partial explanation of how faith, vision, and altruism are mutually influenced.

Activism and Faith

James Loder's work on the developmental transformation of our convictions is especially useful here.[2] Loder sees convictional transformation as a phasic process that includes the crucial culminating step of *testing and revising* our visions in the everyday world. Although a full discussion of Loder's ideas is beyond the scope of this section, I can summarize his thoughts about the imaginative process in order to use this last step—testing the vision—to illuminate the connection between faith and activism in my sample.

Very briefly, then, Loder proposes five "moments" to the imaginative process: *conscious conflict, pause, image* (or *insight*), *repatterning and release of energy,* and *interpretation.* These steps bring us through the *conflict* of not understanding how to "make sense" of something that is terribly important to us. If we can allow the confusion to be felt and articulated, the contradictions that confuse us gain vitality through our grappling. After a pause in which we are still actively involved with the conflict yet not *directly* focused on it, new imagery may emerge that integrates both the old conflict and its new solution, establishing a new equilibrium through which we can resolve many of the disconcerting discrepancies. Sharon Parks notes that "this 'pause' after the consciousness of conflict may be a few seconds or many years; its gift is a unifying image or insight. . . . Seen in this perspective, 'religion' [or 'faith'] is the distillation of 'master images' powerful enough to shape into one the chaos of human experience. Religion [or faith] is the constellation of images appropriated by the soul in its journey toward ultimate transcendence."[3] Following the consolidation that brings insight, Loder believes there is also a great release of energy—the energy that was previously knotted into the confusion of disequilibrium. Thus the new imagery is "seen" with particular clarity, even elation.

The resilient seem to be no strangers to such transformations. Casting the facts of their health, love, and growth against the backdrop of repeated developmental insults suggests that their convictional mettle was sorely tested—and *nobody* claimed to breeze through the pain. Certainly, the accumulated evidence points in this direction. Therefore, we need to look at how they continually "tried" their faith in "lived life" in order to renew it. This brings me to the fifth part of Loder's scheme, which is most germane to this discussion: interpretation—the step that requires us to *test* this new-found reality. Integrating that reality into everyday life becomes, as Parks notes in her highly lucid summary of these five steps, a "public test of the validity [and] integrity of the creative process. . . . [We must] move from subjectivity to public validity . . . and a community of confirmation . . . [searching for] forms to translate or carry the 'transforming insight.' . . . In this way we are saved from subjectivity so it does not substitute for reality. . . . We must bring [what we know] into a community of 'knowers,' . . . into the forum of common experience [in order to] confirm or refute the ability of the image to grasp [an elevated order]."[4]

For my subjects, bringing their faithful visions into the world became a moral imperative. Many felt that if they had no place to hide, they would know that they were *facing* the challenge of realizing their dreams (with firm reference to the many realities that seek to topple or tarnish those dreams). While all sought safety and humanity in the workplace, they avoided that complacent comfort that can be so corrosive to necessary social change. As David describes it,

> Things really manifest themselves through people, . . . something I've been able to give them and share with them. . . . *That* type of credential makes me say to myself, "You know your stuff; you know what you're talking about; you know people." . . . I used to be a schoolteacher; and when I taught school, I believed that it was my responsibility to reach every single kid in my class on that level, that every single kid had something that could move them. . . . And I taught junior high, that age bracket nobody wants to teach. . . . I can get megalomaniacal *[laughter]!* [Now when I'm doing training in my organization,] I believe everybody there can be moved from where they are, and I'll set the environment and tone . . . so that, in fact, it happens. . . . If the intervention can be made, and it's done right, it's a real gift.

Kai also feels that, while he might find a public test of the validity of his convictions in many arenas, his position as the head of a major psychology department *compels* his integrity far more significantly than a smaller niche would. Finding inescapable opportunities to validate or invalidate his vision from such a prominent perch, he feels ethically invigorated—although he has also learned to take frequent respite breaks from its intensity:

> You couldn't keep me away from this kind of stuff. . . . I just feel lucky that I get hit on so many fronts, and I feel lucky that somehow people trusted me to do some of this. . . . There's something about doing this in the public arena that's much more therapeutic than I thought. If I'd just quietly been a psychologist [who didn't have to] interact with so many people or be public with what I do, . . . I think that I would have been much more afraid to face some of that [moral challenge]. I would have been slower to [confront it]. *There's something about having to go public with your character that helps heal and deal with it all.*

Unprompted, Kai emphasizes the healing inherent in testing his spiritual fortitude so publicly. Perhaps the moral imperative of the resilient to realize their visions, as well as the reparative potential of that process, can be understood better if we consider some of the inner dynamics that fuel its intensity.

The Inner Dynamics of Activism

Not surprisingly, the dynamics of activism are complex and interwoven; they rarely appear in isolation. We will examine four common dynamics in turn.

Giving What One Did Not Get.   There are many indications throughout the interviews that most of my subjects are particularly attuned and responsive to others, learning to get indirect nurturance by assuming the role of the "giver" in important relationships.

While their giving does not preclude self-care or the capacity to "*get* well," their tendency is to give more easily than they receive. In this way, they re-create a more ideal version of some essential love that they received only partially, erratically, or fleetingly as children. By giving to others, they vicariously experience some of the parental care that they missed. This basic dynamic eventually shapes or at least informs their work lives, although in no sense can their altruism be reduced to a mere corrective inner dynamic. We can adapt with far less integrity, generosity, and grace.

Joanna, for example, is very explicit about her induction into a "parental role" as a child of eight. At that point, she assumed guardianship of her mother's depression, as if to re-create an earlier light beclouded by her mother's pain. For many, the sense that *somebody* is still giving becomes a crucial reassurance that their small embers of caring concern might one day rekindle the hearth:

> I think I was a kid who felt constantly, in a sense, that . . . life is tragic. Even though [my mother] would never burden me with it [directly], I felt it. . . . I was her oldest kid; she was very family-oriented; she wasn't getting it from her husband, and somehow . . . maybe by osmosis, I thought I could give it to her. *I can remember dreaming or thinking about how . . . I could make her life better. I remember . . . trying to care for other people's emotional needs in the family.* Oh, God! This is a hard subject to talk about *[weeping]*. . . . I was so keyed into their moods. *I was so attentive to how things were going with them.* I swear my mother wasn't one of those people who said, "I had such a tough life as a kid." I *know* she had a tough life, and I bet she hasn't talked to me any more than a sum total of an hour about her childhood, but I just—*it was like a giant puzzle, and I had to make sense out of it.* I think I put it together probably in a fairly accurate way, just because I was so attuned to her, not because she burdened me with it.

Joanna's husband, Kai, echoes her sentiments but feels his

exploitation was more direct. (Most subjects experienced similarly depleting interactions with their parents—or even greater stresses, such as managing parental suicide attempts, trying to raise a passel of younger siblings, fending for themselves financially during their teenage years, stepping in to take blows for a brother, or frequently calling the police to keep the peace.) Kai remembers:

> My mother just dumped all this [depressive] tragedy from her own life on me. . . . My mother's very narcissistic and egocentric, and I think what it's all about is that there was a lot of disappointment on her side with my father's emotional emptiness and I was sort of her emotional ally, and . . . it was done in a way that really didn't take into account my feelings.

Intriguingly, both Kai and Joanna (as well as most of the others) believe that they were inducted *because* they were so attuned, which in turn made them more responsive. They entered the larger world with their amplified responsiveness in the foreground, weaving it inextricably into their career commitments. Now, many souls will spend a lifetime of unrequited yearning, fanning embers that will never reignite a larger blaze. Many will start to smolder themselves in the effort. But others will carry their coals to new hearths, kindling their own blazes. In the case of the resilient, the tattered hopes of childhood found new expression in good love at home and in altruistic community investments. Gifted givers, the resilient eventually ended their indentured servitude to their parents' imposed anguish and began to redirect their empathic sensitivity more autonomously, with great attendant satisfaction.

However—and this bears repeating—it would be inadequate and even insulting to view their activist lives as *merely* attempts to correct a damaging past. The depth of their satisfaction, and especially their delight, transcends the image of the wounded healer, frazzled and sighing, smiling wistfully at those who get the love they only wish they could receive themselves. On the contrary, in a recent study of 340 women in the mental health professions, Diane Elliot and James Guy found that female clinicians had experienced far *more* trauma and family disruption (similar to that of my subjects) in childhood than other female professionals, but they also reported *less* psychological stress (such as depression, anxiety, dissociation, sleep disturbance, and impaired interpersonal relationships) than women in other professions.[5] Remember that my subjects were chosen for this study because they *do* experience great satisfaction in their lives, both at home and at work. Ultimately, their work has become a labor of love, if you will, far surpassing the guilty, trudging overgiving that exhausts the martyred giver and obligates the covertly resented receiver. As Dan declared earlier, "It's become a crusade of joy."

Getting Through Giving.   So in what sense is the social activism of the resilient corrective, and how does it become transcendent? Like most others, Frog attunes himself to some of his deeper needs through his sensitivity to the feelings of both intimates and audiences. His own needs and the needs of others become an interwoven fabric, a nourishing ethic of mutual care:

> They've always been so connected and tangled up—what my work is and what my love is—that I go into theater for the same reasons that I go into relationships. . . . I want to find out about people, about emotions, even about life, and that's the mode I use to . . . *touch people and move people or that I would like people to move in me.* . . . [It's the same] very basic kind of deep desire that I had to [care for my brother and sister by raising them from their midadolescence onward and to give through my theater work], and [it's] why I was a clown. When I was a clown, if I would make a kid laugh, somehow it touched something deep; and I would feel that was good and that was where I was getting a lot of emotional fulfillment: . . .

from feeling that I really somehow made contact through these performances. . . . I wanted something lasting to happen. . . . [I do] what
I wish somebody would have done for me.

Frog's identification with "hurt others" is even more vivid when
he describes trying to reach his adolescent brother and sister during the time that Frog, then a graduate student at Stanford, took
them both in so that they could finish high school. You will remember that, as a baby, Frog's youngest brother was frequently left alone
in a room for hours while Frog was at high school. His sister was
similarly abandoned by their parents. Unable to tolerate their
neglect, Frog took them under roof and wing at the first reasonable
developmental moment in his own life, repairing some of his own
abandonment and neglect in the process:

> That's very vivid to me, that somehow I want to . . . get my brother
> out of that "room." . . . He shouldn't be locked in there and not be
> talking about his feelings. . . . That's what I wanted to do for both
> of them, . . . and somehow get myself out of that room with
> them. . . .
>
> When my sister, Thea, came [to live with me], she was doing
> nothing but drugs and hadn't had a thought in her head for years;
> and she didn't believe in anything—not in herself, let alone any-
> thing outside herself. . . . *I wanted her to just believe in something.* . . .
> So I brought her here. . . . The only model I had was what had
> worked for me, [the theater,] so I brought Thea . . . to the high
> school and introduced her to teachers. . . . Theater was the only
> thing I knew, and she had done a little bit of that before, so it was
> something to cling to that she did have a little love for, although it
> was deep and buried then. [I thought] maybe we could dredge that
> up and Thea would find that she really was good at something, that
> she could have a sense of identity because people appreciated some-

thing about her; and that's how it all worked out. She [eventually] got a sense of identity from something that she believed in passionately. . . .

It was almost too good to be true, that I had this little thought [of how to make it work for her, and it worked]. I had brought Thea here and was really scared. . . . Here I am, with this adolescent girl. I don't have any money—I don't have enough money to support *myself*—what am I going to do? But it all worked out, and . . . when Russ came [a year later], he was in the same kind of chaos. . . . That's probably why I feel so empathic. . . . In some way it's a metaphor for the way *I* was locked in a room.

The Gratification of Symbolic Corrections.   Another corrective aspect of social activism involves the uncommon sense of efficacy that we can experience by helping to repair daunting, defeating, or nearly devastating lives for others when we could not do the same for our families when we were children. As I once exclaimed to my clinical partner, after a session with a courageous client who was emerging definitively from a dismal past by making one of those exponential developmental leaps that come along every so often: "This stuff really works!" We laughed, realizing that I sounded as if I were promoting a laundry detergent. However, after two decades in the field, I am *still* delighted and even amazed that clinical intervention can transform what first appears to be intractable pain, even if it *is* turtle therapy. If you and your client are both motivated and terribly patient, and if your client harbors some capacity for repair, that person *will* get better. In this way, the universe moves incrementally toward its own reconstitution, taking you both with it. This is especially thrilling when your Sisyphean efforts within your family of origin left you perpetually exhausted but still at the bottom of a well-trod mountain.

By contrast, accurately aimed activist efforts often pay off. As

Joanna conceptualizes her own work as a clinical psychologist, she notes that her calm and steadfast efforts with the severely traumatized were reminiscent of

> an African tree that grows underground for years before it ever comes above ground, so that you have the potential for a tree—this elaborate root system—which is down long before the tree comes up. Apparently, in a very short period of time the tree shoots up— seemingly out of nowhere—in the middle of a village in all its splendor and glory, looking as though it comes out of nowhere when, in fact, it's been doing its business all along under the surface.

Seeing your efforts come to *something* (and occasionally come to a great deal) when you could not effect the same changes in your family of origin can be not only corrective but exhilarating. While you must gradually make your peace with the impossibility of *actually* rewriting the past, it is still satisfying and settling to see that you can help set some things straight in similar situations. In fact, setting things straight for others can help you make your peace. Reassured that the capacity to heal *does* reside within you, you find renewed faith that healing really does exist *despite* your original family's inability to make use of your reparative gifts. At the same time, this corrective approach places a premium on the ability to derive genuine comfort from the more symbolic aspects of one's interventions with others.

But why does the impulse to correct the past persist so stubbornly? At the risk of stating the obvious, children are generally eager to please their parents, and that particular hope often springs eternal. They want to be the very occasion of their parents' joy. If you make your mother or father smile, the sun comes out in your own heart. Children also want to admire their parents, and to be admired in return. You *can* kill off the love of a child, but it takes a lot of effort over a very long period of time. In the end, most of them will give you another chance, whether you deserve it or not.

Your offspring often have at least the *impulse* to soften or forgive long after they learn not to seek you out when they sing for their supper and move on to another table. Moreover, any *genuine* effort to reform and repair parental damage is generally met with at least some openness among your offspring, even for the most gun-shy and even after decades of catastrophic disappointment.

Now, since the resilient were thwarted from having the childhood they needed and few live within repaired parental relationships during adulthood, they seem to take some of their reformist impulses into the broader community, as if to say, "If I can't make it right for my family, I'll try to make it right out there." Let us explore the origins of their sense of mission. In the following passage, Grady, a former state prosecutor, describes the childhood anguish characteristic of the attuned, sensitive, and situationally helpless. He repeatedly bore witness to his family's agony and was plagued by his inability to protect them from unbearable hurt:

I wanted my family to be a happy family. I didn't want anybody to be hurt. I mean, I wanted to hurt my father [at times, at least in fantasy], but I also didn't want to see him hurt in the eyes of the community. That was very important to me. I was growing up, and I didn't want to see him not well thought of, because I can recall people saying that when he wasn't drinking he was a wonderful guy and a successful person, charming. . . . When he *was* drinking, . . . my whole world was falling apart—everything was crumbling. I thought everybody in my community knew that I was from a bad family, . . . bad parents, . . . and I must be a bad kid. I can remember lying awake at night doing all I could to rationalize how I was going to be able to carve out this bad part of my family and make everything okay. . . . *That's what got me through.*

My biggest concern then was my mom, [especially when she was hospitalized for months with severe depression and received shock treatments]. . . . I was so worried about my mom; I missed her so

much. . . . I knew she was safe from my father in the hospital—safe
from what he could do to her—but I wanted her to come home desperately. My [immediate] concern was to make sure that he didn't
hurt my brothers. He hit me that night [that she was hospitalized]
for some reason. I don't remember what the reason was, but my
biggest concern was getting my youngest brother to bed, making sure
my other brother was okay by keeping him away from my father. Not
that my brother would have confronted him or caused a confrontation, but my brother might have either walked too slowly or not
reacted fast enough for something my father wanted, and he would
have hurt him; . . . and I can also remember . . . jumping in the way
of a blow for my brother, because I didn't want him to be punished
[for something he didn't do].

Grady's chronic, relatively helpless distress as a child, as well as
his earnest efforts to make things better for his suffering siblings, is
shared by most members of this group. Recall Anya as a young
child, meeting the eyes of other children in the cult while they were
forced to witness infant sacrifices, reaching out to soothe them in
the only manner at hand. Silently inviting these terrorized children
to lock gaze, thus making a human connection in the face of abject
evil, was the only comfort that Anya could possibly offer without
endangering herself or them. But in a squid-ink night you *can* see a
pinpoint of light; and if you have not lost your vision, that light may
penetrate to your soul.

In this manner, most of my subjects slowly settled their own
anguish. Remember that the elegance and challenge of altruism is
that it requires both accurate and empathic comprehension of *oneself* as well as the other. Many subjects spoke of their studious efforts
to learn what they can offer and what they *cannot* offer without
overusing or squandering their gifts, refusing both martyred and nar-
cissistic extremes as the pendulum of activist choices continually
swings. For example, Grady speaks of his decision to steer away from

domestic legal work in his private practice: he found it *too* close to home. At the same time, he is determined to alter the course of disaster for disenfranchised others if he can, even if it is only by a few degrees:

> We don't do domestic work per se [in my practice]. I can't. The divorce work is just awful; . . . it's terrible. But I have taken many cases as offshoots of domestic cases: . . . children who have been abused, care and protection cases, somebody who's been abandoned by a spouse and who's about to get thrown out of the house because it's being foreclosed. I've done things to help that person either avoid that problem, that eventuality, or better cope with it. *[Why? What compels you?]* Probably because I just feel I have that moral obligation. I remember when my mother had the house foreclosed because my father had his problems, and nobody really helped her. [Now] I'll do that [for others]. And not just because it makes me feel better about myself. I just wish that somebody would have helped her.
>
> I feel I have a true obligation to help people. Everybody's so cynical about people in my profession today, and [I know that] I do more pro bono work than anyone I'll *ever* know. I don't want to make myself poor, but I could probably double my income if I didn't take on some of the cases that I've had. . . . So there's an internal memo (of a confidential nature) that's been circulating in the courts that if there's a particular difficult problem, a criminal matter or a domestic matter—not the filing and pursuing of a divorce but a domestic matter with children or an abused person—we'll do the case. . . . There are some cases where we have fronted the expenses and not recouped them. . . .
>
> I do get a true inner satisfaction when I've helped out some people and they say, "Oh, you've been great, you've been wonderful. I'm going to tell my friends." [Then] I say, "No, see, that's the quid pro

quo; I don't want you to tell anybody that I did something or that I did it on a pro bono basis. I don't want that to get out. I'm not doing this for notoriety." I'm really not. To me, that's important.

Thus the elegance of an activist adaptation is that it begins as a corrective impulse, burgeons into an inner vision of how things *ought* to be, and then receives confirmation in the realized altruism of the resilient. While we cannot change the past, we can certainly change our relationship to it through our currently constructed understandings of it as well as our corrective adult activities. If these activities help alter difficult lives for those we are helping in the present, then we symbolically alter a damaged childhood. Obviously, correcting the suffering of others today is not the same as altering our own past, but symbolic transformations can be deeply gratifying. And for those who accumulate a wide range of altruistic successes, helping to turn around a variety of lives that might otherwise have foundered, the accumulated sense of correction is great indeed. Better still, many accompanying achievements—independent of symbolically rewritten scripts—become realized in the bargain.

This was evident to me during a meeting with Shibvon in which she described her spontaneous intervention with two grieving, long infertile parents of premature twins assigned to her hospital service. She had worked with them closely over a few days. Then, on Valentine's Day, they had watched one baby die and the second (still alive but very fragile) fade. Just finishing her nursing shift that day, Shibvon encountered the stricken parents on her way out to the parking lot. Stopping to speak with them, she saw that they had none of the keepsakes that parents normally cherish—a set of footprints, the first lock of hair. She suddenly realized that, although the infant had been sent to the funeral home, there was no reason that these parents should have *nothing* that belonged to their lost baby. Within half an hour, she had gone to the funeral home, explained the parents' anguish to the funeral director, and obtained the talismans. Pleased and relieved, the seasoned funeral director said that he had never come to terms with preparing infants for burial and that he planned give similar offerings to other parents in the future to help them as well as himself. Shibvon quickly delivered the footprints and a lock of hair to the baby's usually contained, now-sobbing parents, normalizing and anchoring their loss. Ten minutes later, she opened the front door of her mother's tenement to find an imposing figure blocking the light at the top of the stairs. Her mother shouted furiously, "Where were you? You're twenty minutes late." In a moment of searing insight, Shibvon realized that, in less than an hour with two virtual strangers, she had communed with more gratitude and mutual satisfaction than she had experienced with her mother in forty years.

This prototypical vignette should also convey that the resilient and other effective social activists would not be as competent as they are, or as highly regarded in their work, if they were not giving others what they actually need, independent of whether or not this symbolically transforms their own childhood experiences. (Let me remind you again that they were chosen for this study for their generally accurate perceptions of others' needs, wishes, and wants. They *know* that they cannot force-fit others into their corrective visions, however similar the plight.) Likewise, the *recipients* of their care would not be so well satisfied with their interventions if those were the equivalent of a well-meaning Boy Scout's rushing an elderly person across the street away from (instead of toward) her destination. In other words, true altruism requires an *accurate* understanding of where one's past is and—most important—is *not* similar to the circumstances at hand, and careful attunement to those differences. The beauty of altruistic actions is that they are genuinely gratifying to both the giver *and* the receiver.

Mourning What Will Never Be.   Effective altruism requires the resilient to understand that symbolically transforming the past can never fully heal one's own hurts. It is very much like the death of a child. No matter how fully you mourn, no matter how many other lives you help to heal, you never quite get over it. In fact, truly effective—thus accurately aimed—social activism is probably *contingent* upon recognizing and grieving over the aspects of a lost childhood that you can *never* reclaim. I will forever weep to see a father of some stature who tenderly and consistently attends to his adolescent son or daughter. I weep for what I can *never* have and for the sweet, swaddling reassurance that it does exist. But I know that I help propel a family in which my daughters have this attentive tie to their father. I also reconnect fathers with their adolescents regularly in my clinical work. Thus we can *all* sadden for what we cannot ever have and still be enlivened by our participation in keeping these coals alive for others. You do not have to have heaven in your own palm to feel its warmth.

Gratitude for What One Got.   Activist action also allows us to express our gratitude for what we *did* receive. As I mentioned in an earlier chapter on the locus of hope in the lives of the resilient, the capacity for gratitude is unevenly distributed in the human race, although we tend to think of it as an acquired grace. Like the protagonist Jean Valjean in Victor Hugo's *Les Misérables*, spared from hanging by a priest's spontaneous claim that he *gave* Valjean the two silver candlesticks that Valjean actually stole from him, we find that a moment of illuminating grace can ignite a long path of gratitude.[6] Virtually all of my subjects feel that they were saved by someone, and they actively sought the chance to return in kind. Here Frog describes dropping out of Columbia University and thereby losing his fellowships ("Somehow I felt like I was losing my soul by being premed"), consequently becoming evicted, and finding shelter with three women who knew him only slightly at the time. These "candlesticks," offered by virtual strangers, reappear in the lives of his own siblings as they seek Frog's shelter; they then light the lives of the many audiences who come to see his plays:

In making a choice of conscience, I lost material support. . . . There was nowhere to go. . . . [I was] really depressed and . . . thinking that . . . I had ruined my life. . . . There were no parents to go back to, . . . nobody that was going to say, "I think you're all right, and I'm going to take care of you." Out of that chaotic time, what pulled me together was work and the love of these people whom I didn't even know, people whom I didn't even have any right to ask to take care of me but who took care of me. These three women who lived in a studio apartment who didn't even have room for themselves let me sleep on their floor while I got these three jobs working in Queens in psychiatric hospitals. . . .

So [a few years later], when [my adolescent brother and sister came], I worked at three different teaching jobs and kept everything going academically. . . . If I [hadn't gotten] the Danforth Fellowship, I wouldn't have been able to have my brother come and live here, so it was really important to work to make all these things possible, . . . *to do for kids what I wished somebody would do for me.*

And now it's wanting to do for *people* what I wish . . . my parents would have done for me. From that central theme, it's mushroomed out into understanding *how* people do for each other what I wish my parents would have done for me, how these families find ways to *create* families, how they get to *be* families, how they create bonds that are based on some kind of laughter and ceremony and celebration. . . . What I'm always trying to do in my work is in some way to make a family, either with a theater company or with a class of kids or with a play that I direct or with the actors in the play or with the audience that comes to the play—*we create this feeling of family there in the theater*—or with the people that I do research about, or even when I write. . . . I want to create that connection between these families that I discovered that are really special and the people that read about them, so that they can connect with that family in some way.

Lest you conclude that Frog lives a life of indirect, attenuated self-care, recall that he and all of these subjects have substantial work and love in their lives. Now forty, he has authored two books and several translations, has received numerous grants to study theater in other cultures, and recently received an offer to head a theater department at an Ivy League university. (He declined, with genuine sadness, after sensing significant internecine currents within the department. These resurrected his longstanding misgivings about losing his soul in Olympic academia—misgivings that originated when he was an impecunious student.) Frog is also truly prized by his loved ones, and he no longer has to sleep on the floor after making decisions of conscience. All of this constitutes a long history of competently caring for himself *while* loving others well. Contrary to dominant cultural assumptions about human motivation, *most* of us can balance both of these effectively if we try.

Similarly, Seagull explains her path toward teaching inner-city children—a path on which her deep gratitude and her connection through activism commingle. Although her own sexual abuse derailed her professional development for many years—a frequent phenomenon among the traumatized—she accelerated her ongoing recovery through social-activist connections with similarly abused and abandoned children. Her gratitude for the chance to make a difference guides her fierce commitment:

> I think I was strongly influenced by my [adolescent] sexual abuse experience and also my experience as a kid, having [repeatedly witnessed] my twin brother being tormented by [parochial school] teachers. I knew that teachers have a great impact on the lives of children, and I wanted it to be a more positive impact than what I had received. . . . *I saw the counseling as a gift that I felt saved by, that saved my life, and I felt like I was a sponge at that point. I needed to make up for all the lost time*—the time that I had lost in dealing with the sexual abuse and the recovery process.

So when I went back to school, I just couldn't get enough; . . . I really just soaked it up. The psychology courses that I took were more focused on children, and then that led me to a degree in education. I felt [that at] my age, [the late thirties,] I needed to do something that I could really sink my teeth into and have an impact quickly, and education was the vehicle that I chose. . . . I love the look in [kids' eyes] when all of a sudden they get something that they didn't get. It just, to me, is very exciting, invigorating, and that keeps me hooked into education, but I also like the feeling that I can make a difference in a kid's life, that I have the chance to say to lots of different kids, "Do you need me to do anything for you? Do you need to talk about something? What's really bothering you today? Do you need a hug?" . . . *[These are] the things that I think would have made a difference in my own life.*

[Once] . . . I was volunteering in my children's classrooms before I went back to school, to make sure that their teachers were nurturing and loving rather than punitive and authoritarian. In my son's classroom, when he was four, there was this little girl that was acting up something ferocious. She was just causing all sorts of disorder in the classroom. The teacher tried to monitor her and get her to do other activities to keep her focused on something. She just didn't give up on the kid and finally said, "Do you need a hug today?" and I started to cry. I was just overwhelmed with the fact that somebody would be that loving, and I thought, "Oh, man! What a difference that would have made in my brother's life, if somebody had ever said to him, "Do you need a hug?" . . . It had such a strong impact on me. . . . I could see the value of a person that has such long contact with needy kids.

Thus the activism of the resilient appears to be guided more by the light that they encountered, both despite and because of the gloom, than by the gloom itself. The resilient live lives marked by gratitude and an ongoing determination to "make the bad better": cleaving to their own convictional mettle, pursuing their visions of a more just human community, robustly giving what they did not get, and returning to "the collective pot" some of what they *did* get, so terribly precious in a drought. Thus they live in active hope, their faith invigorated by the accomplishment of so much of what they correctively envisioned as children. Perhaps the ultimate justice in all of this is that they often ignite a similar faith in struggling others. Illustratively, a Northern Irish woman from war-torn, family-torn Belfast recently wrote to her American therapist: "Hello, 'tis me. Just to say thank you for a . . . new sense of home, one I only dreamed of before [this year]. Revealing truths about myself with your presence very much in mine has been wonderful; many emotions stirred but the most vital one is hope."

Healthy Outrage: Activism's Propellant

In the course of our interview, Kai said, "The one thing I've appreciated out of the last few years, that's also saved my life in terms of my identity as a middle-aged person, is that I'm so challenged now that I can't hide out. You know, the bell keeps ringing, and some big bully is standing there, salivating, saying, . . . 'Let's do psychotherapy that ruins people! . . . It's so easy!' and I just sit there and say , 'No, let's not'" *[laughter]*.

Now, trauma tends to evoke nuclear rage in people, and the resilient certainly carry their fair share. But remember that they are dedicated to *stopping* the family curse and repairing a hurt world, which means that they must find ways to integrate and channel their considerable anger into prosocial forms unknown to their abusive parents. How does this transformation evolve?

First, early on they *named* these hateful human interactions and firmly *dis*identified with them, selectively identifying with more positive parental or surrogate figures. Recall that, in earlier chapters, I asserted that the resilient are well able to propel themselves away from trouble toward the loci of hope in their lives. This requires them to *recognize that anywhere is a better place to be* and determine to *get out*. By adolescence, they sought solace in neighbors' homes, service hitches, romantic love, and nursing shifts that kept them from family turmoil at Christmas dinner. They learned how to stay out of trouble, although their trouble was at home, not on the street. Recognizing that they were furious with their plight—and deciding that did not deserve it—lit the early dawn of their social activism, since they quickly determined to help repair a suffering world as well as their own damaged personal lives. For example, Shibvon realized that her mother's self-referential plan for Shibvon to work in a factory to support the family was something that she had to contradict with equally determined force:

> She shrieked the whole time I was going to nursing school that I should be staying home and working. . . . Probably what sent me off to school so fast, too, was that her role for me was going to work after I got out of school to support the family. . . . Staying [close to home during nursing school] was intentional, because then I could keep an eye on the kids, [my siblings]. So I still wasn't off duty, . . . but I didn't have to sleep there anymore. . . . *I did have a lot of anger*. . . . I didn't know how to [express it]. . . . I wasn't a door slammer or a screecher, *but I had enough anger to think, "I ain't doing this . . . anymore. . . ."* The good part is . . . that I *knew* that I wasn't going to stay there and take it.

Similarly, Kai's fury at his father's bullying forged his early competence in combating misuses of power. While constantly aware of the ways in which *he* might betray others with his own considerable power now, Kai's frequent encounters with his father created a blueprint for avoiding the *mutually* dehumanizing use of force that was so frequent in his childhood:

> I knew my father was a bully; and from a very early age, I didn't trust

him or his anger. . . . I think what I learned from him was that I wasn't going to be bullied in the world. It seems like I could figure out a way around it, and my first things that I learned were cognitive. I learned how to humiliate my father by the time I was seven or eight. I could put him into a blind rage and take some sort of glee out of it, because I could [tamper] with his head. That's the only way I could defend myself, because he was so much bigger than me. . . . I knew that if [my father] pushed me in certain ways, I might do something I didn't want to do. . . . He was so rageful . . . and had such a poor lid on his own anger about that that I just didn't want to be provoked at that level. So I just really never stayed around him then. . . . I didn't give him the chance. . . .

I actually owe him something about this, because he really shaped my willpower. I learned that I could be totally terrified by someone bigger than me, and while that was frightening, I didn't have to feel totally helpless, that I could use my head to . . . take power away from him; and I think I've used that all my life. . . . I'm not going to be powerless around people who have more power around me. . . . I just don't let people influence me that I don't trust. I don't care what situation I've ever been in, I've always been able to walk away. . . . I will not put myself in a position to be dehumanized like that if I can avoid it at all.

Apparently, Shibvon's mother expected her to be much like the Giving Tree in Shel Silverstein's celebrated children's story of that same name, offering herself sacrificially for another's welfare until she was no more than a stump.[7] Kai's father seemed equally surprised that Kai was not inert in the face of his abuse. On the contrary, the resilient give because they care to, not out of martyred self-sacrifice; and ultimately, they all became adept at sprinting away from confrontations requiring them to become subhuman. Concomitantly, they have also learned to transform their considerable anger to avoid the destructive polar extremes of depressive self-attack or sociopathic vengeance against others. Through their social activism, they harness their justifiable but potentially destructive rage into humanizing programs. These programs are often based on the same wisdom. For example, Dan's community mental health agency enrolls inner-city youths in comprehensive therapeutic programs that include training for trades such as auto mechanics. Here furious teenagers smash mangled metal into freshly repaired vehicles. Some of them still become homicidal in the end, but most of them find a genuine start.

Perhaps the most entertaining account of battered rage transformed into social activism appears in Fannie Flagg's novel *Fried Green Tomatoes at the Whistle Stop Cafe*. Flagg's unlikely heroine, Evelyn Couch, is a downtrodden housewife baffled about the sources of her own misery. Unlike the resilient, confined only because they were dependent children, Evelyn has spent her *adult* life avoiding confrontation and internalizing her considerable anger. Her surname conveys the extent to which she has become passive, nearly calcified. She has not had a politically reflective thought in years. But in midlife, Evelyn starts to evolve. One day a brash young punk careens into her in a supermarket parking lot, splattering her groceries onto the pavement. When Evelyn finally tries to speak out, the punk hurls curses most foul. This moment, however, catapults Evelyn into imaginative social activism:

> After the boy at the supermarket had called her those names, Evelyn Couch had felt violated. Raped by words. Stripped of everything. She had always tried to keep this from happening to her, always had been terrified of displeasing, . . . terrified of the names she would be called if she did. She had spent her life tiptoeing around . . . like someone lifting her skirt stepping through a cow pasture. She had always suspected that if provoked, those names were always close to the surface, ready to lash out and destroy her.
>
> It had finally happened. But she was still alive. So she began to

wonder. It was as if that boy's act of violence toward her had shocked her into finally looking at herself and asking the questions she had avoided for fear of the answers. What was this power, this insidious threat, this invisible gun to her head that controlled her life, . . . *this terror of being called names?*

She had stayed a virgin so she wouldn't be called a tramp or a slut; had married so she wouldn't be called an old maid; faked orgasms so she wouldn't be called frigid; had children so she wouldn't be called barren; had not been a feminist because she didn't want to be called queer and a man hater; never nagged or raised her voice so she wouldn't be called a bitch. . . . She had done all that and yet, still this stranger had dragged her into the gutter with the names that men call women when they are angry.

Then she made herself stop thinking because, all of a sudden, she was experiencing a feeling that she had never felt before, and it scared her. And so, twenty years later than most women, *Evelyn Couch was angry.* She was angry at herself for being so scared. Soon, all that belated anger began to express itself in a strange and peculiar way. . . . Thus in her forty-eighth year, the incredible secret life of Mrs. Evelyn Couch of Birmingham, Alabama, began.

Few people who saw this plump, pleasant-looking middle-aged, middle-class housewife out shopping or doing other menial everyday chores could guess that, in her imagination, . . . she was a name feared around the world: TOWANDA THE AVENGER! . . . Towanda was able to do anything she wanted. . . . Towanda went to Rome and kicked the pope off the throne and put a nun there, with the priests cooking and cleaning for her, for a change. . . . Towanda appeared on *Meet the Press,* and with a calm voice, a cool eye, and a wry smile, debated everyone who disagreed with her until they became so defeated by her brilliance that they burst into tears and ran off the show. . . . [Towanda decided that] people would be forced to get a license to have children and must be found fit, financially and emotionally—*no more starving or battered children*. . . . Teachers and nurses would receive the same salary as professional football players. . . . And because of her vision and insight, she became known the world over as Towanda the Magnanimous, Righter of Wrongs and Queen without Compare.[8]

Like Evelyn Couch, the resilient are well aware that they can either identify with their aggressors or they can forge a new vision of social activism. They consciously and studiously choose the latter. They are also relatively unassuming, genial people who do not tilt a crowd on its ear with their confrontational politics. Nor are they strutting coxcombs. This is not to say that they have never had an unpleasant, selfish, small, or hurtful moment. They are mortals, not saints. But they do not live mean lives, and their overall comportment is unusually decent (although their pasts predicted that it would be abjectly *in*decent). Stylistically, they are more the iron fist in the velvet glove, very willing to go to the mat for their convictions but attentive to the referee's compunctions. They are also well aware that social activism and unbridled rage can be tight bedfellows. Dan captures the threat of this potential commingling as he responds to a Thematic Apperception Test card juxtaposing a pensive young boy's face in the foreground against a background surgical scene. Unfortunately, his tale is closely autobiographical:

> I'll tell you a bizarre story. . . . There's a gun leaning against the wall here, and this is a father and his oldest son who have been hunting. . . . They were annoyed at [another] hunter and shot him on purpose (although they'll say it was an accident). . . . They're cutting this person up, and they'll bury the pieces deep, deep in the yard. And the son [in front] knows all this is going on and that his father and older brother are really monsters. . . .
>
> *He* will go on to really straighten himself out, . . . and he'll do

whatever he can to lower the level—the monster level—in the world . . . by helping people who are monsters to vent their rage in more productive ways and to heal themselves in some way. . . . The boy will have a monster inside of himself, and he will use that monster in ways that are also effective. . . . He'll tame it. . . . It'll allow him to be very powerful when he needs to be powerful—not to kill people. It'll give him strength and power, . . . [the] enormous energy . . . that he needs to really accomplish more. That's the good part he'll take from the experience.

In one elegant, dramatic sweep, Dan recognizes his own fury and the way he has channeled it, powerfully transforming potential "bad" into exceptional "good." This is informed anger with a mission. It resurrects and preserves rather than destroys. Thus Dan neither dissociates his rage nor succumbs to it, seeing it as the paradoxical genesis of his own activism. Recall that he is the president of a community mental health organization that now employs 520 staff members. Given the number of clients that so many people can serve, they must collectively be making inroads into the monster level of inner-city impoverishment, with someone who might well have been a monster himself at the helm.

In this manner, Dan and most others in this study manifest a fervent wish to make the world safe.[9] These people keep a vision of human goodness alive. However, none forgets the darkness. All of them saw more exhaustion, pettiness, selfishness, injustice, and cruelty as children than most adults could endure, and their apprehension of the ugliness in life is quite apparent. Looking at it in this light, it is not surprising that they would want to continually counteract the extreme "badness" they have known in order to continually preserve the "good" for themselves and others. Left to fend for themselves so much as children, they typically assume leadership positions and mobilize others who can help them realize their visions, focusing their considerable energies on social reform. As Dan stated poignantly, growing up with constant abuse made him frightened out of my wits. I was just a terribly scared little boy who was always hiding in the bushes, who in school was always trying to find a safe place to be. [Similarly,] the clients we have in our programs are all people who have been battered and abused or have had incredible, catastrophic emotional illness, every one of them. . . . It's no mystery why . . . I feel a tremendous dedication to help these people. . . . [It's] my life's work [weeping]. . . . I'm feeling very emotional about this. . . . I feel very lucky that I've made it—very, very lucky—and I want to give to other people, . . . particularly to help people who've experienced what I've experienced. . . . I'm doing it for me as well as for them; . . . and I know it's possible to be healed with a lot of work, . . . because I stopped the curse in my own family.

Thus it is crucial to recognize that a good measure of mental health—for the resilient as well as those they help—*can* be realized through well-aimed social and political interventions. Truly helping others and themselves, not merely employing corrective dynamics, the resilient feel that it is an honor to bear constant witness to the human capacity for reconstitution and growth. That is why in the previous chapter I integrated the work on faith development: it places the developmental achievements of the resilient squarely in the domain of health and even suggests that some of the more inspiring imagery about our humanity can find particularly fertile soil among those who have known life's most lamentable side as children.

CHAPTER SEVEN

"Struggling Well":
The Sea Beyond the Sirens

And who is to say if the inch of snow in our hearts is
rectitude enough?
— *Charles Wright, "Homage to Paul Cézanne"*[1]

Now, Homer was not the most politically correct fellow, and I have
no wish to promote his image of women as the disastrous
temptresses of unsuspecting men. However, the wisdom of his
metaphor for heroically overcoming life's more compelling treacheries is too valuable to dismiss.

> *Listen with care*
> *to this now, and a god will arm your mind.*
> *Square in your ship's path are Sirens, crying*
> *beauty to bewitch men coasting by;*
> *woe to the innocent who hears that sound!*
> *He will not see his lady nor his children*
> *in joy, crowding about him, home from sea;*
> *the Sirens will sing his mind away*
> *on their sweet meadow lolling. There are bones of dead men*
> *rotting in a pile beside them*
> *and flayed skins shrivel around the spot.*

Steer wide;
keep well to seaward; plug your oarsmen's ears
with beeswax kneaded soft; none of the rest
should hear that song.

But if you wish to listen, hand
and foot, back to the mast, lashed to the mast, so you may
hear those harpies' thrilling voices;
shout as you will, begging to be untied,
your crew must only twist more line around you
and keep their stroke up,
till the singers fade.

What then? [Of the] courses you may take,
and you yourself must weigh them. I shall not
plan the whole action for you now, but only
tell you of [some].

—Homer, *The Odyssey*[2]

These are treacheries that have plagued the human race for millennia, and we still need help. So let us reenvision the Sirens as an androgynous swarm of inescapable *psychic* seductions forming the legacy of abuse. The abused are the mariners tempting fate to sail close to treachery, captivated by its compelling promise. The compulsion to sail *in* versus the wisdom to sail *through* constitutes the struggle of abuse. I will present the Sirens of an abusive past schematically in a moment and then use the rest of the chapter to flesh out the dynamics in detail. My aim is to create a navigational chart of resilient overcoming, thus helping you (or those you help) to pilot similar waters. The resilient negotiate these particular Sirens well, so you will often hear their voices articulating the journey.

As a caveat, I will not attempt to explain all of the dynamics associated with trauma. I urge those of you in search of greater depth in that area to consult the abuse literature—most notably,

Judith Herman's invaluable *Trauma and Recovery*.[3] Also, remember well that the resilient depicted here now spend their professional and personal lives helping people surmount pain. As Herman urges, they maintain moral solidarity with traumatized people who still struggle more fundamentally with the often devastating effects of abuse. They take care to invite and inspire, not retraumatize others dealing with similar pasts with a punitive standard of overcoming that many are not ready to meet. They do not see themselves as an elite but as luckier than most, and they are eager to include—rather than exclude—their fellow strugglers. Remember, too, that they have spent *years* grappling with their travail, although I am condensing the process here. They describe far less struggle and more true satisfaction over time, as their measures of mental health suggest.

Why is the metaphor of the Sirens so instructive in understanding the hurts and yearnings forming the legacy of abuse? The reasons are complex. Most crucially, the Sirens look absolutely delicious. Most of us can spot trouble when it arrives toothless and pocked. But Homer was more perceptive than that. He made the Sirens thrilling, stirring our deepest yearnings for the touch and the taste and the sweet glory of having *it*. If *it* were not so very compelling, we would not be tempted to risk smashing ourselves on sea-boiling boulders to obtain it. What the Sirens offer may be the long-thwarted chance to be an effective daughter or a loving son, reconciling your estranged parents, reforming an entrenched alcoholic mother, sustaining a single conversation with two parents who are truly interested in your concerns, or any equally unlikely but precious wish. It looks like the best you will ever find, and it is something that you desperately *need*—at least you did as a child. The *intensity* of the quest may be as compelling as every other aspect combined—intensity often confused with actually having what you need. Why else would you risk your psychological integrity to have *it*?

But Homer admonishes us to learn well or perish. Shivering and swooning, whooping and stomping, you listen to the promise of it, thinking that your ship has come in. Instead, chasing it crashes you onto the Sirens' shores. Pursuing it turns out to be a perpetual growth-retardant. That pursuit is often dangerous, sometimes ending in spiritual or literal death. Most of us, thirsty for the heart's long-lost essentials, do not want to see the bones around the water-hole. It seems too terrible to relinquish love's sweet promise. You think, "Maybe they will relent. He will be what I need him to be for me. She will let me be what I want to be for her." You are tempted to enslave yourself to a life of unrequited love so that you do not have to relinquish love's *failed* promise, ignoring the evidence that you will *never* get what you need from these shores and may well perish in your quest. Odysseus, lashed to the mast, strains against his ties, commanding his unhearing crewmen to turn toward the treacherous shores as the Sirens sing:

> This way, oh turn your bows,
>   Akhaia's glory,
> As all the world allows—
>   Moor and be merry.
>
> Sweet coupled airs we sing.
>   No lonely seafarer
> Holds clear of entering
>   Our green mirror.
>
> Pleased by each purling note
>   Like honey twining
> From her throat and my throat,
>   Who lies a-pining? . . .
> Sea rovers here take joy
>   Voyaging onward . . .
>
> Charmed out of time we see.
> No life on earth can be
>   Hid from our dreaming.[4]

So what were their more dangerous enticements, those compelling and potentially fatal Sirens in the journey of the resilient? I will refer to the dynamics of these enticements metaphorically and then explain the symbolism more fully. They include the Sirens of the mythical family Walton, the Sirens of basic badness, the Sirens of the schoolmarm stance, the Sirens of unrestricted interaction, the Sirens of denied or derailed victimization, and (not least) the Sirens of reflexive forgiving and psychological ignorance. I will weave humor throughout this discussion, because the resilient frequently laughed and wept as they talked with me about the graver moments in their lives and because humor has been so instrumental to their overcoming. The humor is also meant to illustrate that pleasure and perspective can be wrestled from great pain and to make the Sirens more memorable. The resilient use serious laughter, among other strategies, to hoist themselves up from what would otherwise be insurmountable pain.

Although I offer these challenges in sequence, they do not necessarily unfold in stages. Rather, these developmental tasks are negotiated in a series of shifting foreground and background concerns, ascendant and descendant issues that dart and dodge over time as overall personal progress unfolds. While there is some inherent logic to the Sirens' progression, I am not claiming that the sequence is invariant, inclusive, or even normative. In fact, I actively discourage stage-theorizing about them at this point (although a longitudinal prospective study with many traumatized groups might answer this question more definitively). Instead, please see these Sirens as singing a dark chorus with significant leitmotifs—or developmental challenges—reappearing throughout the score as the life's work progresses. While nobody in this study feels that he or she is entirely beyond the Sirens, all feel that they hear more distant developmental echoes. If the volume swells on occasion, the resilient feel relatively confident that they can steer clear of familiar seductions, employing considerable insight and a well-practiced navigational repertoire. They welcome fellow travelers on these easier azure seas.

The Sirens of the Family Walton

Traumatized people—and certainly their abusive family members—
are frequently plagued by the temptation to maintain a bankrupt
filial fiction. They want to believe that the past was harmonious
and loving, or at least "just fine," continually overlooking evidence
to the contrary. This insistent family mythology is commonly sustained through rationalizations, minimizations, or outright denial,
evidenced by such statements as "It wasn't that bad," or "What's
the big deal?" or "Those things never happened," even in the face
of well-documented, severe abuse and neglect.

"Well, if my childhood was 'good enough,'" you muse, "why do
I feel so terrible, especially when I'm around my family?" As
Melville reminds us, dark undercurrents often belie smooth surfaces:
"Warmest climes but nurse the cruellest fangs: the tiger of Bengal
crouches in spiced groves of ceaseless verdure. Skies the most efful-
gent but basket the deadliest thunders: gorgeous Cuba knows tor-
nadoes that never swept tame northern lands."[5] Adaptively, you
begin to *catalogue* the bones around the waterhole in order to combat this Siren. Repeatedly shocked that interacting with your family feels poisonous or at least defeating, you gradually become a
more observant, initially mournful but ultimately committed pale-
ontologist, reconstructing your family relationships in the undeny-
ing light of *acknowledged* abuse.

The resilient seem to see through the family's denial of its abusiveness sooner than most. They are more like the proverbial child
who courageously claims that the emperor really *is* naked, although
they, too, struggle to accept the whole truth. Perhaps they question
the mythology sooner because their abuse was so blatant. Perhaps
they are unusually gifted seers. Perhaps their surrogate care ignited
alternative visions earlier. Perhaps many are "wired" with less capacity for dissociation or denial, those guardian angels of entrapped,
terrorized children. Whatever the reasons, the resilient, too,
struggle to hold on to genuine goodness while relinquishing the

mythical goodness of their families of origin, ultimately relieved to pass these Sirens and see their families in an accurate, albeit sadly limited, light.

But why is family mythology so compelling? Why do we reflexively wax rhapsodic when the cook says, "It was my grandmother's recipe"? How quickly we leap to the mythic meanings of filial love. Maybe the manna is from heaven or maybe it is mediocre; regardless, even *terrible* family recipes, rites, roles, and rituals can stand the test of time, revered. As Donald Henahan once said in another context, "Nothing is harder to kill than a good myth. Beat on it with hard facts, and it will hardly notice. Chop off its head, and it will grow another one by nightfall. Nothing, it seems, can put an end to a myth but its replacement by another myth."[6] Since most of us desperately *want* to come from a loving family, yearning to be effective daughters and sons, our childhood idealizations of our family remain stubbornly tenacious. What child would not choose to love and be loved well within the family? It is especially agonizing to give up what in many respects you never had, no matter how fruitless your search. It requires a heroic vision and the courage to seek it.

Unfortunately, norms of family interaction that promote the mythology seem invented to fit families clustering in the middle of the bell-shaped curve. Healthy family loyalty, continuity, stability, accessibility, and ongoing interaction presume that the family is decent enough to its members—and certainly not actively abusive. Normative models also assume that members will be *responsible* for their impact on one another. By contrast, the norm of peace at *any* price, connection at *any* cost, is a travesty among abusive families, often retraumatizing its members. It only tempts people into a Sisyphean struggle to get what they can never have.

For example, years ago Joanna, a trauma psychologist, invited her eruptively alcoholic older sister Maxine (now in good recovery for many years) for the weekend. Maxine drank, staggered, passed out onto her Mexican dinner, and then attempted to seduce

Joanna's husband as the couple guided her to the guest room. The next day she lost track of Joanna's young children in a supermarket: while waiting with her in the long line at the deli counter so that she could get her lunch, the children lost patience and wandered off; not wanting to lose her place in line, Maxine did not look for them. To what norms of family interaction should Joanna appeal as she decides how to proceed next?

And what do you do when your sociopathic brother, dying but remorseless, wants to pay an eleventh-hour call to you and your family? Do you overlook the fact that he knowingly infected numerous unsuspecting gay men with the AIDS virus, remains unrepentant, and ignores the plight of several young boys he sexually abused? Do you consult Emily Post? Reread the parable of the prodigal son? Do we ask the victims of convicted rapists to break bread with their attackers during Thanksgiving dinner at the penitentiary? But what if the rapist is your father? What if he raped your child? Family abusers of any stripe occupy a position outside the universe of "good enough," straining our ability to use what we consider a reasonable mode of interaction with them. They miscarry simple justice—twisting, manipulating, and foiling the rhythm and tempo of family ties. Usurping relationships to their own advantage, they make the abused become invisible. What navigational map do we consult to pass *these* Sirens?

Normative expectations are especially painful when traditional bonds of loyalty and affiliation cannot be observed without endangering oneself or one's offspring. Life in the tails of the bell-shaped curve requires us to rewrite the ground rules; the junctures of the foundation no longer meet. Norman Rockwell, the Hardy Boys, and even the Cosbys left us ill-prepared to cope with families such as these, even though they did offer an invaluable, albeit simplistic, blueprint for what is *possible*. As Dan discovered when he and his twin returned from seeing *The Wizard of Oz* and threw a bucket of water on their mother, difficult family members rarely melt away gracefully. Perhaps this is why the resilient turned as children to classics such as Greek mythology and the works of Dickens and the brothers Grimm. Off in the extremes of family functioning, abuse turns the traditional norms of interaction into undulating fairground mirrors. The norms are inadequate because they are only partial and often unjustified. They overlook complexities too checkered to count.

Thus the resilient face a particularly thorny challenge to developmental differentiation as they contend with their defeating families of origin. They must creatively construct a model of family membership that allows them to protect and preserve the integrity of their own psychic functioning while honoring their ethics of loyalty, love, and participation in the human community. Not surprising, they often experience a significant sense of challenge trying to negotiate seriously competing, if not irreconcilable, claims as they grapple with the dilemma of continuing participation in their families of origin.

Under these conditions, many of the abused eventually realize that family membership *cannot* be considered an inalienable right. Although family circumstances are largely out of their control, they feel pained, aggrieved, and guilty that they cannot make family life work in the usual way. Why? If we are loving and loyal, we feel that maintaining robust family ties is basic to the human condition. We can barely imagine denying those ties to a blood relative, no matter how badly that person has behaved. Nor does the culture provide much acknowledgment that some individuals *cannot* integrate or reciprocate our love—perhaps too full of hate to try or too damaged to know how.

Ultimately, the resilient must synthesize two apparently polar sets of questions: First, can you be healthy *without* maintaining ongoing interactions with your family of origin? Is restoration of filial relationships essential? Possible? Your responsibility? Second, by contrast, can you be healthy *while* maintaining ongoing interactions with a Siren family? What if the family is collusively protecting a severely abusive member, refusing to hold him or her accountable? What price do you pay for participating in a denying network that implicitly demands that the maltreated overlook its destructiveness, blaming or sacrificing the traumatized to preserve family unity? Deadlocked in old family mythology, the abused are often subordinated yet again to relationships that preclude both justice and growth.

Reweaving the fabric of family functioning entails great loss and sadness, attendant fits and starts, bargaining and despair, and, with effort, a new beginning in relationships that are more norma-tive. It requires that we gradually relinquish the myth of the fam-ily and instead embrace the reality of who our family members are. Since this process is far from a smooth trajectory, I will discuss other inescapable temptations toward which the resilient drifted before becoming more appropriately confrontational and self-promoting with their difficult, if not dangerous, families of origin. Please remember that these tasks seem to occur simultaneously—rather than sequentially—for the resilient throughout adult development. At any given point, some may be in the foreground while others are in the background; but they are mutually influenced dynamics. The Sirens may also unfold in a different progression for various individuals. If I were to discuss them as they occur, however—that is, simultaneously—I would create a cacophony. So on now to the Sirens of self-hate.

The Sirens of Basic Badness

As W.R.D. Fairbairn noted, many of us are quietly convinced that "it is better to be a sinner in a world ruled by God than to live in a world ruled by the devil."[7] More colloquially, most abused children would rather see themselves as a bad child in a fundamentally good world than as a good child in a fundamentally bad world with no hope of safety, control, or redemption. Thus a typical belief of abused children—including the most resilient—is that if they could *be* more or *do* more, they would finally get the responsiveness that they so sorely need. As children, they typically blame themselves, rather than their parents, for their own troubles, even though they can describe their lives as rough in a factual sense. Thus they characteristically struggle with exaggerated self-reliance, self-accusation and recrimination, intense self-scrutiny, and nearly punitive perfectionist standards (although these soften considerably over time).

The first manifestation of this sense of "basic badness" revolves around their historical difficulties with emotional vulnerability. Since most of my subjects were systematically attacked or neglected—usually both—as children, it should not be surprising to find that they struggled to remain open to their own deepest experiences. As Margaret, a novelist, said cryptically, "If you're living in a house of cards, you don't slam the door." As I have noted, the resilient are profoundly empathic in many respects; we know that they have remained open to *others'* vulnerabilities. Most of their adult growth revolves around allowing *themselves* the same compassion that they extend to others. This is still possible only because they have never hardened their hearts to human suffering.

Perhaps the most direct evidence of this openness to their own suffering is the fact that nearly all of these adults, men and women alike, wept during the interviews, even though many of them were just establishing rapport with me. We might attribute this to a reasonably "good fit" between us, since they often intuited that I share a similar corner of the universe. However, locked hearts do not open easily, no matter what companionship we provide. It is just as likely that they shed tears because the pain of their lives, like the radiance of their overcoming, is never far from hand. In fact, most wept just when they were describing their part in curtailing some of the cruelty in life, as if an oddly compelling tension between hope and despair pulled their tears.

At the same time, many indicated that they had previously made an overdetermined ethic of emotional self-sufficiency, turning necessity into a virtue. While most saw this as a hazard now, interfering with healthy intimacy, they said it had been difficult to rest their defense. Brenda, a psychologist, describes the roots of her struggle:

> When I was a kid, I used to think I was invisible. . . . I was always . . . someone who did everything and took care of everything, but I wasn't a separate person. . . . I always used to be amazed when someone would remember me, because there was just this sense that I wasn't there for my own purposes; I was there for someone else's purposes. . . . There was always a sense with [my family] that you kept at it. It didn't matter how bad it was or how awful it was or how hopeless: you were never allowed to quit. You just had to keep going and going and going and going and facing tragedy after tragedy, and you were certainly *never* allowed to laugh about it. [I was not to] deserve or need anything separate from that. . . .
>
> But there's a whole other part of me that says, "That's not true!" and "That's not fair." . . . It's kind of a struggle on my part between how much I want to let the part out that says, *"You cannot assume responsibility for every single part of it; you do deserve more!"*

A similar inner landscape characterizes David's past and explains his ambivalence about leaning emotionally on others. He recounts losing his job as a business consultant a few years ago and genuinely needing help that he could not provide for himself. He struggled to lean, knowing that it was reasonable and healthy but terrified that he would be shamed or abandoned:

> [When I have a deep conflict with someone I love now,] I go inside real deep first and go away. . . . I have to go away and observe before I can come back, . . . because I may go someplace where it'll allow me to cry or something, which I've learned to do in the past few years. . . .
>
> I'm [also] learning that I can draw on my credit line if I want. . . . When I've gone through stuff, I've had all kinds of credit

lines out there that I can draw upon, but no, . . . not me! I've got to do it myself, . . . a lot of times because I'm embarrassed. That unemployment reminded me of the first couple of times my father was hospitalized [for manic-depressive psychosis]. . . . We went through a lot of hellish experiences in the middle of the night, . . . rampages for three days. . . . But when I walked out that door to go to school it was: "Hit the boards when the rubber meets the road." No teachers knew. Guidance counselors. Nobody knew. It wasn't the day and age. There wasn't any parents' hotline. It didn't exist; . . . you didn't take your family's stuff outside. . . .

One time reading poetry [in Mrs. Carron's class], I just started crying at my desk; and I went up to her and said, "I just really don't know how to do this work." I remember feeling naked, so there were few times it came out.

Similarly, Marie, an attorney, packs up her troubles while watching her fragile mother motion toward a squat, ugly orphanage that they drove past from time to time, sighing to her children, "I did consider putting you all in an orphanage; . . . there's Glendale." Marie realizes that her mother was essentially saying, "There's where you might have been, but for the fact that I kept you." Since she knew that this was a serious consideration on her mother's part, Marie learned not to lean:

If you're a kid, you behave! After someone tells you [you might end up in an orphanage], it's a pretty good incentive not to press your luck. So there's always been that sort of feeling of treading on a lot of thin ice and feeling a disproportionate sense of power to . . . either upset or destroy people, which makes it very difficult to find a comfortable way to modulate your feelings in such a way that you don't get hit or abandoned.

Thus even subjects who are actively grappling with allowing others to help them negotiate their deepest vulnerabilities still possess abundant insight into the roots and folly of their extreme ethic of self-reliance. Almost all the people in the study described working toward a softer and more compassionate approach to themselves and intensely valuing those who extend open hands to their neediness and pain. During his first interview (at thirty-two), Frog speaks well for them all:

> Why does love matter? Why does love matter? I can't answer that question. It's just because it *should* matter. . . . Just a few months ago, I cried for the longest and deepest time that I've cried . . . in my life. [Diana was completely there for me; she let me be as I was.] . . . I'm really terrified, . . . but I've done most of the unusual things that I've done in my life on blind faith and just the instinctual feeling it was right to do. . . . You really have to take the risk. . . . That feeling of deep connection that we have . . . is so wonderful that you feel you'd risk anything to keep that going.

The depressive experience of "basic badness" also takes the form of excessive guilt—a form of rage turned inward. Abused children develop an inner conviction that if they could only behave in a manner more consistent with their wishes for themselves or their ideals, then they could obtain inner security. Fairbairn calls this the "moral defense" and sees it as an outgrowth of the child's splitting off rage toward disappointing and frustrating parents and then internally experiencing this rage as disappointment and frustration toward the *self*.[8] As Shibvon said, "I used to think nothing good could come out of me." Such self-hate is based on an especially sad false premise: that the child has brought neglect upon him- or herself. In reality, of course, the parents simply could not, for whatever reason, supply more care.

Therefore, the methods they use to rectify the difficulty as children—sterling behavior and the parenting of siblings, for example—do not address the basic problem: we can be "as good as can be" and still not change the status quo. Unfortunately, we cannot be *more* than we are in order to motivate caregivers. They must rally

themselves. However, the resilient child's schemes for self-improve-
ment and unusually high sense of responsibility are so often
rewarded by parents, the child's social network, and the prevailing
cultural milieu that the moral defense usually remains intact. Thus
we end up with a group of delightful people who are generally gratifying to others and a fair amount of trouble to themselves (through
self-reproach and excessively high standards). Dan summarizes his
gradually transformed view of himself:

> I [slowly] began to feel that I was a good person. . . . Up until [my
> forties], I'd always felt that I was a really bad person because, if I
> wasn't bad, why was I hit so much? [This persisted] even when I
> knew *intellectually* that I wasn't bad, . . . that my father was drunk,
> . . . and that he was very angry and had his own issues. . . . *But if I
> was hit so much, I must have been bad,* and he would *tell* me I was
> bad. . . . It wasn't until a couple of years ago that I decided that I
> really was a good person, and then I could begin to think about
> things like having fun. . . .
>
> It was a whole lot of things, not one single thing. It was getting
> a lot of appreciation from a number of people, seeing my children
> do really well, and seeing them old enough now so that they're really
> making it in life in some significant ways, [being happily married and
> working at jobs they like,] and realizing that I had succeeded as a
> father . . . and I'd stopped the curse. . . . Hearing a lot of people tell
> me they loved me, hearing that a lot, . . . I started to believe them.
> There were too many people telling me they loved me. . . . Also,
> feeling that I was saving some people's lives and being told by these
> people that I had saved their lives . . . [helped me realize] I couldn't
> be all that bad, . . . and crying like I'm crying right now without any
> shame, [realizing] that I can still feel okay about myself. . . . It's hard
> to fight the evidence.

To fight their inner conviction that they are very bad children,
the resilient launch what I refer to clinically as the "guilty lamb of

God defense." They redress real or imagined grievances constantly; they strain to right wrongs they never committed; they become overly good to counteract their underlying conviction that they are unutterably bad. This reaction may occur even when there are many solid layers of effective social and personal functioning above this core conviction of "basic badness"—levels at which they are appropriately self-confident and self-promoting. As psychologist James Manganiello once said, if someone accused these souls of killing Kennedy, they would look around the room for a place to hide the brain—even though they know it was a crime they could not have committed.[9] Anya certainly fits this description when she sighs and says that, although nobody else sees her as a mean person, *"I think that the smallest thing that I do is hurtful."* Characteristically, others see her as *particularly* caring, and she is slowly absorbing their wisdom about her. Similarly, Ariana, a social worker, slowly jettisoned a

> giant load of guilt. . . . I think that my guilt in the past took the form of a certain amount of depression, although it wasn't a deep, dark depression. It was a type of ongoing depression. . . . I actually carried around the guilt consciously, beating myself with it all the time, so that even if I wasn't doing something, . . . I would find places to put it, or reasons for feeling it. . . . [I had a litany of complaints about myself, such as] "I'm not good enough. I'm not bright enough. I'm not fast enough." . . . I take responsibility for a lot . . . in relationships, in expectations, in life, and I just feel guilty if things don't work out the way they're supposed to. . . . I think it's very typical of children who have the type of life I've had to feel a tremendous amount of guilt and carry it with them. . . . There's also the Irish Catholic background [adding to the load]; . . . and as the oldest of nine children, I had a tremendous amount of responsibility that I couldn't possibly ever live up to, and an incredible superego that wouldn't quit. . . . *I'm a lot more forgiving of myself now.*

Mounting the "guilty lamb of God" defense against imagined hurtfulness is promoted in childhood by parents who assume little or no responsibility for their impact, even actively blaming the child for *their* abusiveness. My clinical partner, Carol Taylor, characterizes this dynamic as, "Let's both ignore my 99 percent of the responsibility and focus on your 1 percent." It takes years of adult awareness to realize that you have been duped into absorbing responsibilities that were never yours to begin with and then slowly to reassign the percentages so that others assume their fair share. You gradually realize that you are paying off a Kafkaesque mortgage for which you never applied. As Joanna notes about herself and her traumatized clients,

> One of the things I've been absolutely struck by with my survivors of severe sexual or physical abuse is that basically all the ones who come to see me are people . . . [whose] trauma was so unbelievably horrendous that at some point it became clear to them that they just had to make a choice. They were either going to be those who hurt or they were going to be those who made sure, as best they possibly could, that they would *not* hurt. . . . "You can't miss this lesson" is what I'm hearing from these people. . . . These are the trauma survivors whose behavior tends to be impeccable, yet they're afraid they're going to turn into mass murderers because they got gruff with the postman! . . . But their behavior's impeccable! They're so afraid they're going to do something bad when they've chosen such decent, contributing lives.

This is one of the more compelling reasons for the resilient to see themselves as victims at some point in their recovery (an issue that I will discuss in more detail in a moment). To be healed, you must first see that you were terribly hurt and fully recognize the extent of the damage. You need to get furious and outraged about your maltreatment in order to place responsibility where it belongs and stop internalizing the rage and guilt that form the nearly inescapable legacy of abuse. You then gradually learn (and trust) that you can become *appropriately* confrontational without becoming a reincarnation of the very abusiveness you eschew—perhaps the most haunting fear of the resilient. By reassigning appropriate responsibility to those who hurt you, you shift the excessive blame you have internalized against yourself. Then you develop a greater sense of agency and influence over your own destiny, feeling that you can delimit future hurtfulness because you finally believe that you did not *deserve* your abuse. In an odd sense, you have to forgive yourself for crimes you never committed, continually refocusing on the *abuser's* culpability. As Joanna concludes in one of her Thematic Apperception Test responses,

> The woman in this picture . . . will have a very hard struggle to overcome her sadness, and she'll never completely overcome it. . . . It won't always be the struggle with blaming herself, . . . feeling that had she been more responsible or better, . . . she would have been able to prevent this from happening. As she gets older, she'll realize that she probably couldn't have prevented it; and although she won't get over the sorrow completely, she will get over the self-blaming guilt.

However, once you have determined that your abuse was *not* your fault, it is often tempting to put inordinate effort into reforming your family or electing stand-ins who trigger the same revivalist dynamics. Thus the lure of the next Sirens—those of the schoolmarm stance.

The Sirens of the Schoolmarm Stance

The schoolmarm stance is the cousin of codependency. Having established that you were not at fault for what went wrong, but still feeling responsible for orchestrating a happier ending, you will be forever tempted to enroll your psychologically unenlightened family members in a class for slow learners. Semester after semester, they fail to catch on to the curriculum. You fuss and fume during this fruitless enterprise, brandishing your ruler and retaining them each year as you repeatedly explain basic concepts of sharing, fair play, open exchange, and common decency. You repeat yourself ad nauseam: prompting, cajoling, nagging, and hoisting cue cards that spell out the "D-O-G" basics. You begin calling through a megaphone, in the manner of a person shouting at someone who speaks a foreign language. You insist that the unyielding will ultimately affirm you and embrace your wisdom. Eventually, you realize that if you have to explain it more than a few times, you are *not* dealing with a hearing problem.

On the contrary, the problem lies in other areas. It may be minimization. It may be denial. It may be a lack of a structure for comprehension. It may be a tenacious worldview that will never conform to your own. You gradually recognize that you must mourn the loss of the understanding that you will *never* achieve with your family (or at least some of its members). You need to tolerate your sorrow about the communication and connection that will forever be beyond your reach. You learn that you cannot legislate love *or* understanding. You realize that if your family cannot graduate from the class, *you* can find a new position. You slowly don your black robes and retire your ruler, saddened but full of anticipation about an easier future. Here Alison, an art teacher, feels that giving up her efforts to reform her severely alcoholic parents became a threshold experience for her:

> I feel like for so long I held onto the hope or the notion that they would change, that I would be able in some way to have the power to make them change. What feels right over the threshold for me now is, in a much more profound sense, a real acceptance that I don't think they *can* change. . . . They are who they are, and whatever contact I'm going to have with them is going to have to . . .

abusive and collusive families continually deny the need to delimit their *ongoing* abusiveness. They often shoot the messenger, making that person feel bad and wrong for trying to change the status quo. Some claim that the challenger is victimizing *them*. Yet my subjects found that challenging these Sirens became pivotal to their own development and often ushered in critical periods in their own growth. They now realize that although the meek do not inherit the earth, neither should the mean. They have determined to set firm, sane, and clear-cut guidelines with their families that preserve their safety without repeating the viciousness that was inflicted upon them. Maintaining certain important aspects of family connectedness while identifying and delimiting more toxic elements is a great art—not unlike delicately balancing a globe of mercury between thumb and forefinger. However demanding, that challenge is a welcome relief from pursuing hauntingly unrequited love or simply being haunted by abusive family members. Balancing the mercury becomes a more promising labor.

How did the resilient achieve this over time? Why did they plunge forward despite the protestations of those Sirens denying their very need to set definitive limits? What were the consequences? Let me return to Joanna's dilemma, in the aftermath of her sister Maxine's most recent disruptive visit. While Joanna might have tolerated some aspects of this episode without a confrontation, her sister's casually losing track of the children in the supermarket finally made Joanna push some psychological "total" button, and a cash drawer of energetic possibilities flew open. She sat down to write Maxine a nonnegotiable agreement for future contact:

> I wrote a letter to her basically telling her the effects that her drinking had on me directly and [saying] that I could no longer put up with those effects. . . . This wasn't a moralistic [maneuver]. This was just an awareness of my own limitations and what I can and can't do at this point in my life. . . . [I insisted that she had to ensure] from that point on . . . that I was never brought into the picture [of her

alcohol abuse]. . . . Basically, after that letter, to the best of my knowledge she had few or no drinking episodes. There may have been one brief setback, but . . . she gave up drinking.

[As a result of your letter? . . .*]* Well, it seems too simple to think that one letter from a sister would have that kind of effect, and there may have been other things going on at that time. . . . On the other hand, . . . I'm absolutely certain she's been sober [since that time]. . . . My father also stopped drinking around then, and we now have a *wonderful* relationship. But I *never* thought I would have a reasonable relationship with my sister. And in the last year, I'm beginning to think that maybe, . . . just maybe, no big hopes, but just maybe, . . . we might be able to have . . . a decent relationship.

Now, I do not mean to suggest that Joanna's experience is typical of those who confront alcoholic loved ones. Most in this group have suffered years of anguishing incidents and self-doubt, as Joanna did, and only some have finally mustered the courage to set definitive limits despite their considerable guilt. However, far fewer have encountered the positive response that Joanna received. Knowing this, Joanna was astounded to find that her limit-setting not only established saner boundaries for herself but may have jump-started her father's and sister's sobriety (although she confronted her sister with only the former goal in mind). But her courage in confronting their destructiveness has led to an unusually satisfying adult relationship with her father and one on the mend with her sister, restoring Joanna's sense of dignity and influence.

When I asked Joanna whether she had been inspired by any similar experiences in the past, she readily recalled an earlier round of healthy familial iconoclasm. This serves as a good example of resilience building on itself over time, since her previous success gave her faith that she could set *further* limits and make her life improve considerably. She recounted that, after a final postcollege year at home, she refused to go back for more than short stays and would not spend any more time with her parents as a couple. While both parents had become either truly enjoyable or at least tolerable as individuals by then, they were still poison as a pair. Joanna felt that her sentence of bearing witness to this folly should end at the inception of formal adulthood, and she refused to relent:

> I just couldn't bear living in that house [or being with them as a couple]. . . . This is a very conscious decision on my part; and I really realize I broke a family tradition by basically making it clear that I will never again do anything with the two of them as a pair, to the best that I am able to accomplish that. I haven't said it in a mean way, . . . *and I sort of horrified people, but I don't regret it for a minute.* I've just basically said, "It never works for me when I'm with the two of you together, so I won't do this anymore." . . . They didn't literally drop their jaws the first time I said it, but it was clear to me it had the same effect: "Oh, my God, do you really mean this? . . . What does this have to say about us? (You think we're having *trouble?*)" *[laughter]* . . .

This stand also speaks to Joanna's revision of her previous notions of "goodness." That is, until her declaration of independence from her parents' relentless marital hostility, she thought her lot was to soothe and scrape, bow and bend endlessly, although she found that this strategy was useless:

> It's very interesting that in growing up, I always thought if I were more conciliatory and more understanding and more accepting, that things would get better; but it just didn't do any good. Things didn't *ever* get any better. So . . . the story of my adulthood has been that [the more] I set limits and I'm clear about my own boundaries, and [declare] what I will and will not put up with, the better they behave. It's the opposite of what I spent my childhood doing— which got me nowhere. What I seem to be doing as an adult is setting limits and standards for my own treatment. . . .

It's a very painful realization for a nice person to have, because there's a way in which you feel a really solid moral ground [when you're trying to fix your family], and you think it's the only way to be a good person. Then you learn that the definition of goodness is really different, and morality is different than what you thought, and of course your adaptations have to be very different. It probably has changed my image of myself as a person more than anything. It's sort of shifting from that notion that if you're good enough, your goodness will simply spill over and other goodness will ensue. . . . It's *still* goodness, but it's got to be enlightened goodness.

Thus Joanna steers a course among these conflicting perspectives with clarity and integrity. She defines a new filial ethic of goodness based on preserving herself and delimiting what she believes are inhumane encounters with her family, or at least refusing to participate collusively in what she abhors. Relinquishing her former efforts to *reform* her parents, she becomes increasingly determined to sharpen the boundaries around her interactions with them. This strategy has served her well for over twenty years. Joanna, like many others, also feels that her stand both reveals and facilitates her own development. That is, by retiring her "guilty lamb of God" efforts to tolerate and understand her family's destructive interactions without really holding them accountable for their impact on her, she liberates herself into a more detached, autonomous stance. She begins to define her *own* life, deliberately creating a cooperative and respectful marital niche with Kai.

Another crucial reason to confront destructive family dynamics is that, if you continually collude through silence, you feel progressively more divorced from any sense of your own authenticity. Both Joanna and Kai spoke of the gradual leeching effect of not addressing deeper grievances with their families. For many of the resilient, ongoing contact became trickling and anemic; they felt increasingly empty, remote from their own heartfelt concerns. At some point, this deterioration occasioned confrontational epistles or challenging conversations from many subjects. Here Kai explains that, in the years before he wrote a landmark letter challenging his parents' maltreatment of him,

> they'd call once or twice a month and we'd talk for five minutes. Who's died, that kind of thing. . . . [There was] no real connection on my part, no real feeling. . . . There was a real conspiracy of silence in the family about this stuff. . . . [In the letter, I] basically said if I didn't [confront the past with them], I could never have a relationship with them, because I'd be hiding the truth about a part of me.

These critical junctures typically yielded a well-defined hiatus in contact and eventually some form of improved interaction with family members, although there was usually great sound and fury in the process. Most subjects stressed that their aim was not to be mean, vindictive, or bitter but to make their outer interactions with family members more fully consonant with their inner lives. The prior gulf had become an intolerable growth-retardant as well as a continuing offense to their integrity. This may be why the resilient are so fierce about the truth. Joanna describes this process:

> I guess I could feel bitter toward them, but I don't. Not out of any magnanimity; I just don't feel it. I feel anger and I feel a sense of loss at times about what happened and what didn't happen, but it almost feels, . . . very simply, that we're either going to move on from this and have a real relationship or we're not. But I am *not* going back to the old way. I am *not*. If that's the rule for any member of my family—that we're going to go back under the old terms—then I simply do not, will not, cannot, have a relationship with them. That's clear to me.
>
> [*Why is that stand so crucial to you?*] Oh! It just takes such a terrible toll. It basically means my acting all the time. What it feels like basically is, "Joanna, in order to have a relationship with them, you

have to invent a you that they can have a relationship with, which means they really don't want a relationship with you, so why are you pretending?" It just feels that basic.

Thus many subjects linked authenticity, confrontation, and developmental progress when they recounted these Rubicons. While they were usually in their late teens or early twenties when their particular critical event occurred, their recollections now are as vivid as if the event had occurred only an hour ago. Most seized a critical moment—one that was the embodiment of all that they abhorred about their historical family interactions—to have an unequivocal showdown. As terrified as they often felt at the time, all of them were careful to maintain their own standards of fair play; and in retrospect, *none* of them regrets the confrontations. In fact, they look upon these as pivotal stands for selfhood, generally seeing them as having benefited the entire family system, prompted new phases in their own growth, and ultimately altered the trajectory of their development. Their subsequent path has been far more autonomous and self-determined.

When I asked Grady if there was such an event in his life, his reply was like the report of a gun:

Christmas of 1978. I had my first house, my first holiday in it, and my son was three. . . . [I was] twenty-six years old. . . . This isn't me doing something crazy, or letting my hair down so that somebody would say, "Oh, that's not him; he's so tightly wrapped." *This was, in large measure, when I found myself.* And that's how this story unfolds. . . .

There's one holiday that's really important to me, and that's Christmas. [Growing up,] there were some terrible Christmases where [there was] heavy drinking, gifts not getting there because of stupid, crazy stories, lies. . . . I knew it—but couldn't confront it before—so just some really bad, hard recollections. I always wanted that to be a happy time for my family—not so much religious, but just happy. We don't have that crazy emphasis on a million gifts; it's just that . . . *we're all here*. It's an important time, and it's a family time; I always get back to that. I really push that. I know I'm over-compensating, to a large degree, in my own mind; but I want the kids to understand it's important we're happy and that's what we do.

[Well, on this particular Christmas,] I talked to my father and told him he was welcome to come over. We were going to eat at two o'clock sharp. Now, the control that he exerted for twenty years was, "When I get there, it will happen." So at two o'clock, quarter to two, . . . I'm carving the turkey, and I'm doing the roast beef. . . . It's time to sit down, and he's not here. . . . I said, "I don't give a damn if he's not here; we're eating. *This is my house, and we're going to eat.*"

Thus, like so many of the resilient, Grady was the family icon-oclast. Occasionally, the resilient inspire a similar leap of faith in their siblings, but that is not usually their aim. In Grady's case, his other family members were too frightened to take a stand. Some actually discouraged his confrontation. However, Grady saw him-self take an emblematic stand, heard his words coming out of his own mouth and going into *his* ears (despite what anyone else heard). In this transformative moment, he repossessed himself:

I remember my brothers [saying], "Whoa!" and I said, "Hey, I'm twenty-six. We're going to eat," and everybody was sort of appre-hensive, and I said, "Let's sit. We're going to eat now," and I was determined. It was just going to happen, and so we sat down. Now, my mother was already divorced [from him], but she was petrified, and my brothers were nervous. . . . There was just tension, and there shouldn't have been.

At three o'clock, he showed up, and he had been drinking. . . . I could tell, and I said, "You're not welcome here. You've been drinking. *That's not going to ruin Christmas in my family,"* and he said, "Well, I had *one,"* and I said, "Fine. But if you come in, you're not going to drink." I thought we would have a confrontation there, and we didn't. It wasn't an argument; it wasn't yelling. . . . But he *knew,* and he hated it; he hated it! He came in, and he was completely wild. He was inwardly wild. . . . He didn't do anything, but I could tell he was in a rage. [He fully expected] that the thirteen other people in the house should have waited for him and never said anything. We had just started to have dessert. . . . My mother was saying, "There's turkey over there," and I was apprehensive that there would be a problem at the house. *Since then, he's always come on time.*

I had some anxiety, but I was tickled pink. *I was happy and that, in large measure, became a defining moment for me.* . . . *It was a rite of passage;* . . . *the evolution finally happened.* . . . And that's a very clear recollection. This was going to be *my* life. . . . "He's not going to bully me. He bullied me when I was young. He's not going to bully his grandchildren. . . . He's not going to bully my wife." . . . [By eating at two o'clock, I was saying,] "You aren't going to control me anymore. You're not welcome here if you're not going to abide by the rules of the house."

In sum, although nobody relishes Samurai limit-setting, my subjects all feel that their spiritual integrity depends on it. When they first refused the old regime, *their* visions suddenly waxed ascendant. They refused to brook compromise. They determined, if necessary, to spend a lifetime posting "no trespassing" signs to preserve the sanctuary of their healthy connections. Eventually, they enjoyed a new, elevated order in which Passover or Christmas or simply supper evolved into what those occasions *ought* to be: reasonable, humane, reverent, communal, hilarious, touching, kind, and *safe.*

Now, as these limits solidified and were elaborated over time, and as the resilient grappled more *internally* with how they were treated as children, how did their view of past hurts evolve? Did they come to they see themselves as victims? In what manner? What does this mean to them? What are the hazards? Let us take a look.

The Sirens of Denied or Derailed Victimization

Ariana describes her confrontation with the Sirens of victimization:

> I just understand . . . that I was coping with a situation that was an impossible situation, and the fact that I survived . . . and survived as well as I did is the miracle. *[But] I don't like to think of myself as a victim.* . . . I've learned to take responsibility for what goes on in my life. . . . I might have been a victim as a child, . . . but I feel as if I survived that. It's over. I feel as if it carries on within me, but today I'm the survivor, not the victim. *Victim was a part of me, is a part of me, but is not who I am;* . . . [and] I wasn't the only victim in this situation. . . .
>
> [Anyway,] I just don't *want* to be a victim! . . . I think it's something I just choose not to be. It leaves you feeling too vulnerable. And I feel as if . . . it's something that I've left behind and something that I've gone beyond. . . . *Because as a victim you don't have control, and as a survivor there's some control. As a victim you're acted upon, and as a survivor you're acting.* . . . It's not as if I can't look at my past and realize that it was horrendous, and no one should have to go through it, *but it was just a part of me.* It's something to be survived; it's something to . . . move toward the light, to just make sense out of. . . . [The goal of it all is] the integration, . . . keeping it all integrated and keeping it all whole.

These Sirens offer the polarizing tendency to either deny that you were a victim or become derailed by assuming the *role* of a victim. These are often competing claims, requiring heroic integration over time. The resilient indicate that such a synthesis is possible, although it entails gradually constructing and then deconstructing a view of themselves as victims. I will make very careful distinctions between these two concepts throughout this section, since the resilient replied, rather uniformly, that they do *not* see themselves in a victim *role*. Characteristic replies came from Ariana, quoted above, and Kai. At the mere mention of the word *victim*, Kai declared emphatically,

> It ticks me off! It ticks me off; and I can laugh about it now, but . . . the idea of thinking of myself as a victim was so foreign to my thinking that it *actually took being in this project the first time to realize that I was*, but I still don't *think* of myself as one. What's a victim? It's sort of an interpretation of a situation.

So in what sense *are* the resilient victims and why are they typically disidentified with the *role* of victim? Before addressing those issues, let me offer a grave caveat: do not misinterpret this discussion as an attempt to blame victims for their own abuse or to minimize the damage done to them by their offenders. Both are anathema, only perpetuating the original abuse. In a legal and ethical sense, the abused are *always* victims, because they were targets of serious maltreatment or even criminal injustice. While the resilient may have solid control over their adult lives, most know they were victims as children. They regard this undenied knowledge as a keystone of their remarkable recovery. They seem to subscribe to the Israeli motto, "Never forget," so germane to all who were ever victimized. They understand that when they were young, they were *unable* to challenge their abuse due to their inescapable dependency and developmentally limited degrees of freedom. Although virtually all of my subjects have emerged into firm identities as *non*victims in adulthood, their abusers do not graduate from being perpetrators any more than the resilient stop being victims as children. The perpetrators are always culpable, no matter how well the hurt recover. By analogy, *attempted* murder is a serious crime, even though the victim survives or even thrives. In fact, surmounting effectively may even mean suing one's offender, although none in this group happened to pursue that route to mental health.

In sum, although the resilient take full responsibility for their own *recovery*, which may in time lead them to disidentify with the *role* of victim, they know that they were once victimized and that their perpetrators are *always* responsible for the *abuse*. Margaret, a novelist in her forties, addresses the complexity of these issues when she says with great conviction,

> I can accept that I'm responsible for everything I've done as an adult, but I'm *not* responsible for what happened to me as a child. . . . [Several years back,] I looked at my life and how I felt about it, and I thought, "Well, other people are satisfied with their lives. How do *they* do it?" and I forced myself to look at things that hadn't been considered relevant [by my family], to test out other ways of looking at my life, other than the brainwashing I'd been given. *I just forced myself.* I said, "You can either be a nonthinking person like your mother, who avoids truth and reality, or you can face everything that comes along. It won't all be relevant, but some of it will. . . . I remember once reading something in the newspaper and thinking, "I don't have to look at that," and then saying, "No, you *do* have to look at that, you *have* to read it."
>
> That was the kind of thing that changed me—pulling myself back from the way I had been trained to avoid, to deny, even to manipulate, to turn myself away from that and say, *"You must look. You must ask yourself these questions. You must answer them honestly, and it won't kill you."* I kept saying that to myself . . . so that I consciously made myself change.

Margaret, like so many of the traumatized, continually *faces* her childhood abuse and consequent mistrust even though her family modeled nothing but cast-iron denial and minimization. In typical resilient fashion, she keeps trudging on, supported by her bedrock faith in growth itself even though she is frequently terrified through her mid thirties and yearns to quit the world, quivering in her home:

> [In the past,] I just had lots of anxiety, [but I thought] "You're not going to be afraid. And if you are, you're just going to keep on going." . . . There were times when it was just strictly willpower to go on with this, to say, "You have to do this. You cannot hide in fear in your home," because there was one day when fear just over-whelmed me, and I was terrified. I think . . . the only [thing that] triggered it was a late notice from the library. I was just terrified, and I spent the whole day cowering in fear. . . . I kept saying to myself, "It's all right, Margaret, you're going to get over this. You're going to get over this," and I did. . . .
>
> But sometimes *it was just willpower, that I could be normal, [that] I could live like other people, [that] I could be all right,* . . . [the willpower just to *try*], because I knew if I didn't make it, the alternative was to be like [my family], and I wasn't willing to do that.

Thus the great challenge of robust recovery is constructing a compassionate model of self that honors the genuine, often heinous hurt that you endured while encouraging growth, control, progress, and responsibility for *overcoming* your abuse. You are constantly tempted to succumb to the Sirens of denied or derailing victimization in the process. Let me try to hold both sides of this developmental tension as I explore how the resilient bypass these two defeating alternatives. Their struggle to integrate their victimization outside the *role* of victim occurs in a few critical areas: increasing their self-compassion, heightening their internal locus of control, and including rather than excluding themselves from the broader fabric of human suffering.

First, *healthy self-compassion* is one of the critical achievements of well-recognized and mourned childhood victimization. As I suggested earlier, if you are able to make your abusers the locus of responsibility for their abuse of you, then you begin to jettison the extensive shame and guilt that plague the victimized. Gradually, rage is aimed outward at your assailants rather than inward against yourself. Characteristically, Seagull, a forty-year-old inner-city teacher, first realizes in her mid twenties that she is not bad when she reads a brief news article in 1975 naming her experience "incest":

> *I felt validated* that there was a name to it and that it happened to other people, so that was a major, major impact. . . . *The sense of feeling alone and bad and dirty started to open up a little bit, and I started to see myself more as a victim rather than as a bad person.* [Before that] I had a great sense of aloneness through all of it, and knowing that other people had experienced the same thing that I had experienced and that they were healthy was comforting. It was almost that ounce of hope that you need, that there was a light at the end of the tunnel. . . . And I also think that its being public . . . was a bigger message, that it was in the newspaper for lots of people to read, and that maybe someday, somewhere, there would be somebody that I could connect with. To me, it was very hopeful that it was being talked about. . . . It couldn't be as bad as what I had made it, because people were talking about it.

Virtually all of my subjects said it was also crucial for them to hold particular family members accountable for their harmfulness, whether or not the hurtful *assumed* their rightful burden of culpability. Sometimes that assignment of accountability even took place in the absence of confrontation or communication, especially when abusers were deceased or too dangerous to confront. Critically, they resolved that their hurtful family members were *in fact* responsible for the harm they inflicted. Irene, for example—a college student in her early twenties—feels that shifting the locus of responsibility for her abuse away from herself was the cornerstone of her recovery:

> People tell children all the time, "This is your fault. *You* did this." But abused people have to realize, even as adults: It is *not* your fault. It was *never* your fault. I had no control over the situation at all. . . . [This helps me] really take that blame off myself. . . . If I want other people to respect me, then I have to start respecting myself, and in order to respect *myself* I have to get a grip on myself and say, "Look, it wasn't your fault. There was nothing you could have done about it. Quit beating yourself around the head and the shoulders with it; . . . start again."

Most subjects also said that their overcoming hinged on *fully* recognizing how bad the past was and bearing extensive witness to their abuse in the attentive company of trusted loved ones and/or a respected therapist. They learned to heighten their self-compassion on those occasions when they lapse back into punitive standards, self-blame, and depressive self-attack. Paradoxically, they also learned to *forgive themselves* for their abuse. Although they realize intellectually that self-absolution is completely unwarranted, the process of forgiving themselves eventually raises self-esteem. Over time they learn, like Marty in the 1955 film by the same name, that "dogs like us, we ain't such dogs as we think we are."[11]

Another important outcome of recognizing prior victimization is *heightening your internal locus of control*. That is, once you see what you could not possibly control as a child, you can also honor what you *are* able to control in adulthood—primarily yourself and your own reactions to external events. Most subjects said that they balk at the idea of being victims now because they refuse to accord such control to anyone else. They pride themselves on proceeding with a strong sense of agency and efficacy. They feel that, because they fought so fiercely for their own sanity, integrity, and autonomy, they were able to *do* something for themselves. Thus even as children they never felt entirely helpless or hopeless. Speaking for many others, Anya links her fighting spirit to her self-definition as a thriver, not a victim:

> I know I was a victim, but I feel like I was always fighting. I never stopped fighting, so that I was always in the mode of surviving [something] or thriving . . . rather than in the mode of being done in by it. It almost doesn't matter how much they actually got to me, how terrified I was or how much it hurt or how much under their control I became. *Each layer they went in, I felt like I rallied up somewhere inside of me*—at least that's how I looked at it; . . . and you know, they have to convince me that I was a victim. It's very strange, but I just never . . . I just never gave in, and that, to me, is the difference.

Thus, after such a childhood governed by chaotic, uncontrollable elements, the resilient resolve to put their fate in their *own* hands. To do this, they are willing to take great—although carefully calculated—risks to reshape their lot. They find the *role* of adult victim frightening, since it gives away power and control to others, subordinating the victim. By contrast, by shifting their locus of control and responsibility onto *themselves* as adults, they are more likely to exert considerable control over events. Some feel at the mercy of their own defensive strategies at times, but they do *not* feel subject to those who originally hurt them. This creates a great sense of freedom from *externally* oppressive circumstances. Here Margaret explains why she cringes at the thought of using the word *victim* to describe herself now:

> I don't like the word *victim*; it makes me feel vulnerable. It makes me feel, in some ways, remiss, that instead of dodging left, I dodged right, and that I should have been better prepared or whatever. Now, I know that's not true. I recognize that, in part, . . . parents train their

children to be what they want them to be [and] . . . that my mother
. . . trained me to take maltreatment. . . . You [finally] realize that if
that's the only treatment you've had from people who are close to
you, you don't know that it isn't normal. You have to be told, and
there wasn't really anybody there to tell me. My family was very
good about presenting . . . a good face in public. So being a victim
means being taken advantage of, being used, being kept ignorant,
not being recognized, having your basic identity and character as a
person denied, . . . being put down. [It's] just a very negative [term].

Thus Margaret, so characteristic of this group, emphatically
states that she now sees *herself* as the locus of control in her life and
cherishes being its author:

I could still be taken in my thirties, but not in my forties. I'm not
paranoid about it, but I'm careful. I'm much less likely . . . to be
taken than others are, I suppose. Well, I realize that sometimes I *do*
get taken, or used or set up, and I resent it; but . . . *I don't think anybody can do to me today what was done to me as a child.* . . . I'm very
careful; . . . I'm a fairly strict judge of people, because I'm simply not
willing to take the risk. It just would create so much turmoil in me,
. . . [but] *I assume that if it happens to me, I let it happen, and I have to
be more careful.* I recognize that there's no such thing as a perfectly
normal, healthy person, so we're all going to have encounters that
are less fulfilling than others, but we need to use as much precaution
and foresight as a reasonable person can expect to have. [But my
abuse did teach me that] if I'm pinned against the wall, . . . I *will* fight
for my life.

Yet Margaret and my other subjects realize that their determination and stamina couple with good fortune to render them
autonomous now. They know that many others are less lucky, able,
or wise. Margaret says, "I feel bad when I meet somebody who's
been taken as an adult, because I know that person must hurt so

much. . . . I can really sympathize with the shame, because it takes years to get over that, and you get stronger each year."

The final area in which the word *victim* can be problematic for the resilient involves their sense of *inclusive versus exclusive suffering*. Now, a sense of exclusiveness—of the uniqueness of their suffering—may be a necessary phase in recovery for many; retreating and healing one's own wounds before trying to make solid connections within the human community can be a path of great wisdom. The resilient, however, appear to be healing their wounds *within* the company of suffering others. They see that they are not the only ones who have been deeply hurt, and they have the strength to reach out. In fact, they responded more effectively to others in their early years of recovery than they did to themselves, although their responsiveness is more balanced now. It is as if they were saying, "I am a part of human hurt and hope, unique but also integrated into a larger collective." Their professional lives and their fierce social activism are a testament to this experience of being included in the fabric of human suffering and thus humanity itself.

By contrast, the battle cry of the *abusive* seems to be, "I own all the pain in life, and the rest of you own all the responsibility." In many cases, the parents of the resilient justified maltreating their children on these grounds. Disidentifying fiercely with this self-serving rationalization, the resilient consider themselves immensely responsible for reversing the suffering of others as well themselves, not propelling it. They generally despise their abusers' sense of entitled monopoly on the world's pain. For example, when I asked Anya if she had ever considered taking legal action against the cult, her response evidenced greater concern about the public welfare than her private welfare:

> I've often thought of lawsuits, although there's nobody to sue; . . . but . . . I wouldn't do it for reparation. I would do a court case so that it would just add to the public knowledge that [cult abuse] goes on, because I believe it has to stop. . . . I would do *anything* that I can

that's . . . preventive or . . . anything that'll make it public knowledge for people to feel free to speak out so that there's prevention,
there's education, a raising of consciousness about this. I'm sure I'm
going to do it at some point, but that would be the reason for me to
go to court, not to get money or send somebody to jail necessarily,
. . . [although] I would want to send them to jail if they were the
kind of people that are going to keep on perpetrating and injure lots
more people.

Thus the resilient have an inclusive model of human suffering.
They do not feel that their serious maltreatment entitles them to
hoard all human hurt. Nor does it justify hurting others, although
they endured the kind of abuse that is sometimes used to defend
inflicting injury on others. At its preposterous extreme, this took
the form of the so-called Twinkie defense in the late 1970s: a defen-
dant claimed that excessive sugar intake impaired his judgment so
much that he subsequently slew a prominent political figure. Others maim with more compelling excuses. However, such definitions
of victimization—those that their parents employed to rationalize
serious child maltreatment—are repulsive to the resilient. Having
a bad snack or a bad past simply does not justify hurting others. This
specious reasoning only continues the plague. Locked within it, we
all become Montagues and Capulets, and an eternal curse on *all* of
our houses ensues. Thus the resilient enlighten us about stopping
the cycle of abuse. Their deepest conviction is that we *all* carry
scars, yet we have no right to be *scarring*. Their ethic is extremely
powerful when you recall that they have as much reason as anyone
to smash, slash, and disappear.

Now, once you have integrated the fact that you *were* a victim
in childhood but no longer are, other Sirens beckon. Arm in arm
with the Sirens of denied or derailed victimization comes yet
another heroic struggle: the pressure to forgive and remain ignorant. Since most of the resilient said that they were more compelled
to make the past intelligible than to forgive it, I will combine the

Sirens of reflexive forgiving and the Sirens of ignorance before moving on to the sea *beyond* the Sirens.

The Sirens of Reflexive Forgiveness and Psychological Ignorance

These Sirens invite the folly of forgiving hastily and unreflectively, without requiring your abusers to embark upon what might be termed the three R's of restitution: recognition, remorse, and reparation. The folly may include feeling compelled to forgive at all. While I am not attempting a comprehensive philosophical treatise on the ethics of forgiving, it is important to understand something of these complex matters from the perspective of robust overcomers. The resilient have spent enormous amounts of time and energy coming to terms with their mission to be humane in the context of their membership in highly damaging families of origin. While many of them feel that navigating an ethical course through this turbulence has been a titanic task, most feel relatively resolved about it now. Thus their struggles in this area may help others with similarly challenging families of origin who are still caught in these fierce currents without a navigational map.

What dilemmas do the resilient face in regard to the matter of forgiveness? Unfortunately, many (if not most) abusers feel entitled to an easy pardon. Stated simply, they have no problem *being* "bad"; they just don't want to *look* "bad." Accused of wrongdoing, most either minimize or deny it outright. Those few who acknowledge it generally expect or even demand to be forgiven. They seem to ask for Evelyn Wood speed salvation. They prefer to skip over all the difficulties of recovery—intense personal anguish, self-doubt, and soul-searching—to which the abused typically devote years and small fortunes, if not their lives. These abusers are an insurance industry's dream, expecting to wash their hands of the process in a few counseling sessions or—better yet—without ever coming to therapy at all. Implicitly, they want the abused to labor at their own recovery as well as the abusers' debt. The resilient are not suckered in: "First I'm expected to recover from your abuse of me; then I'm expected to help *you* recover from your abuse of me? Hercules had less to do."

Let me address four serious ethical flaws in reflexive forgiveness: allowing abusers to assume that they can avoid the extensive work of obtaining forgiveness from their victims or their deity; implicitly colluding in abuse; thinking that the work of recovery can be avoided by extending unearned forgiveness to the abusers; and putting inordinate amounts of energy into forgiving abuse or abandonment when it could be invested in self-growth. These Sirens called to the resilient; but the resilient ultimately healed primarily through *understanding* themselves and their abusers, not necessarily forgiving them.

Abusers and the Work of Forgiveness

Genuine forgiveness is not obtained easily. Most religious traditions consider ultimate forgiveness to be a concern between the transgressor and his or her deity, bypassing the sufferer completely.[12] The errant have to *earn* forgiveness, and not easily. Thus those of the resilient for whom extending forgiveness was of concern generally outlined several nonnegotiable conditions for the abuser, typically covering what I referred to earlier as the three R's of restitution: recognition, remorse, and reparation. Recognition involves a deep and thoroughgoing understanding of what the abuse was and what its extensive, prolonged consequences have been. Remorse entails genuine regret, sorrow, and empathy toward the one you hurt. Reparation requires concerted efforts to repair the damage through empathic interactions or financial efforts (or both). The resilient, like most maltreated people, rarely encountered *any* of these within their families. In face, they were usually thwarted at the first level: their families rarely acknowledged any hurtfulness at all.

As an example of all three R's gone awry, Shibvon describes

confronting her mother about her extensive abuse after a few years of therapy, when Shibvon was in her late thirties. If you recall from her earlier case vignette, Shibvon endured years of serious maltreatment. When Shibvon finally spoke out, her mother at first denied the abuse entirely and then acknowledged only minimal aspects of it. Then she flew to her parish priest and evidently gained rapid absolution—in one ten-minute confession, a lifetime of annihilating abuse forgiven. Her mother nearly bragged about it to Shibvon. Soon after, Shibvon all but stormed the confessional, irate.

> She ran to the church to be forgiven, and I think that's what's done me in with the church. . . . The hardest part, too, is the fact that a priest could sit there and tell you that she is forgiven—if she's truly sorry. I said [to him], "Where does that leave me? . . . You're telling me someone can torture a person all her life, and because she's saying now she's truly sorry, it's okay?"

I then asked Shibvon what, in her estimation, forgiveness should entail and whether forgiveness is a viable concept for her. Again, remember the cultural assumption that we should forgive family for nearly anything; in contrast, consider whether any of these pressures would have been placed on Shibvon if a *stranger* had treated her so horrifically. ("You know, you really *should* see the prison pastor and tell him that you've forgiven your sodomist.") If you assume that all parents offer their children something that counterbalances their maltreatment, remember that Shibvon's mother provided as little love as a stranger, and far more abuse. Thus Shibvon does not consider forgiveness to be a reasonable expectation at all:

> I don't think it's viable. . . . I could be a bitter person and spend the whole rest of my life ramming it down her throat, saying, "You're a bad person." . . . [I won't do that, but] I haven't forgiven her. She wants that desperately, because she had the priest get involved in

it. . . . I told him to stay out, that he had no right, and if the same forgiveness came to her, then I'll be forgiven because I didn't forgive her. . . . But he said that . . . she's looking for me to tell her it's okay, and I won't.

It'll *never* be okay. How can you ever in your life say that that's okay? There's no excuse for this. This wasn't a one-time accident. It wasn't an "I didn't realize that guy came through the window" [incident]. . . . This is worse than a guy who slipped in and did it and the mother didn't know. *My mother knew.* She's always known. . . . *It was ongoing,* . . . and I think it was to keep [her lover] with her, for whatever reason. And I just can't forgive her.

At the same time, Shibvon does not feel preoccupied by the forgiveness issue. She offers generic contact to her mother, including access to her grandchildren on circumscribed, ceremonial occasions. But Shibvon feels that *she* drafts these rights now, in reference to her *own* revised ethical constructs:

I don't spend my life now thinking about forgiving her. It's just not an option. And it won't be. I'll see her when I have to. I'm not downright cruel. I haven't cut her off. She said the other day, "I've lost my three grandchildren." Well, they were never hers to have. She lost that right. She can go to their social events . . . if I'm comfortable with it. But there are certain things that I'm not inviting her to anymore. . . . I don't have to. *She lost that right a long time ago.*

Just because somebody came out of your body doesn't give you inevitable rights to destroy that person. Our job is to protect [our children]. She's lucky that [my siblings and I] are as good as we are, and she doesn't realize that fact. Whenever we see her, . . . we imagine her on "Oprah" saying, "Well, I did the best [I could at this and that]," and it would be, "I, I, I, I." *I don't think you'd ever hear an "I did wrong." There's an excuse for everything.*

When I pressed Shibvon to consider under what conditions she might *ever* forgive *anyone* who hurt her this seriously, and what that person would need to do to be redeemed, she gave a complex reply:

> I forgive the people who could have helped me and didn't—the teachers and medical personnel—because I forgive the fact that they didn't know [*weeping*] at that time. If it was 1992 and it happened, I wouldn't forgive them; but I haven't even crossed that path with her, to forgive. . . . *I don't know if it's worth the energy to even put into thinking about it.* You get deathbed confessions and all that. . . . I don't even know if I could deal with that. I don't plan to. I don't plan to be put in that spot where I have to tell her I forgive her. And I told the priest that. *There are certain things that are just so unforgivable.*

Thus Shibvon's unyielding stand is based on her mother's complete lack of recognition of her extreme abusiveness, as well as her absence of remorse or any reparative efforts. While Shibvon feels that she has learned a lot about herself during her recovery and through therapy, she realizes that her mother is locked in time like the vengeful Miss Haversham in Charles Dickens's *Great Expectations*, spiritually frozen and embittered, learning nothing about either empathy or compassion over the years.[13] Shibvon also knows that her mother would easily sacrifice Shibvon's children if given the opportunity—which Shibvon will never allow. Ultimately, Shibvon links her freedom from the very *question* of forgiveness to her currently high level of differentiation from her mother. She feels that she has earned her final reward: ownership of her own life:

> I think that she could expose my kids to abuse. . . . If she had the choice tomorrow of offering one of my kids to get a better end for her, I think she would. But the wonderful part, and that's what I wish I could tell everybody, is that . . . it's so good when you tell them that it's over for them, as far as their right to be in your life, that *you* can

now make the right. . . . I truly feel like I've *earned* that right. . . . *The tables are turned, not in a vicious way, but . . . I own this part of my life. I have a right to it.* I didn't have a thing, and now it's my turn. . . . If I can get ten minutes of pleasure versus ten minutes of abuse talking to her, then I'm taking the pleasure—reading a book or socializing with somebody!

Shibvon's descriptions are typical of what most of the resilient encounter with their unyielding family members in adulthood. Many subjects said that the question of forgiving was not even *relevant* to them. They did not think it was their work to do.

The Complicity of Reflexive Forgiveness

Some of my subjects said that reflexive forgiveness was tantamount to complicity. As Poet, a psychologist, notes, "I think that there are things that shouldn't be forgiven. I think if we forgave the Third Reich, we wouldn't be doing anybody a favor. . . . Maybe we can *understand* what made . . . Hitler [or anyone like him] do what he did. . . . We can even assume that there must be reasons for this, but the *actions* are not forgivable."

Anya, another psychologist, extends and amplifies Poet's words when she reflects upon her parents' involving her in systematic and prolonged cult abuse:

How can you forgive evil? Only God can do that, if there is one. *There's no forgiveness.* It happened; it's horrible; who can explain it? But it's not a question of forgiving, in my view. It's a question of all kinds of things. It's a question of surviving. It's a question of speaking out against it. It's a question of . . . living your life in opposite ways from that, . . . looking to the good side and finding what you can that's worthwhile and focusing there. . . . There are lots of things to do that are worthwhile that might be considered good values, but forgiveness . . . *[sigh]*—the only way I could picture forgiveness . . .

would be, in my situation, if my parents were alive, if they felt contrite and guilty and horrible, then I could imagine forgiving them. But otherwise, I don't. It's not a question.

Even subjects whose parents were less premeditatedly evil or less outright abusive (but more immature and incompetent) feel that they necessarily revised their view of their parents' underlying intentions over time. While they now feel that their parents were not as *deliberately* hurtful as they once thought, these subjects still refuse to overlook the extensive damage that was done to them and their siblings by significant parental neglect or egocentrism. While these subjects might not have been as angry as others who were treated with conscious meanness, neither do they minimize their parents' actions because "their intentions were good" or "they did the best they could." They give credit where credit is due without turning a blind eye to the consequences. For example, several years ago, Joanna relinquished her belief that her parents' hostility and abandonment should be subordinated to their good intentions when she and her then-four-year-old son saw the animated movie *Dumbo* together:

> My son and I were watching *Dumbo*, and there's a scene in *Dumbo* where the mother—who has already heard a bunch of indignities heaped upon her son for his huge ears—hears [yet another]. A young boy comes along and makes fun of Dumbo. The mother picks the kid up by her trunk, throws him over the rope, paddles him, and he goes running and crying for help, at which point the ringmaster and the guy setting up the circus rope tie Dumbo's mother down and take her off to elephant jail *[laughter]*. And Dumbo is left by himself.
>
> I turned to my son, . . . and I don't remember what my exact words were, but clearly my intent was to elicit from him some appreciation for the mother's gung-ho determination to set things right for her son. I don't know how I worded it, but I wanted him to agree

with me: "Wasn't this a loving, caring act on the mother's part?" He turned to me and said, "No, actually, it was really bad." He basically said, "She did something that got her taken away from Dumbo." He didn't say this, but I knew what he meant. *She did the one thing that he could least afford to have happen to him. She got herself taken away from him*, and now he's left holding the bag *[laughter]*. Then I thought, "Oh, yeah! Good intentions aren't enough!" I mean, good intentions are great; it's better than nothing. [But] good intentions are *not* enough!

Reflexive Forgiveness and the Hard Work of Recovery

Several subjects also said that reflexive forgiving was often a way to bypass some of the hard work of recovery, allowing forgivers to avoid the buried fury and even hate that abuse engenders. This seems to be yet another manifestation of the "guilty lamb of God" defense, in which you rush to paper over your hurts because you cannot tolerate the sense of shameful, guilty badness and disruption that accompany massive anger. As Seagull realized a few years ago, her recovery was contingent on her refocusing on her *own* feelings about her sexual abuse rather than continuing that common derailment of healing—making the perpetrator focal. This realization ultimately enabled Seagull to feel forgiving toward her brother, in the sense that she was no longer preoccupied with him, finding his actions intelligible in light of their strongly disconnected family climate:

> *For a long time, it kept me silent.* I just wanted to . . . deny that . . . the sexual abuse was a big issue. I just wanted to get to the forgiveness stage. . . . Instead of dealing with the raw feelings, it was easier to say, "I've dealt with it, and it's over, and I'll forgive him." I think that I did get hung up on the forgiveness aspect of healing. [But] when I was able to stay focused on the hurt and the pain, to the exclusion of other people—be it my husband, my kids, my family members,

my siblings—when I was able to just stay with how *I* felt for a long enough period of time and just go through the pain and forget about the forgiveness, forget about the perpetrator, . . . [then] *I* started to heal within. Many years later, I realized, without even thinking about it, that the forgiveness had come.

Is that clear? [The central aspect of my healing was] that *I really needed to forget about the forgiveness*. I don't think the perpetrator's feelings or situation should be considered for a long time in the healing process.

Reflexive Forgiveness Versus Self-Growth

Most of the resilient feel that they achieved their independence by working through their unavoidably intense feelings so that they *could* refocus their energies on their own lives, gradually creating a measured detachment. While avoiding darker feelings was a detour for everyone in this group at *some* points, the resilient are very well aware of how utterly furious and sad their abuse made them feel, not to mention their anguish about losing any normal sense of family as a consequence. Yet, while their legacy of abuse is always in the picture, it is finally a background rather than a foreground concern. Most are not directly focused on these matters now. Thus my subjects' current levels of differentiation and autonomy from their families of origin may explain why many do not feel compelled to even *address* the issue of forgiveness. This concern assumes a more active relational connection to the past. Instead, their energies are poured primarily into their own current families and their socially active work. They are so busy healing themselves or helping others heal from similar hurts that they do not consider grappling with the question to be a worthwhile use of their time. Margaret is especially eloquent about this process. Having embraced her own fury and sadness for some time, she is determined not be mortgaged to her own rage toward her mother for colluding so thoroughly in her sexual abuse as well as deliberately sabotaging Margaret at every developmental turn:

> You hear that you're supposed to forgive, . . . and I struggled with it, and I struggled with it, and then I realized that forgiveness does *not* mean that you go back into the same old situation and are willing to go through it again. That's not what it means. *Forgiveness means being free of anger, being free of any desire for revenge, and being willing to let those who have harmed you just go on and live out their lives in their own way. It means the end of any desire to alter the future because of the past.*
>
> When I wrote my mother and siblings this past Christmas [and explained the abuse from my point of view], I didn't say, "I forgive you . . . ," to my mother. I said, *"Despite all that has happened, I wish you well," and I meant it.* I felt genuine goodwill toward her, but I recognize that she's the same person, and I'm not willing to go through it again, so I have . . . forgiveness in the sense of *I hold her no grudge. It's over. But forgiveness does not mean that she can go on treating me the way she has.*
>
> [*And as a result, you're in no ongoing interaction with her?*] No relationship at all. I got a letter from her. . . . She still doesn't understand what she's done. . . . I'm not going to argue about it. I hope she works it out. I don't wish her ill, but I'm not interested in spending the rest of my life tied up over this, and I'm not interested in continuing to be her . . . her victim. That's just not for me.

However, *understanding* the psychological underpinnings of abusiveness—not to be confused with forgiving or condoning it—unquestionably helps the resilient heal. Thus they put monumental effort into making their parents' or other perpetrators' inner workings *intelligible* to themselves, thereby shattering the Sirens of ignorance promoted by most abusive families. They make the horrific comprehensible—as much as it *can* be made so—by recognizing, reading, reflecting, analyzing, and speaking out about human pain. They believe, as I have noted, that remembering is an act of loyalty and affiliation to themselves and abused others. Anything else constitutes abandoning the suffering. Here Diana, a trauma psychologist, captures the sense of resolution she has achieved by differentiating from her parents through *understanding* rather than forgiving them and by making an unromantic but humane distinction between them and those she openly loves:

> I don't like the word somehow, . . . *forgiveness*. . . . I can't forgive them for what they did. That's very clear to me: that I never will forgive them. Yet I really feel like whatever harm they did to me, I've transcended. I mean, it doesn't seem relevant anymore. I would never say to either of them that I loved them, yet in some fundamental way I do. I feel related to them. I wouldn't want to invite them to my house for lunch, but I wouldn't refuse them in a time of pain. I don't want to have any social encounters with them, but I feel like they're my family and I belong to them and they belong to me. I don't forgive them. But neither is it anything that's relevant to discuss; and I don't feel poisoned by that.
>
> I feel like it's much more important for me to stand my ground about how horrible things were for me. . . . Because many people, you know, to whom I might have explained my family situation would say, "Oh, come on, . . . they're your parents. They can't be that bad," and that's kind of what my parents said to me. They really had no tolerance for any feeling or any opinion. I could barely get two words out of my mouth in their presence. They minimized my experience. One of my mother's favorite things to say if I was upset about something was . . . "It's just a stage. *It doesn't matter*." *But somehow my feelings that I came from a kind of toxic environment* matter, *and*

they'll always be part of my identity. But it doesn't feel to me like they're
my whole identity; that was my past.

Like most others in this group, Diana has put considerable effort into understanding herself and her parents in order to make sense out of what happened to her. Whether the resilient are trained clinicians or not, their comprehension of abuse and its consequences is highly sophisticated. During the interviews, they offered a wide variety of complex explanations for why their parents were so damaging to them, ranging from the colloquial to the biblical. They saw them as people shackled in pain they did not understand, inflicting it on their children wittingly or unwittingly, unable to rise above their *own* pasts as their resilient offspring determined to do. They often described their parents as sad, even pitiable figures, defeated in old age. As Kai concluded,

> My parents had young kids, and because I was a young kid in that system, I got abused by it; but as soon as we didn't have needs that were dependent on them, they became better. . . . Forgiveness isn't part of it. I don't like what they did sometimes, but I don't feel that they were psychopathically mean. . . . I think they were overwhelmed and immature and had no inner resources and did bad things because of that. Had I felt a malignant, pathological meanness [*a great evil?*], yes, then I would see it differently. I didn't experience it that way, and I still don't. It's still hard not to picture my father as a stupid bull, . . . but he's so old now and decrepit that it's not like you worry about it.

If not yet dead, the abusive parents of the resilient will soon die as they lived: many small, withered souls, a few revitalized. They devastated many of their other offspring, who typically struggle in very fundamental ways, even in midlife. The wreckage of the abusers' lives abounds. Dry-docked schooners, halyards hissing and mainmasts swinging, they might continue to batter, but the resilient are now well out of their reach. While my subjects harbor no illusions about their families' continuing capacity to hurt them if they allowed it, they also mourn the senseless loss of human possibility that surrounds their lives.

Perhaps this is why so many of the resilient are therapists. While the profession offers no guarantee of mental health, it at least offers the resilient a saturated exposure to psychological wisdom and insight—ways to make sense of the senseless. You are constantly dealing with others' disclosures, revelations, pain, joy, grappling, and overcoming. You come to understand human suffering and surmounting. Yet you *cannot* do it well if you are not open to your own suffering, making concerted, bounded efforts to negotiate your past. Thus, through their professional experience as well as their own personal evolution, resilient therapists eventually arrive at a "detached comprehension." They find their own earlier hardships explicable if not forgivable. They are no longer so guiltily or ragefully or sorrowfully entangled with the past. They are not preoccupied with their families of origin. They are careful about ongoing interactions with family members, engaging in only carefully circumscribed and orchestrated contact. They feel that the second half of their lives is *theirs* and that they can *choose* whom to love. They are determined to sail steadily in sunnier seas.

The Sea Beyond the Sirens

As I said earlier, sadder but wiser is simply not good enough if you have lived an abusive early life, so the resilient seek a southern exposure and hold on to it with great determination. Although they *never* forget, and in the distance they hear the Sirens' continuous calling, they refuse to settle for a life of chronic sorrow. They appreciate the fact that, unlike many others, they are lucky and stubborn and talented enough to have a choice. Here Robert, a fifth-grade teacher, characterizes the resilient:

I think that probably the analogy that [describes] my life best . . . is

e ties [that have] teachers and apples and school buses on them
make people laugh, that make kids comfortable. I think when
have a sense of humor, it allows you to be free, to be yourself;
ything that you can do that allows people—adults more than
-to just be themselves and to drop all their masks that they
is really precious].

ally, Seagull and others in this study maintain their humor
ism while they continually confront trouble. These days,
h belongs less to them and more to those they help; but
ill actively engaged in revising human hurt, not perpet-
ng themselves on some remote rock. Paradoxically, their
ork is also the wellspring of their joy, because they see
d *possibilities* embedded in pain:

her in an inner-city public school, I see kids [who struggle
. It's difficult for me to get beyond their eyes a lot of days,
hey have such pained expressions or such sadness. Some-
class of twenty-nine kids, my hunch is that twenty of them
abused physically, emotionally, sexually; they don't have
eat; they're not sleeping. I'm often providing the comforts
d be provided at home: food, or a pillow and a blanket and
eep on. I always allow a kid that's tired to take a nap.
me is more important than a kid's mental well-being.

eir faces and the way they look at life and their
-[that] to me is also inspiring. When you see a kid and
Oh, man, what are you going home to? And you come
y day ready to go to work? . . ." How can I say they're
they got a C or an F on a test? To me, it just doesn't
heir *strengths*. Man, they can put one foot in front of the
ey often have a smile on their face. . . .

umor of the resilient is integrated with their past

a card game. We all get dealt a certain h
left might get a better hand and the per
worse hand, but . . . [all people are] re
cards to the best of their ability. I th
because I can also say that, with one ex
my life get better every day.

Because for the resilient the over
what was overcome, I do not want t
struggle without elaborating on the
You have already seen some of the
dant throughout the interviews,
overcoming. Most subjects cons
finding true pleasure despite the
them that they always engage, a
as a way of enjoying themselve
allows them to attain, as adults,
asked Seagull if she feels proud
been through and how she lives
gives her validation that she l
masks of inauthenticity that c

I think the thing that right
proudest of is that I have a gr
I can still get sad and depre
see life as pretty joyful. . . . [
delicious. I really believe th

I think [my sense of h
validation is the thing tha
that indicated] that you
[behavior was] good or b
me to just be me. If I'm
sunglasses. I have an ass
that I think pulls them

I ha
that
you
. . . a
kids—
wear

Cruci
and optin
the angui
they are s
ually sunn
yeoman's
the *profou*

As a tea
so much
because
times in a
are being
enough to
that shoul
a rug to s
Nothing t

But th
resilience—
you think,
in here eve
bad because
fit. . . . I see
other, and t

Thus the h

struggles and the current struggles of others. It is joy despite and because of disaster.

Most subjects also said they were simply happy to be alive, grateful that they survived. They savor the simpler pleasures of life with a gusto heightened by knowing *how it was*—and *how it might have been* if they had not survived so well. Diana, a psychologist who struggled throughout her twenties with serious depression and never dreamed she would marry and have her own sons, says with slight amazement:

> When I hop out of bed in the morning, I'm really happy to be awake, and the list of the things that are there for me looks good. Going to Harvest Market is fun. I took [my two-year-old], Ben, to Harvest Market this morning and bought him his first box of animal crackers—you know, the age when kids get too old just to entertain themselves . . . and you can no longer play peek-a-boo under the cart. He sat there with those animal crackers, looking at them, going, "Lion, lion," trying out all his new words. I was just in heaven.

Virtually everyone in the study also feels that living well is a near mission. Negatively inspired by their parents' misery, they seized the reins and cantered toward satisfaction. Because they see themselves as agents in shaping their own future, having had enough success in challenging their abusive parents and the Fates themselves that they developed confidence in their instincts, they have resolved to live well. For example, even though Stan co-directs an effective inner-city mental health agency and is steeped in others' consuming troubles during the work day, he is adamant about having a positive focus in his life:

> I'm not going to be sixty, seventy years old and saying, "God, what did I do? Why did I waste my life?" I'm just not going to do that. I hold the belief that you have control of your own environment and existence and that you can either set yourself so that you're

enjoying life or not enjoying it. . . . If that is in fact true, then I'm just determined not to [be miserable]. I don't like being unhappy. I *do* like being happy, so I try to structure things so that I spend most of my time having a good time.

Thus, unlike many other professionals, the resilient said they are insistent about taking time to cut their motors and ponder, muse, laugh, and simply enjoy themselves. Many said they take time off religiously. While they *learned* these enjoyment skills consciously, they are now postgraduates. Much of their pleasure comes from the fact that they can finally *sustain* their enjoyment, and they share it with people they love. Here Dan realizes that his especially arduous passage is largely behind him, his days now propelled by a spinnaker at full billow:

Last Father's Day, last spring, my kids—they're not kids anymore, obviously; they're in their twenties and thirties—took me for a sailboat ride. We anchored off this little island and we rowed in, and they had made this whole picnic for me, and they had this wonderful present, which was a picture that I could hang on the wall in my office. I was sitting there on the blanket, a little bit teary, realizing . . . how much fun they were having doing this wonderful thing for their father, and how they were all totally into it, and how they were delighted with every step of making this the most perfect day for Dad and doing all the things they knew I would just love. . . .

And . . . I just realized, My God! am I lucky to have children who love me so much and all of them are children I can be so proud of; they have wonderful qualities. Again, they're not perfect. . . . Nobody ever does anything perfectly, and if I could do it all over again, I would do some of it differently; . . . but I've got wonderful kids, just wonderful kids. . . . [Now I can finally see and enjoy] what I did right.

Now, in earlier chapters I mentioned the uneven distribution of gratitude in the human race, and the robust capacity of the resilient for it. It is nowhere more evident than in their remarks about self-pride, in which they reveal their feeling that "there but for the grace of God go I." The resilient know they are in the minority. Their siblings are among the lost and maimed. Those they help are often on the edge or barely off the bottom. They have no illusions about their invulnerability. At the same time, they understand that they are beyond much of the misery that defined the past, and they are beginning to exhale. Joanna eloquently summarizes her recent arrival:

> I think there's something in my life that keeps saying, "Are we there yet? Are we there yet? Is it okay to feel safe? Is it okay to feel good? Is it okay to be proud?" [laughter]. But at some level, I think turning forty helped enormously, that somehow I said to myself, "Hey, you know, in all likelihood you really are entering the second half of your life here, and isn't it about time to sort of notice what you've been doing all these years and maybe relax a little and enjoy it and appreciate it and be proud of it and stop and smell the flowers? Notice that you actually like the person you've become, and are proud of the person you've become. . . .

No longer locked in basic struggles with the Sirens of this chapter, Joanna and others have begun to experience a renaissance. Their self-esteem is continually on the rise, their growth ballooning. Joanna sustains an articulate view of herself as worthwhile and important, dignifying others with the same regard:

> I think the fascinating thing that happens—and this is, I think, almost unexplainable to somebody who hasn't experienced it—*is that growth becomes exponential*. Then there's a level of refinement of the capacity for self-worth and self-dignity and good treatment of

others that's just wonderful, because then it really feels like you're just doing . . . the fun work. This is going to be an odd thing to say, but it relates to discovering that you've entered the realm of genius when all you ever thought of yourself before is that you were sort of a smart person; but then somehow, by sheer diligence—not native ability, but *sheer diligence*—at some point what you do is really extraordinary and maybe you didn't even know it at the time. . . . You know how you get to a certain point in any sort of learning where *you just sort of take off*, and it's just a remarkable experience?

At the same time, Joanna feels herself to be a smaller, but no less significant, part of the vast mosaic of life itself, hushed and reverent:

And yet, [in the face of life's mysteries,] once you feel solid about being big, you also get to be little and humble. . . . This is what happens to astronauts; this is what happens to mountain climbers. . . . They go into space [or climb up Everest] and they become philosophers; *they come to believe in God.* My whole thinking now about myself and life and the meaning of life and the work I do with patients and what I'm capable of [has changed]. *I felt like I was going down a tunnel for years, and now I feel like I'm looking at this vast, expansive, limitless track of possibilities that's just exhilarating.*

CHAPTER EIGHT

Recommendations from the Resilient

> Therapists [and educators] need to know that people
> with these kinds of childhoods not only can be
> healed but have an incredible set of gifts to offer the
> world. . . . They're often talented, creative, and
> [substantially] self-made.
> —*Kai, director of a Yale teaching hospital psychology department*

Abuse is a plague that should occasion universal sorrow. Miraculously, some of its victims do not lose their radiance. This is a book about how some love well despite hate. It is ultimately intended for the legions still struggling to overcome and those who are trying to help them. It is not meant to blame *any* victim for his or her current place in the effort. Rather, it offers travelers some navigational charts for how they might get to where they have a right to be. Sadder but wiser is but sorry comfort for the terribly treated. Thus I offer this work to help the struggling renew their promise of a larger future.

Although there are now a variety of essential volumes on helping the traumatized recover, it seems useful to explore those assumptions and interventions that flow directly from the previous chapters on the *resilient*. Thus I will summarize here some of the prominent themes that emerged in my data, addressing specific recommendations to either the potentially resilient or to clinicians, educators, or more informal (*but no less important*) surrogates. I will call the potentially resilient "sufferers," "strugglers," or "surmounters"; I will refer to clinicians, educators, and other surrogates (all of whom have something valuable to offer the traumatized) inclusively as "helpers" or "healers."

Remember that these deceptively simple recommendations are a composite of what helped my *subjects* the most. Recall that several of them are senior clinicians, yet they reiterate here the value of basic, humane interventions, thus inviting us to embrace the fundamentals more deeply. Although much of what worked best for them occurred spontaneously or accidentally, you can certainly nourish by *design* if you thoroughly understand these reparative forces in the lives of the potentially resilient.

I will also integrate some of the more useful insights and approaches informing my own clinical and educational work and that of close colleagues in the past decade, since our work is devoted to identifying and nourishing the resilience inherent in *most* lives. I assume you will encounter some familiar recommendations here, but my aim is emphasis not novelty, utility not pyrotechnics. Remember that my forty subjects were chosen for their extremes of past hurt and current health. However, they overcame their trials by employing *human* capacities that lie dormant or unamplified in many of us. You do not have to be a card-carrying resilient to recover well. As Shibvon concludes,

> Not all of us are in a real mess, you know. . . . People often associate anyone who's been abused with "There's no hope for that child." . . . *Tell people that we can do it.* That you can survive all that and be a fully functioning member of the community. Don't give up on that kid at age seven and say, "Oh, he's been through so much; he's never going to amount to anything." . . . The abused are labeled. *But you can change somebody around.* . . . So for that teacher who might be thinking, . . . "I think this kid's going through something terrible," maybe [knowing that *we* did it] would give her that gumption. Or

for the teacher who put out for that kid and wondered if it mattered: *tell people that it does matter. . . .*

I'm not standing out in the middle of Town Square saying, "Guess what? I was abused!" but I'm very comfortable [disclosing] now, if I feel it will help somebody out to hear it. . . . They might look at me and say, "Oh, Shibvon's okay. . . . She does well at work; she [cares well for her kids]." *I think that's been the shocker [to many people]: . . . that we can be normal.*

Underscoring Strengths and the Lifelong Capacity for Growth

Resilience, like growth itself, is a developmental phenomenon propelled by vision and stamina. It evolves over time. *Facilitating resilience is more a matter of orientation than explicit intervention.* It assumes that many of the maltreated are motivated to overcome hardship, whether they were raised in a familial inferno, an emotional limbo, or by parents too depleted to care for them. It requires a firm refusal to join the ranks of the sour and dispirited. It also assumes that, if the traumatized seek you out and form any relationship with you, the two of you already have a toehold on their surmounting. It insists that you hold a broad developmental view of growth and change, realizing that there are always untapped degrees of freedom for the motivated to mobilize. Remember that many subjects in this study stated that they would *not* have met the study criteria in their earlier developmental eras, although they were recruiting others' invested regard and spawning their vision—thus sowing the seeds of overcoming—from early on. They *cultivated* progress, toiling hard with rake and hoe. Their health blossomed over time. As Dan exclaimed to me,

You've known me only in my adult years. If I could transport both of us back to that time, you at your present age and level of understanding, me back to when I was eighteen, . . . you would be saying,

"Oh, boy! I've got a really sick guy here." If you were to enroll me
in the study then, you would probably end up hospitalizing me, . . .
totally unglued.

Thus, while chronological age is obviously no guarantee of
progress, since people frequently deteriorate or ossify over decades,
growth *can* and often *does* occur throughout the life span. The more
determined, propelled by insight, stamina, and recruited love, can
use the press of development to overcome even staggering odds.
You can accompany them. Motivation and faith—yours as much
as theirs—rank as high as your credentials or your competence in
determining whether the relationship is transformative.

How can you help them? Stop hanging crepe, for starters. It is
essential to focus on how human beings self-right, not on their
floundering. Helpers need to know the whole history of their strugglers' surmounting; we need to catalog their capabilities with the
exquisite concern we normally reserve for their weaknesses. How
have their strengths emerged over time? Why? Without sacrificing
subtle attention to the slights, hurts, and hates that injure any soul,
you must also know their triumphs—writ large, writ small, or not
written at all. These triumphs deserve more than honorable mention. How did this person negotiate his or her troubles with coherence and competence? Why is this person not doing *worse*? By
overemphasizing ideal standards of where we *ought* to be, we often
neglect what went right in a life. For example, since the majority
of abused adults do *not* abuse their children, we need to explore
how they *stopped* that curse with the same intensity that we explore
their derailments. Here Dan defines the orientation of the many
subjects who are actively intervening in *others'* lives, explaining his
massive mental health agency's steadfast focus on client strengths.
The agency's focus, deceptively simple, is not common enough in
the field:

We try to catch people as early on as possible, but we have programs
that run from early infancy all the way up through the chronically

mentally ill adults so that we cover the entire life span. We have an enormous substance division, offering lots of substance abuse programs of very different kinds. One of the philosophical concepts of the agency is to *focus on what people do well, on their strengths, and to build on the strengths rather than obsess on the weaknesses*. We do it with staff [as well]: it's not "Aha! I caught you doing something wrong"; it's "Great, you did that right!" There's a very positive kind of a focus in terms of staffing. People don't have to go around feeling fearful of their jobs. Instead, they feel good about being thanked or rewarded or praised for doing good things. There's a very nice morale in the agency because of that, because of the positive focus.

It's the exact focus that I apply to the clinical work. . . . If you're dealing with people who are chronically disabled and who have such catastrophic emotional problems, *if you had to make them perfect, you'd never do it.* . . . But if you can focus on their strengths and help these individuals to do something that they already do [well] even better, then [they end up] feeling good about it, and feeling much better about themselves, because you've taken that thing that they do well and enhanced it and made it a that much more important part of their lives. [Of course, you proceed] with the understanding that some people are just so disabled that you're never going to heal it all, *but there's a way of finding hope and strength and what it is they can do well.*

We get high school kids. By the time we get them in the residential school, the kid, let's say, is twelve years old and maybe has been beaten every day of every one of those twelve years. . . . We have so many kids who have been abused in these ways. . . . But maybe he's wonderful in the metal shop, and he can pound things out with that hammer; . . . and he can go on to do the most wonderful job as an automobile-body mechanic, pounding out all that metal as he goes rather than hitting other people. . . .

We have a very practical, down-to-earth approach to these

things: . . . we find what people can do well, where they're good, where they have some self-esteem, and we build on it. That's the philosophical base. If we had millions of dollars for every client, then maybe we could do better, but . . . it's sort of a practical kind of a thing there, and we've got some really nice success stories that come out of it.

Thus to plumb resilient potential effectively, you need to explain and amplify the past and present strengths of the traumatized, clarifying the adaptive strategies that keep them farther from the bottom rather than focusing on why they are not closer to the top. You need to acknowledge and celebrate how far they have come, and how well. *You need to let them know about their own strong overcoming—any scrap of it—and let them hear it often.* This does not mean that our interventions should not also identify how people can do *better*, holding them accountable for what needs to change. Why would people seek help if they were not trying to alter their own developmental trajectory? Yet we *cannot* help if we neglect the history of strengths guiding their lives, if we fail to honor each modicum of decency, good judgment, self-protectiveness, and just plain skill that they developed against the odds.

Now, I tend to think of human experience as a long series of Rorschach cards, ambiguous inkblots stretching across life like so many boxcars on the Boston and Maine Railroad. We interpret our experiences as we chug through them. My favorite live Rorschach regarding the balance of hope and despondence involves the panoramic view outside my office. Although our building itself is nondescript, the view is dominated by antique architecture, a cobblestoned park, a patch of sea, distant hills, New England church spires, and expansive skies. The day we moved in, one of the movers—evidently discouraged by life—stopped for a moment to gaze outward. Suddenly squinting and peering, he pointed to a glistening heap in a small section of the vista. "You know, . . . you have an auto graveyard right in the middle there. They're dragging in

another accident. See it?" I fear that too many potentially reparative relationships interpret the scenery of troubled lives in this manner—consumed by the twisted heap, ignoring the surrounding
health that might heal it. *Do not overlook the phoenix for the ashes.*
Otherwise, you neglect the very resources that are your best allies
in forging a firmer future. Above all, let your strugglers laugh (or
help them learn how). They need to laugh as much as they need to
weep and rant—not to laugh off their grief but to embrace their joy.

Understanding the History of Hope in Challenged Lives

Denial of abuse abounds. It operates intrapsychically, interperson-
ally, and culturally. It constitutes a far greater hazard to overcoming than ignoring a sufferer's strengths. However, for those who can
tolerate bearing witness to trauma's *full* catastrophe to help the hurt
heal, it is just as essential to honor the history of *hope* in their lives.
Where was the light in this darkened life? Where is it now? What
surrogate figures did this struggler internalize? Is there a singular
shepherd sitting on some inner slope, quietly awaiting recognition?
What vision did that shepherd embody and protect? How did this
sufferer form core images of decency and kindness? How do the
resilient maintain faith that they were "made for more"? Recall that
all but four of my subjects encountered potent surrogates who
became beacons of possibility in their lives. Most were taken aback
to recall their deep and intense gratitude toward these figures and
to realize how much they were influenced by them. Larry, an engineer, repressed the most positive era of his development considerably until I asked him where the light shone in his life. Once his
memories were kindled, he ignited with grateful warmth and animated intensity. Thus we not only repress what is potentially annihilating; we sometimes also inter what is life-preserving. Our
professions seem similarly repressed: an excessive emphasis on
pathology in both psychology and education, justifying both

intervention and reimbursement, has led us too far from the light in people's lives. The dark and the light need to be resurrected *in equal measure* to help people heal. Melville seemed to understand this when he wrote: "Gazing down from his boat's side into that same golden sea, Starbuck lowly murmured: 'Loveliness unfathomable as ever a lover saw in his young bride's eye!—Tell me not of thy teeth-tiered sharks, and thy kidnapping cannibal ways. Let faith oust facts; let fancy oust memory: I look deep down and do believe.'"[1]

Thus several subjects in this study, especially therapists, strongly recommended that those of you who touch the life of a child constructively, even briefly, should *never* underestimate your possible corrective impact on that child. The more resilient the child, the more mileage he or she will gain from your help. In fact, one of the strongest leitmotifs rippling through the interviews was the reparative power of simple, open availability. As I said earlier, you do not have to pull a dove out of your sleeve to make a difference. Recall that so many of the resilient emphasized that their hope was continually buttressed by the sudden kindness of strangers, integrated into the broader fabric of resilient faith over time.

Furthermore, never forget the immense contrast between simple, *sustained* kindness and the horrendous abuse described in this volume. Certainly, there is no substitute for intervening appropriately (especially if you are a mandated reporter) and challenging abuse with all the leverage at your disposal. But remember the gratitude with which the resilient recall their surrogates. Enormous reparative potential resides in the bread-and-butter basics of caring about the young and listening closely to their lives. You can do this in *any* capacity: babysitter, teacher, therapist, neighbor, relative, clergy, coach, butcher, baker, or candlestick maker. As the chapters on finding love in more and less likely places reveal, no particular *stripe* of helper holds a monopoly on surrogate love.

Remember, too, that the surrogates of the resilient were generally available for only small amounts of clock time, and some faded after a limited developmental exposure. Yet their positive impact persisted for life. Just as abuse poisons by small acts in brief moments, so can we sow antidotal seeds through our gestures of caring concern. While the latter certainly do *not* neutralize the former (merely counteracting to a limited degree its effects) and should never be used to justify it—perish the thought—we must look to these *constructive* interactions while fully honoring the *destruction* in a challenged life. They are the wellspring of resilient vision, the faith that finally life might be lived in the sea beyond the Sirens.

More specifically, it is crucial for you to comprehend just *how* surrogate relationships wield reparative influence in the past and present. As Melville reminds us, "Not seldom in this life, when, on the right side, fortunes' favorites sail close by us, we, though all adroop before, catch somewhat of the rushing breeze, and joyfully feel our bagging sails fill out."[2] You can assist sufferers by helping to create an inventory of those characteristics and dynamics of their unofficial caregivers that they have emulated—those breezes filling out their bagging sails. If you are working directly with children or adolescents, you can also assist by encouraging and helping to secure their continued access to surrogate figures. You should help both surrogate and child understand the vivid influence that surrogacy can have on a troubled life. The singular strengths of gifted surrogates—such as their quiet availability, inspired capacity for fundamental positive regard, and talent for helping children avert impossible loyalty conflicts—also need to be dignified with *thorough* recognition.

Since surrogacy is the polestar of resilient overcoming, its relational role in promoting the vision of a better life should also be fully understood. Just how did the surrogate help shape a struggler's sense of possibility? How did that surrogate's vision become selectively internalized and embellished so that it became an integral part of the surmounting self? How do actual and imaginatively sustained relationships continue to be a source of faith-renewing sustenance? Looking closely at their heroic figures—either symbolic or real—will help strugglers honor their own visions of who they *are*, who they might *become*, and *how* they can get there. Exploring their guiding metaphors should also help them celebrate, elaborate, and thereby strengthen their attachment to their ideals. If the potentially resilient strengthen their internal locus of vision, then they can revitalize their own ability to shape and *live* their hopes. As long as a sufferer is still alive, hope commingles with the despair in their lives. Why *are* they still here? What gives them any sense that life is worth living? What embers, however modest, offer promise? Recall that Anya, the psychologist pulled into ritual cult abuse as a young child, found hope by gazing kindly into the eyes of other terrified children and constructing an inner pantheon of benevolent guardians to shepherd her. From these shards she gradually built a sanctuary of resilient love. Like any good cathedral conservator, you need to help your strugglers assemble *their* shards into sanctuaries.

Therapeutic Ties: Clinically Sensitive Teaching and Formal Clinical Relationships

All that I have already recommended is, of course, germane to both therapy and teaching. There are aspects of these more formal healing relationships that deserve some pointed attention now. (These comments are relevant to more informal surrogate relationships as well, however.) My recommendations, to be elaborated in a moment, include valuing what you do and openly caring for those you help; honoring the reparative capacity of effective loving and social relationships as much as you value executive competence; recognizing that the more fully resilient are pros at surviving who will lean on you when and *if* they decide that you are trustworthy— they do not need to be pressed to absorb reparative light; learning to hear, undenyingly, the very worst about a struggler's life in order to stop any ongoing abuse immediately and help the person heal from egregious past insults; maintaining your bedrock faith in even imperceptible growth; and finally, closely examining your assumptions about whether adult mental health can take place only within—or *without*—ongoing interactions with the family of origin. This survey, gleaned from the resilient lives in this study, is suggestive ruther than exhaustive.

First, remember that the maltreated typically lack genuine appreciation and open admiration at home. Yet a healthy capacity for self-love and self-promotion does not spring automatically from human beings. We are a dependent social species, learning to love *with* someone else before we can extend love to ourselves and others. Thus, while not shirking the joint enterprise of holding the maltreated closely accountable for their recovery—especially the ways in which they continue hurting themselves or others—you need to establish a high standard of genuine self-regard *with* them. This is particularly crucial for those many decent strugglers who give themselves far more trouble than they *ever* give anyone else. Here Dan summarizes the impassioned faith in simple caring stressed by all of my subjects. When I asked him what recommendations he would make to clinicians or educators trying to encourage resilient potential—especially those interventions that brought *him* along—he replied,

> [Clinicians and educators] need to have both technical knowledge and ability; but in addition, I feel it's absolutely essential for the person to be highly developed as a human being: capable of caring for others, capable of loving others, . . . a realized person. You cannot get good work done by defective individuals who just have the right credentials. A successful therapist must work on her- or himself as well. [The] people who helped me the most helped me partially because of who they *were*, modeling for me how to be as a human being. It just doesn't work to say, "I read it in a book and I'm going to say this." [Healing stems] partly from just sitting there with someone who you can see in all these nonverbal ways is comfortable, who has a sense of self-worth, cares for others, isn't focused on himself, is

focused globally [rather than self-referentially]. It's expressed in so many ways you can't fake it. . . .

Caring openly about sufferers within the boundaries of your therapeutic or academic relationship with them is essential. You express that caring not by declaring your love or talking like a greeting card but by being attentive, concerned, and intensely valuing. If your caring keeps their needs and purposes—not yours—in the foreground, your high level of fundamental positive regard can ultimately be as healing as those early surrogate relationships in the lives of the resilient. Recall that the resilient did not feel exploited within this care; rather, they felt valued for who they were *independent* of meeting the surrogate's immediate needs. They thrived on their surrogate's quiet admiration and genuine investment in their welfare. Eventually, this allowed them to model the regard that they could not originally extend to themselves.

Since the resilient in this study were quite used to boundary violations and exploitations at home, earlier surrogacy also helped them recognize when later relationships became distorted or destructive. By adolescence or early adulthood, they learned to avoid the sexualized and the sentimentalized. They learned not to trust anything that felt exclusive or secretive. *Thus it is critical for healers to communicate their regard clearly. Many of the abused have little sense of what a positive model of human interaction involves, nor do they necessarily realize how bizarre their childhood treatment has been.* Many even lack any media models of comparatively decent family interactions. Prototypically, Dan first noticed that his family was odd when he went to friends' houses as a teenager, surprised to discover that the parents did not beat the children and have sex with them:

This may sound strange, but for the longest time, I had no concept that what was going on at home was any different from other people's lives, because we didn't, as a family, associate very much with other families. . . . We were very isolated, as happens in families where a lot of abuse is going on. They become isolated. So it wasn't until I was quite well on in age, fifteen or sixteen, before I began to realize that what was happening to me was different from other children.

We had no television at home, . . . none at all, so I couldn't see any comparison there. [But when I first visited friends,] I noticed that other people's parents would sort of laugh and joke with each other and they'd touch each other in sort of loving ways and so forth. . . . I just couldn't quite understand what was going on. I mean, they were laughing together and having a good time. I'm waiting for the hitting to start and nobody's hitting anybody. . . . I'm thinking, "Gee, it's so different!" There weren't any fights going on. I'd go to visit somebody, and I'd be there three hours, and there wasn't a single fight the whole time. . . . I was dumbfounded. I'd sort of think, "When do they fight? They don't fight in the afternoon; when *do* they fight? Maybe they fight at night."

We must remember that, while attaining high self-esteem is the ultimate goal and responsibility of sufferers, *they cannot know what it is if they find little or nothing of it in their own experience.* They may encounter it for the first time when you, as a therapist or teacher, extend gifted regard and model basic decency. In doing so, you may help ignite a resilient life.

It is also essential to openly value the loving and concerned social relationships across the lives of the potentially resilient as much as you value their *executive competence*. (In fact, love— broadly construed—needs to be central to the study of psychology in general and clinical work in particular. Too long relegated to the domain of "women's work" or "women's experience," love must be accorded a firm place in the pantheon of human overcoming.) Recall that my subjects generally performed well at school and in their careers. Many found surrogate love in teachers and coaches who saw that they were suffering despite their high performance. While many of them went to marginal schools, some still encountered some remarkable care; others did not. (Of course, many of the less-resilient abused perform poorly because they are *suffering*, not because they are incapable.) In any case, the reparative role of good relationships, not just scholastic or athletic performance, is a crucial consideration; such relationships clearly saved the day for the resilient.

Loving and caring relationships should also be far more valued in schools, since it is difficult to learn anything at all without enough love in your life and far more enjoyable if you have it. Because school is the only probable source of surrogacy for many children, we need to ensure the availability of caring there.

Thus in both clinical and educational settings, you need to become very curious about the love—or the lack of it—in any life. Is this National Merit Scholar overfunctioning to salvage her sadly sagging self-esteem? Is that quiet child in the back of the room dissociatively numb from maltreatment? Is this girl unable to formulate ideas because, having been silenced on one subject by her perpetrator, she has been rendered globally silent? Is this boy prevented from succeeding because none of the envious adults at home can tolerate his emerging competence? Few of the resilient were identified by schoolteachers or guidance counselors as troubled, let alone taken to therapists, because they were not the easily identifiable, disruptive figures that gain adult attention immediately. As a result, most of my subjects stressed that clinicians and educators need to be closely attuned to the *quality* of relationships in children's lives—particularly the children who are too quiet or too eager to please; they need to consider whether or not love is failing *outside* school. Seagull, now teaching in the classroom herself, summarizes for many others:

> I think all through my elementary years, grades one through eight, I was such "good girl" that I did get lots of positive feedback from

my teachers; but I [paid] a price for that . . . I think the approval of others became such a monster in my life that I lost sight of myself. So when I look at kids as a teacher, I often think about [whether] they're doing this just for me. We often need to say to kids, "You should be proud of yourself. . . . *Are* you proud of yourself? How do *you* feel about what you did and didn't do?" . . . and let them have ownership of their work.

I think anytime you have a child in your classroom that's an overachiever, that has to be the best at everything, you need to be a little bit concerned about . . . [that child's] inability to just relax and be a kid. Why [is this kid] so driven? I do think many kids do this to themselves, and it's not always a sign of sexual abuse, but it's a sign that somebody's putting a lot of expectations on a kid. For myself, my fallen grades—going from a 95 to an 80 in one year—should have waved a red flag. My wanting to please so much should have waved a red flag. To me, that's really symptomatic of somebody that's either denying or defending or keeping a secret.

Also, I see it in some of my babysitters—this idealization of parents, . . . treating parents like they're gods. To me, these are extremes [that suggest] a parent that's holding too much power over a kid for whatever reason, and it frightens me; . . . or being really too enmeshed with their parents at a time when they should be more involved with their peers. . . . I think so much of what I did, I did for my parents' approval. I wasn't encouraged to be an individual or to think on my own; and by not thinking on your own, you don't think that you *can*, so that you always need that reassurance from a parent that you're okay rather than being encouraged to make mistakes on your own. . . . I never saw that I had a voice.

Those of you who are teachers or guidance counselors, recall that many of the resilient found school to be the only *systematically* safe place they encountered. While they hardly went to choice schools (since many were poor), the contrast with home was extreme. Those who were good students probably got the best of what their schools had to offer; but for all of them, school was an ordered world, a place to be competent, a universe in which the junctures met. They could predict what would happen there. In fact, for many of the resilient, it was tantamount to a therapeutic milieu, providing most of the coherence they encountered in their early years.

That my subjects vividly recalled gifted teachers many decades later indicates that educators can also be a profoundly important source of focal surrogate care. This phenomenon warrants both funding and training for its largely unofficial but critical reparative role in the lives of the abused. For example, Seagull's inner-city classroom holds about thirty young children, many of whom leave each afternoon to reenter unrelentingly bleak and tearing circumstances. For many of these children, Seagull provides the only environment restoring some dignity and sustenance to their lives:

> I think it's important as an educator that we tend to a lot of their needs. Kids that are hungry just can't function. We can't expect them to, so I keep a bowl of fruit on my desk that they're welcome to every day at snack time; or if they have no lunch that day, they can take something at recess time, or lunch time. And they know I always have a closet full of cookies.

> To me, kids need to feel validated. The most important thing that ever happened to *me* was being validated. "Your feelings are real; . . . you're not going crazy. There's a reason that you feel this way. I don't know what it is. I don't have all the answers. Life's difficult sometimes, but I'm here if you need me." I always have fresh flowers in a classroom, from my garden or a florist. *[What are you saying to the children?]* That they're important to me—that they're important enough to me to bring in something living—that there's hope, that I'm here for them in a lot of different ways. To me, any-

body can teach material, but you have to help them feel good about themselves to learn.

Now, before closing, let me address several comments and recommendations to therapists in particular. You, too, provide an invaluable and in many respects unique reparative niche for the potentially resilient. Recall that most of my subjects were in therapy for prolonged periods, far beyond what the insurance industry covers. They are adamant that therapy was *essential* to their recovery, particularly during earlier adulthood (when most would not have met my study's criteria for mental health). In fact, most said they struggled fundamentally during those years, in the manner of most traumatized individuals. Thus the extraordinary recovery in this volume rests in crucial part on solid clinical work. *If the best mental health outcomes associated with childhood abuse require such careful clinical attention, it is obviously essential to the recovery of most traumatized individuals*. The best news is that it often *works*, especially for the motivated.

Aside from your pivotal underlying role in recovery, what are some specific points to remember? First, it is important to recognize that your abused clients, especially the more resilient, are often already pros at surviving. You may not have surmounted as much or as well yourself. Kai was adamant that the coping styles of survivors need our full respect—especially their use of adaptive strategies, which render them far healthier than their earlier experiences would predict:

> People who have had traumatic childhoods have got to explain things in their own time, in their own way, and that has to be valued. You have to . . . acknowledge and give respect for the way people cope. I don't care about the *symptoms*; . . . people don't heal or trust a therapist until they feel that that person can appreciate *the way* they're compromised, because there was no other way to survive—period. . . . You really have to appreciate the integrity of

someone who's survived his childhood. . . . [It may be worth] suspending theory a bit and . . . really learning to appreciate that person's life, . . . *appreciate what it took to survive, to hang in there in the world. . . . These patients are professionals at certain things that the therapist isn't a professional at because they've been in battle.* . . .

[Therapists have] to get that across: that they respect the *professional* coping skills that the patient has that *they* may not even have. They may not even have been able to cope with the same situation the same way, and I think that patients who don't believe that [the therapist realizes this] will distrust the therapist. If they feel like the therapist is always trying to keep the upper hand or be the arbiter of what's a good coping mechanism all the time, or what's appropriate or what isn't, [that alienates clients]. . . . Sensing that, I think, turns off a survivor. It's just easier to do it yourself. You don't need to take care of a therapist *[laughter]*; . . . it's not your job just to educate them. I don't think that the therapist has to be a professional coper the same way that a survivor is. But a therapist has to be open. . . .

[What's most crucial to survivors is] being with them and *witnessing* . . . this war that they've been through. This is really probably the most important thing that therapists can do. . . . Hang in there as a human with them while they're re-creating the war that they've been through. Interrupting that process too much or trying to pass judgment on it or focus on some theory really just gets in the way. . . .

Remember that all efforts to stay alive in the face of potentially annihilating torment have their own logic. But some adaptations are elegantly and unexpectedly humane. So you need to appreciate the remarkable sturdiness of a person who could be doing far worse; you need to maintain a sense of friendly wonder and respect for your client's overcoming while not devaluing the additional help that you can offer.

Aside from these clinical assumptions, how can you help more directly? Well, although the resilient seem to preserve much of their own health and autonomy by maintaining great clarity of perspective about their parents' folly, they also sacrifice some degree of intimacy if they cannot yield to the support and wisdom of healthier mentors. You might provide this support. Yet their histories have taught them an immense amount about life's shadows, particularly shadows that lurk in gifts from Trojan guides. So if you are going to invite resilient adults to share their reins, you need to encourage them toward greater vulnerability while maintaining a profound respect for how remarkably well they have "made themselves." Crucially, do not push the overly self-reliant to rely on *you*. They are well aware of how easily others crumble when sufferers openly reveal need or want. As Kai stated, "Professional survivors and copers *know* who to lean on and who to trust." Rather than pressing them to trust you, it is more useful to remain curious about their ethic of self-sufficiency, considering how it might be a virtue born of necessity with aspects that are now overdetermined and outdated. Thus, while you can negotiate healthy interdependence as a therapeutic goal, you might also think of working with late adolescents or adults as more of a collaboration, recognizing *with them* just where and how they might rest their defense of overdetermined self-sufficiency. They are generally relieved to share the reins once they trust your sense of direction. In any case, the journey is always *theirs*, no matter how devotedly you guide them.

The resilient therapists in my study avoid pressing clients to trust them or urging them to take up a particular path. Yet they have great faith that if they are invited to guide, they can be of service. Not the least of their credentials is their own surmounting, implicit but probably powerfully *experienced* by their clients. Here, as Joanna and I discuss her model of trauma intervention, she realizes that it is much like the Lewis and Clark expedition. She believes that, while neither the guide nor the guided can entirely know what terrible uncharted territory they will enter, the guide taps deeper knowledge that will keep both of them on track. Yet they must *both* decide independently that the expedition is necessary if the sufferer is going to heal:

> It goes back to something you and I were talking about earlier: this phenomenon of conveying to people that it's their job to do but that you have faith in them that they *can* do it. I think, to some extent, that's what my grandmother did for me—although it never got said. This is the most extraordinary thing. . . . It was *never* talked about, but I've always had the sense that by her allowing me to watch how she did things and treating me as though she thought I could be like her, there was a message: "You can do this. Somewhere in you is all the right stuff. You've just got to find it, and you'll do it, and I'll love you. I'm your grandmother, and so I'll be there; but . . . this is your job, and you can do it and you *will* do it."

> I think that to some extent that's what is the most affirming in trauma therapy. The Lewis and Clark metaphor basically says this is such a long, scary journey, and you can't be expected to know all the guideposts, so I will accompany you; but it's *your* journey, the client's journey. . . . I use the analogy in trauma work because it's really uncharted territory for the client. [In the more grizzly cases,] it's uncharted territory for me, too. At times I'm Lewis or I'm Clark, and the client is the other. . . . At times I'm just sort of three steps ahead—I'm not very far ahead, but I *am* three steps ahead—*but I have faith that collectively we're going to do this*, not because the environment isn't hostile and dangerous and unknown *but because this is what we decided to do;* and we both have to see to it that we have it in us to keep going down the path. Because that's the only alternative at this point, and because it's the *best* alternative at this point, and because it's what we want.

> I think there has to be strength and humility at the same time. The strength to say, "I'm going to do this with this person. I *choose* to do it with this person. I'm in it with this person. I'm not going to wimp out at this point, but I'm not going to take this person's job

away; . . . I'm going to watch my ego so that I don't take on this person's job." I do think, because I tend to be a pretty nurturing person, I have to watch to make sure it *doesn't* become my job—that basically, ultimately I cannot walk in another's shoes. I do say this to my patients a lot: "I'll never know the *same* pain. . . ."

> Keeping your own role in focus is central. I think that probably the two greatest pitfalls in trauma work are either being afraid you don't have enough courage or wisdom in yourself to do it, or thinking you've got enough to supply both of you. Both of those things are pitfalls. . . . Probably this whole analogy of going into the wilderness is that *if you're going to do that, you hire the best guide you can possibly hire*. But the best guide you can possibly hire is basically saying, "Look, you're paying me to do this. It's your experience. I'm going to try to help you be as safe as I can and help you get the most out of this, *but it's your trip.*"

Most essentially, you as a therapist need to be able to hear the entire grim tale if your clients are going to heal. In her invaluable book *Trauma and Recovery*,[3] Judith Herman is particularly eloquent and impassioned on this point. Anything less than bearing witness to the full catastrophe can be silencing, no matter how well intentioned you are or how subtly you convey your fear. If *you* can bear it, they might bear it. Your bravery may lead clients to relinquish their solitary, ashamed anguish. While this puts a tremendous burden on therapists to tolerate far more atrocity than most of us *ever* bargained for, seeing human hope reborn potentially transforms *you*. As Joanna recently realized, one of her greatest strengths as a therapist is this: "I have a huge tolerance for other people's emotional pain, as well as my own." Similarly, Dan's organization carefully scrutinizes prospective staff members for their capacity to tolerate their clients' agony:

> In the therapeutic process, since we're focusing on people who are battered and abused and who have been traumatized, I think it's so

essential that therapists be able to sit with the worst . . . and not say, "Okay, now I get the picture, . . . no need to talk about the beatings any longer." Now, they wouldn't probably say that in words, but rather nonverbally: "This is getting too heavy." For example, . . . in my own psychodramatic experiences, it was necessary—dozens of times—to go through a reenactment of the beatings. *Dozens* of times. And to do this with a therapist who was sufficiently realized as a human being and sufficiently secure in herself so that *no* intensity was going to overwhelm her. And again, this is putting a great challenge on the therapist, being capable of not being frightened, being comfortable enough with herself or himself to be able to sit with that, to live with that, to deal with it. But that seems really crucial.

It is also imperative that clinicians help clients recognize their true childhood victimization while respecting their intolerance for the *role* of victim. They need to help all self-attacking trauma victims see that you cannot stop your accusing self-hatred unless you *fully* understand how utterly helpless you were to prevent your own past abuse. Strugglers need to develop a deeply compassionate view of the hurt child that they *were*, no matter how self-sustaining and sturdy they are *now*. In addition, any stand for stronger selfhood that clients took during their abuse needs to be recognized and explored so that the abused can see that, within the confines of their developmentally limited predicaments, they were doing *something* to protect themselves. Remember that few of these resilient people challenged their abusers until midadolescence. When they did take a stand, they felt reclaimed. So help your clients recall and explore any forms of healthy self-preservation and examine together just what wisdom guided the encounter. What were they fighting *for*? Did they carry some core conviction that they were "made for more"? What "more" did they know about? While honoring their helplessness as abused children, constantly underscoring how much they were *not* at fault and how wrong the abuse was, you also need to help them see how much they struggled to preserve themselves then, even in minute ways. Even their determination to *grow*—to have a friend, go to school, read a book, or love a pet—is vastly courageous when a child is under assault.

In regard to particular therapeutic modes, several subjects stressed the importance of matching an intervention to a developmental moment and noted how helpful it was for them to encounter therapies that offered insight, trustworthy companionship, and a safe expressive outlet for their anguish. Once again, Dan summarizes well for the others:

> I found that I was helped greatly by two very diverse therapeutic techniques. One was having a classical analyst help me to understand from childhood on up through the years—some comprehensive understanding of what happened and what it did to me. You know, good old-fashioned insight. I think the two years [from twenty to twenty-two] I spent with Dr. Levy, the psychiatrist, really had a profound impact on me. . . .
>
> There were a number of things that he did that were really quite wonderful. One of them was . . . I saw him three times a week, and I probably spent thirty of the forty-five minutes crying, week after week, day after day after day. It got to the point where I would arrive for my session and . . . sit down, and he'd just look at me and I'd start to cry. . . . For whatever the reasons were in his own makeup, he was able to sit with that, with my sadness. Sometimes I'd just sit and cry for three or four minutes. He would hand me Kleenex periodically and wait until the crying kind of abated, and then we'd begin to talk; and then the tears would come again. *It was all right to cry as much as I wanted, and . . . it was so very clear that not only was it all right to do that, but he was never going to hit me, no matter what I said. I was safe, he was never going to hit me, and it felt like he cared about me.*
>
> I think he genuinely did care about me. It wasn't just a therapy

relationship. I mean, here's this young guy who had a really tough situation in his life, and I think he genuinely cared about me. I suspect that I was probably one of the patients—if he was talking to a colleague, he'd say, "Well, I'm treating this young man who's had a really profound amount of abuse in his life, and he's doing very well." I think he . . . I can feel his interest in me, and his caring for me, I guess, and that was just terribly important, and what he did was he helped me.

People sometimes put down Freudian analysts so much, . . . but he helped me to go back to as early a point as possible in my life and begin to put it all together again and make sense out of it, and then to say to me, "The things your mother did were wrong." I remember him saying very clearly, "Little boys shouldn't have to be treated in those ways. She probably had tremendous problems of her own, but she shouldn't have treated you this way," so my thinking was, "If he says that, then it must be so." So he was giving me a whole new set of values. . . . It was a very significant two years, and I devoted so much of my energy to the treatment. I was working and going to school and doing other things, in and out, during this time, but the treatment was extremely important. Nobody has three-times-a-week therapy nowadays, as you know—this isn't done—but damn it—. Initially, my parents paid for it, and then I paid for it after that. . . .

Dan and others said that finding an utterly safe expressive outlet for their distress was invaluable. Some deliberately enacted their feelings *outside* therapy but with a therapist's guidance, ripping cardboard while enraged, shouting and hurling stones into the ocean, or going to the graves of their perpetrators to have a final sobbing say. However, others chose to remain *within* the safe companionship of trusted others; these said that the affirming companionship of an expressive therapist—and even other witnesses, as in the case of group therapy—helped them understand exactly how abusive, bizarre, and unfair their childhood treatment had been. Dan discusses the cathartic processes that he found therapeutic:

> By itself, analysis wouldn't have done it. It would have been half a loaf; I wouldn't have made it in the way that I would have liked to have made it, but I found that it was invaluable to have it to start with. What I had to have in addition to that [during my thirties] was to . . . participate in therapeutic processes where I could achieve a full, toe-curling catharsis. For example, I'm standing there [in a psychodrama session] dripping wet with a tennis racquet in my hands and I'm beating the bed, expressing to my father how I feel about the time that he punched me in the stomach, you see. Not saying, "Oh, that was upsetting, and I think I was probably angry with him doing that" [laughter]. Instead, I'm [symbolically] beating him to death. Physically beating him to death for all the beatings he gave me, you see, and I'm going to do that not only that time, but the following week I'm going to find myself beating him to death again [laughter]. And the following week, once more beating him to death, and then following that, I'm going to lie on that bed shaking in fear, absolutely shaking in fear with a therapist who can say, "Go with the feeling; . . . shake some more. You've got more fear in there." Trembling and shaking, terrified, you see, and really experiencing the terror and then weeping for twenty minutes. . . . [And then she and I would talk] about . . . what that was all about. "Okay, that was the fear you felt as a small child." But I couldn't probably have gotten to that as easily or as well without first the insight therapy to kind of understand the framework and then . . . the more difficult reenacting of it in the Gestalt way or a psychodramatic way. . . .

I asked Dan if he thought that there was something about the developmental timing of his therapies that was important. That is, if he had switched their order and plunged into a more dramatic, expressive mode first, would that have influenced him differently?

I wondered if he needed to know that he was *entirely* safe from reen-acting his parents' abusiveness in his own life in order to benefit from these symbolic, therapeutic re-creations of the abuse when he was older. He quickly replied,

> It might have been too terrifying to switch it, . . . because I wouldn't have understood [the difference between what was symbolic and what was real] when I was younger. But it wouldn't have to be [some-one's] twenties [as opposed to] thirties; it could be even six months of getting some insight and then getting into more active work.

Although the developmental time frame varied from person to person, it seems that some combination of insight-oriented and more expressive work was especially beneficial to some of the resilient, giving them active ways to rework traumatic experiences within the safe containment of a therapeutic setting. By the time they did more expressive work, they knew that they would not extend these enactments into their actual lives and thus repeat the parental plague that they had gone to therapy to heal. In any case, settings that encourage depth of feeling while containing the more destructive potential of such feeling—that delicate high-wire work of all therapy—seem especially reparative to the resilient.

Therapists also need to believe in imperceptible progress. While the resilient tend to move faster than others, most underlying change is plodding (human character being fundamentally conser-vative). Thus it is important to notice small changes constantly, telling your struggler about the differences you see and helping bear witness to growth. Remark that one tight bud looks slightly more open of late. As gardeners are well aware, plants are repotted only one size up; otherwise, the extra pot space will swamp their growth. You may both yearn for time-lapse photography to speed the process, but all genuine progress takes *time*. Most of the resilient in my study are in their late thirties and early forties and *known* for their tenacious industriousness. As my clinical partner, Carol

Taylor, analogizes, doing trauma work is like serving as midwife for a client in the throes of psychological childbirth. She reminds clients that hard labor alters your perceptions. Time distorts; you feel you have been at this your entire life. "It goes on forever and ever and ever and you still don't have a baby; and you've been in pain far too long and you're *sick* of it. You don't want to go any further. 'I can't do this,' you say. But if you have a competent midwife, she will say, with steel-hard, warm certainty, 'You *are* doing it. You *are* doing it.'" So when her trauma victims say, "I can't do this," Taylor replies, "You *are* doing it. You *are* doing it." She reassures herself with the same words: "When I get into that panicky state of 'Oh, my God, they're no better now than they were three months ago or six months ago,' then I have to say to *myself*, 'You *are* doing it; you *are* doing it.' I think that as long as you don't see the baby, you're afraid you don't have anything to show for it—and then whoosh! *[laughter]*—you have a birth."

Finally, it is essential to examine carefully your own assumptions about whether mental health can occur only within or without ongoing interactions with the family of origin during adulthood. While our job is to support our clients in their choices about continuing, delimiting, or even ending these interactions, many of them need to realize that they actually *have* a choice. This is a novel discovery to many clients. *If your therapeutic model of mental health assumes that ongoing family interactions are essential, you may be doing your clients as much of an injustice as a therapist who assumes that the lot should be fired.* You need to realize that, at times, it is simply too physically and psychologically dangerous to "work it out." Recognize that resolving the past does not necessarily *assume* ongoing interactions. Sometimes family members are either too toxic or too unrelenting to allow any healthy resolution, necessitating thoughtfully attenuated, suspended, or severed contact for adult mental health to flourish. If you have not considered that sometimes growth can occur *only* outside ongoing contact with members of the fold, you will have difficulty helping many of the maltreated. You need to help them understand that they have a wide range of viable choices; if you fail to, you are effectively taking their choices away from them—to their detriment.

Remember, too, that most people are desperate to be effective family members. This is certainly true of adults who love well, such as the resilient. Most of them *would* "work it out" with each family member if they could. They see limiting or leaving interactions as the court of last resort. However, *they are not the only ones who have work to do*. "Loving well" is a *joint* enterprise; like any other mutual activity, it requires capable and willing participants. Since families often bypass their own recovery work, even the most diligent over-comers may be thwarted in their attempts to render these relationships viable. They find that their adult mental health is predicated on having little or no ongoing contact with family members. Therapists need to embrace this possibility, offering it to clients who are in defeating and unyielding familial circumstances as an alternative that might be chosen with integrity.

In closing, those of you who have the strength of conviction and stamina to help the hurt heal should remember to celebrate your own courage. You are being asked to summon all of your talents to descend into Dante's hell while reaching for the heavens, fully embracing both savagery and possibility in a challenged life. Whether you are teachers, clinicians, or those invaluable informal healers that rise up quietly without a drum roll, you are the sturdy crew helping to row the potentially resilient toward the sea beyond the Sirens. The resilient know they cannot get there alone; thus their gratitude toward helpers like you billows on.

Over a decade ago, I embarked upon a penetrating exploration of the soul's capacity to soar. I wanted to know how the terribly treated are launched *at all*, let alone surmount so much so well. I wanted to know how they find—or create—a Shaker peaceable kingdom, an oceanic realm well beyond the Sirens' call. While human resilience retains a sense of miracle and mystery, it *can* be explicated and replicated. Thus I offer this work as a set of provisional navigational charts for effective overcoming. I welcome fellow cartographers.

Above all, remember that the resilient yearn for more of the hurt multitude to join them in their relative health. Most of us have dedicated our lives to stirring hope and encouraging some means of surmounting in the many who still struggle. And so, if your own hope is a baby born blue, cold, and still, recall that so many of us also came of age in the dark. Yet we did find a way to grasp a shaft of the sun. By speaking out, we press our palms against your dimmed hope's chest so that its wail will crack hurt's silence and *your* song can be sung.

Resources for Researchers

This summary outlines the research design, instruments, and findings of my work.

Sources of Data

The data for this study were gleaned from a four-hour clinical interview guided by a standard set of questions. These questions explored early events and current relationships. Total interview time was 180 hours among forty subjects (five original subjects were reinterviewed). Screening criteria included DSM III, Axis IV (Severity of Psychosocial Stressors), Axis V (Highest Level of Adaptive Functioning, Past Year); major parental psychopathology; my criteria for "loving well" (see the Preface); and Vaillant's Hierarchy of Defenses. Subjects in the first group also completed the Thematic Apperception Test, the Family Environment Scale, the Relationship Inventory, the Early Life Events Checklist, and the Subject-Object Interview. I focused more of the second group's time on themes that emerged in my thesis work regarding locus of hope, defining current relationships with the family of origin, current work and its meaning, conceptions of victimization and forgiveness, and specific recommendations for promoting resilience in others. However, the second group also completed the Family Environment Scale and Early Life Events Checklist.[1]

Demographics and General Characteristics
of the Sample

Unless otherwise stated, the characteristics described in this section apply to a combined sample of both subject groups.

- *Sample size.* The total sample of forty subjects breaks down as follows: Group 1 (1984), $n = 23$; Group 2 (1992), $n = 17$; Group 1 reinterviewed (1992), $n = 5$.

- *Sex.* The group was made up of twenty-two women and nineteen men.

- *Age.* In Group 1, the average age was thirty-eight (ranging from thirty-one to sixty-five, clustering in the mid thirties); in Group 2, the average age was forty-one (ranging from twenty-three to fifty-eight, clustering in the early forties).

- *Religious/ethnic background.* Approximately 18 percent of the subjects were brought up Jewish, 40 percent were Catholic, 40 percent were Protestant, and 2.5 percent were other.

- *Racial group.* The subjects were predominantly white, although concerted efforts were made to recruit other racial groups. It should be noted, however, that this concentration of white subjects is an unfortunate artifact of the referral process, *not* an indicator of lesser resilience in any other population.

- *Current socioeconomic status.* This was a predominantly middle- to upper-middle-class group with an 80 percent upward-mobility rate (demonstrating a much higher level of education and income than their families of origin).

- *Sibling order.* There was no particular pattern to the sibling order among the subjects.

- *Siblings' current level of psychological functioning.* Most subjects reported significant current psychopathology in one or several siblings (for example, severe substance abuse, psychopathy and other personality disorders, severe depression and suicidality, and/or sexual and physical abusiveness toward their offspring).

- *Therapy experience*. Eighty percent of the subjects had been in therapy for at least two years (typically far longer). A few started therapy before the age of eighteen.

Documentation and Nature of Background Stress

All forty subjects' backgrounds were judged by the screening psychologist or psychiatric social worker as well as the primary investigator (and, for Group 1, two other reliability observers on a representative sample of cases, $n = 6$) to be either "severely," "extremely," or "catastrophically" stressful during at least one major developmental era on the DSM III list, Severity of Psychosocial Stressors (Axis IV).[2] Virtually all were judged to be facing such stress for most of their childhood and adolescent years.

In addition, there was a history of major psychopathology in at least one (generally both) parent(s) during at least one (usually all) major developmental era(s). These parents were judged to be at a "poor," "very poor," or "grossly impaired" level of functioning for five or more years when the subject was anywhere from birth to eighteen years old. In almost all cases, this compromised parental functioning extended throughout most of the subject's early childhood and adolescent years.

The Early Life Events Checklist and clinical interviews gave a suggestive clinical picture of specific stressors that subjects encountered.[3] Noteworthy findings include a high incidence of the following:

- Serious physical illness in self or family (68 percent)
- Major changes in financial status (63 percent)
- General difficulty making ends meet (77 percent)

- Chronic family discord; parental fighting (82 percent)
- Long separation from infancy caregiver (35 percent)
- Parental alcohol/drug abuse (50 percent)
- Serious childhood illness (27 percent)
- Parental mental disorder, including mental deterioration associated with significant substance abuse (100 percent)
- Persistent/harsh parental discipline (68 percent)
- Absent father or mother (43 percent)
- Loss of parental employment or sporadic employment of breadwinner (38 percent)
- Repeated sexual or physical abuse, usually both (58 percent)

The subjects' level of background stress was also evaluated using the Family Environment Scale (FES).[4] The FES *normative group* (n = 1125) includes a national cross-section of single-parent families, multigenerational families, and ethnic minorities. The FES *distressed family group* (n = 500) includes families with alcohol abusers, general psychiatric patients, an adolescent or child in crisis, runaways, delinquent children or adolescents, and children being placed in foster care.

In this study, Group 1 subject families of origin conformed to the profile of the FES *distressed family group*: they had significantly less cohesion, expressiveness, intellectual-cultural orientation, and active-recreational orientation than the *normal family group*, and far more conflict and control. In fact, they had significantly less cohesion and expressiveness and more conflict and parental control than the FES *distressed family group* (greater than one standard deviation).

Group 2 subject families of origin also conformed to the profile of the FES *distressed family group* (although they did not exactly match the first group): they had significantly less cohesion, expressiveness, independence, intellectual-cultural orientation, and active-recreational orientation than the *normal family group*, and far more conflict and control. In a slightly different configuration of extremes, they had significantly less expressiveness and independence and more conflict and parental control than the FES *distressed family group* (greater than one standard deviation).

Documentation of Adult Mental Health and Growth

As in the previous section, all discussion applies to both subject groups unless otherwise indicated.

Overall Levels of Mental Health and Growth

The referring clinician and I (and two reliability observers for the 1984 group, both psychologists) also judged each subject to use predominantly mature defenses, including altruism, anticipation, suppression, sublimation, and humor.[5] Since J. Kirk Felsman and George Vaillant's subsequent work on adaptive strategies finds that those employing mature defenses are dramatically more likely than those using immature defenses to sustain warm relationships with a wide range of people, ego functioning becomes a correlated measure of "loving well."[6] Each subject also demonstrated "superior" to "very good" adaptive functioning in the year prior to the interview. In addition, high levels of ego functioning were established in the 1984 group using Robert Kegan's Subject-Object Interview. This measure was not repeated in the 1992 group in the interest of allowing more time to pursue other questions in the interview protocol.

All subjects met screening criteria for overall functioning that can be rated as either "superior" or "very good" on the DSM III list of Highest Level of Adaptive Functioning, Past Year.[7] In addition, all met screening criteria for an adaptive style that can be characterized as "predominantly mature" within Vaillant's Defensive Hierarchy (exhibiting altruism, anticipation, sublimation, suppression, and humor).[8]

Group 1 (1984) was assessed using Robert Kegan's Subject-Object Interview, as I noted earlier.[9] This instrument correlates well with other measures of ego development, such as Lawrence Kohlberg's Moral Dilemmas and Jane Loevinger's Sentence Completion Test.[10] All subjects reached at least Balance 3 on Kegan's scale (indicating that they are able to empathize with others' perceptions, wishes, and needs as well as their own). Additionally, over half were shown to be operating at higher levels of ego development (Balances 4 and beyond), although they did not receive sufficient parental nurturance to explain these levels of growth.

"Loving Well"

The average length of time the subjects had spent in a satisfying marriage or other long-term committed relationship varied between the two groups:

- *Group 1 (1984).* Twelve and a half years (ranging from under one year in a relationship for a person age thirty to twenty-seven years in a relationship for a person age forty-nine). This average includes an additional eight years of marriage for four of the five individuals reinterviewed from the 1984 group.
- *Group 2 (1992).* Eighteen years (ranging from five years for a person age twenty-three to thirty-five years for a person age fifty-eight). Given this group's average age of forty-one, many of the subjects have been in these relationships for nearly half of their lives.

All met screening criteria for "loving well," as measured by the question, "Do they form and maintain friendships (at least three for as many years) marked by a considerable degree of mutual satisfaction and reciprocity, despite whatever difficulties in communicating and cooperating they might encounter?" Reliability observers judged a smaller subgroup ($n = 6$) on a variety of criteria for "loving well" and agreed that all subjects met these specific criteria. The aim of this further testing was to establish credibility of the screening criteria and clinical interview data.

Working Well

The average level of education of the total group was as follows: 70 percent had a master's degree or a doctorate; the remaining 30 percent had a bachelor's degree or some college; only one had a high school equivalency. Roughly 70 percent were more highly educated than their parents. All had above-average to superior intelligence based on educational level, type of institution attended (many attended highly selective colleges and universities), and caliber of verbal responses in the interview.

The work of 85 percent of the subjects involved social/political activism or some sort of role as a change-agent (jobs included, for example, clinicians, teachers, nurses, community organizers, and community physicians). Roughly 50 percent were trained psychologists or social workers.

Regardless of their profession, the subjects expressed sustained work satisfaction in the field for which they received specific training (for example, engineering, teaching, machinery operation, education, psychology, nursing).

As a correlated measure of work success, Vaillant's research also links mature defensive strategies, characteristic of my group, with above-average income and low rates of unemployment, at least for men.[11] This is true for the women as well as the men in my study.

Chapter Notes

Opening Epigraph

1. B. Russell, *The Autobiography of Bertrand Russell* (London: Allen & Unwin, 1967), 9.

Chapter One

1. D. Russell, *Sexual Exploitation: Rape, Child Sexual Abuse, and Sexual Harassment* (Newbury Park, Calif.: Sage, 1984).
2. J. Herman, *Father Daughter Incest* (Cambridge, Mass.: Harvard University Press, 1981). See also J. Herman, *Trauma and Recovery* (New York: Basic Books, 1992).
3. J. S. Wodarski and S. R. Johnson, "Child Sexual Abuse: Contributing Factors, Effects, and Relevant Practice Issues," *Family Therapy* 15 (1988): 157–173.
4. D. Finkelhor, *Child Sexual Abuse: New Theory and Research* (New York: Free Press, 1984).
5. M. Belenky, B. Clinchy, N. Goldberger, and J. Tarule, *Women's Ways of Knowing* (New York: Basic Books, 1986).
6. C. Hartman and A. Burgess, "Sexual Abuse of Children: Causes and Consequences," in *Child Maltreatment: Theory and Research on the Causes and Consequences of Child Abuse and Neglect*, ed. D. Cicchetti and V. Carlson (Cambridge: Cambridge University Press, 1989), 95–128.
7. Cicchetti and Carlson, ed., *Child Maltreatment*, xiii.

University Microfilms International, 300 Zeeb Road, Ann Arbor, Mich., 48106; telephone 1–800–521–3042; dissertation number 85–23328.

55. R. Kegan, *The Evolving Self* (Cambridge, Mass: Harvard University Press, 1982).

56. D. Quinton, M. Rutter, and C. Liddle, "Institutional Rearing, Parenting Difficulties, and Marital Support, *Psychological Medicine 14* (1984): 107–124. See also "Long-Term Follow-Up of Women Institutionalized in Childhood: Factors Promoting Good Functioning in Adult Life," *British Journal of Developmental Psychology 2* (1984): 194–204.

57. Rutter, "Psychosocial Resilience and Protective Mechanisms," 324.

Chapter Two

1. R. W. Emerson, *Essays* (Boston: James Munroe, 1841).

Chapter Three

1. D. W. Winnicott, *The Maturational Processes and the Facilitating Environment* (Madison, Conn.: International Universities Press, 1965).

2. R. Kegan, *The Evolving Self* (Cambridge, Mass.: Harvard University Press, 1982).

3. L. Rogers and R. Kegan, "Mental Growth and Mental Health as Distinct Concepts in the Study of Developmental Psychology: Theory, Research, and Clinical Implications," in *Constructivist Perspectives on Developmental Psychopathology and Atypical Development*, ed. D. P. Keating and H. Rosen (Hillsdale, N.J.: Erlbaum, 1991).

4. *Quotable Women* (Philadelphia: Running Press, 1989).

5. G. Vaillant, *Adaptation to Life* (Boston: Little, Brown, 1977); G. Vaillant, "An Empirically Derived Hierarchy of Adaptive Mechanisms and Its Usefulness as a Potential Diagnostic Axis," *Acta Psychiatrica Scandinavica 71*, supplementum no. 319 (1985): 171–180.

6. Rogers and Kegan, "Mental Growth and Mental Health as Distinct Concepts in the Study of Developmental Psychology."

7. Rogers and Kegan, "Mental Growth and Mental Health as Distinct Concepts in the Study of Developmental Psychology"; G. Noam,

"Borderline Personality Disorders and the Theory of Biography and Transformation," *McLean Hospital Journal 11* (1986): 19–43; G. Noam, "A Constructivist Approach to Developmental Psychopathology" in *Developmental Psychopathology and Its Treatment*, New Directions for Child Development, no. 39, ed. E. D. Nannis and P. A. Cowan (San Francisco: Jossey-Bass, 1988).

8.   Winnicott, *The Maturational Processes and the Facilitating Environment*.

9.   Kegan, *The Evolving Self*.

10. Kegan, *The Evolving Self*, 116.

11. Kegan, *The Evolving Self*, 116.

12. Kegan, *The Evolving Self*, 19.

13. E. Werner and R. Smith, *Vulnerable but Invincible: A Longitudinal Study of Resilient Children and Youth* (New York: McGraw-Hill, 1982), 136.

14. C. Kaufmann, H. Grunebaum, B. Cohler, and E. Gamer, "Superkids: Competent Children of Psychotic Mothers," *American Journal of Psychiatry 136*, no. 11 (1979): 1400.

15. N. Cheng, *Life and Death in Shanghai* (New York: Penguin, 1986), 327.

16. H. Harlow, M. K. Harlow, and S. J. Suomi, "From Thought to Therapy: Lessons from a Primate Laboratory," *American Scientist 59* (1971): 538–549.

17. R. Rhodes, *A Hole in the World* (New York: Simon & Schuster, 1990).

18. R. Kipling, *The Jungle Book* (New York: Macmillan, 1892).

Chapter Four

1.   S. Parks, *The Critical Years* (San Francisco: HarperCollins, 1986); R. Kegan, *In Over Our Heads: The Mental Demands of Modern Life* (Cambridge, Mass.: Harvard University Press, 1994); R. Kegan, *The Evolving Self* (Cambridge, Mass.: Harvard University Press, 1982); L. Rogers and R. Kegan, "Mental Growth and Mental Health as Distinct Concepts in the Study of Developmental Psychology: Theory, Research, and Clinical Implications," in *Constructivist Perspectives on Developmental Psychopathology and Atypical Development*, ed. D. P. Keating and H. Rosen (Hillsdale, N.J.: Erlbaum, 1991); R. Goodman, "Myth and Symbol as Expressions

of the Religious," in *A Clinical Case Approach to Religious Experience in Psychotherapy*, ed. M. Randour (New York: Columbia University Press, 1991); G. Noam, "A Constructivist Approach to Developmental Psychopathology," in *Developmental Psychopathology and Its Treatment*, New Directions for Child Development, no. 39, ed. E. D. Nannis and P. A. Cowan (San Francisco: Jossey-Bass, 1988); M. Basseches, *Dialectical Thinking and Adult Development* (Norwood, N.J.: Ablex, 1984); A. Fleck-Henderson, "Moral Reasoning in Social Work Practice," *Social Service Review*, June 1991: 185–202; B. Speicher, "Adolescent Moral Judgment and Perceptions of Family Interaction," *Journal of Family Psychology* 6, no. 2 (1992): 128–138.

2. Kegan, *The Evolving Self*.
3. Rogers and Kegan, "Mental Growth and Mental Health as Distinct Concepts in the Study of Developmental Psychology."
4. J. K. Felsman and G. E. Vaillant, "Resilient Children as Adults: A Forty-Year Study" in *The Invulnerable Child*, ed. E. J. Anthony and B. J. Cohler (New York: Guilford Press, 1987), 289–314.
5. R. White, "Motivation Reconsidered: The Concept of Competence," in *Functions of Varied Experience*, ed. D. W. Fiske and S. R. Maddi (Homewood, Ill.: Dorsey Press, 1961), 278–325.
6. G. Vaillant, *Adaptation to Life* (Boston: Little, Brown, 1977), 300, 210.

Chapter Five

1. *Holy Bible*, Revised Standard Version (New York: American Bible Society, 1884).
2. S. Parks, personal conversation, June 1991.
3. S. Parks, *The Critical Years: Young Adults and the Search for Meaning, Faith, and Commitment* (San Francisco: HarperCollins, 1986); S. Parks, "Faith Development and Imagination in the Context of Higher Education" (Th.D. diss., Harvard Divinity School, 1980).
4. S. Parks, "Faith Development and Imagination in the Context of Higher Education," 36.
5. J. Fowler, *Stages of Faith: The Psychology of Human Development and the Quest for Meaning* (San Francisco: HarperCollins, 1981).
6. S. Parks, "Faith Development and Imagination in the Context of Higher Education," 36.

7. B. Bettelheim, *Surviving and Other Essays* (New York: Knopf, 1979), 296.

8. R. Niebuhr, *Experiential Religion* (New York: HarperCollins, 1972), 39.

9. Niebuhr, *Experiential Religion*, 39.

10. Fowler, *Stages of Faith*; J. Fowler, "Stages of Faith and Adults' Life Cycles," in *Faith Development in the Adult Life Cycle*, ed. K. Stokes (New York: Sadlier, 1982); Parks, *The Critical Years*.

11. Parks, "Faith Development and Imagination in the Context of Higher Education," 32.

12. A. Walker, *The Color Purple* (New York: Washington Square Press, 1983), 122.

13. Walker, *The Color Purple*, 187.

14. V. Frankl, *Man's Search for Meaning* (New York: Washington Square Press, 1959), 58–61.

15. Parks, "Faith Development and Imagination in the Context of Higher Education," 212.

16. Parks, "Faith Development and Imagination in the Context of Higher Education," 202.

17. Frankl, *Man's Search for Meaning*; N. Cheng, *Life and Death in Shanghai* (New York: Penguin, 1986).

18. Niebuhr, *Experiential Religion*, 39.

19. H. Melville, *Moby Dick* (New York: Library of America, 1983 [originally published 1851]), 1335.

20. S. Parks, personal conversation, June 1991.

21. E. B. White, *Charlotte's Web* (New York: HarperCollins, 1952), 184.

22. Cheng, *Life and Death in Shanghai*, 315.

23. Melville, *Moby Dick*, 1349.

24. Melville, *Moby Dick*, 1285–1286.

25. P. Gallico, *The Snow Goose* (London: Michael Joseph, 1951).

26. A. Frank, *The Diary of a Young Girl* (New York: Washington Square Press, 1952), 237.

27. Cheng, *Life and Death in Shanghai*, 346–347.

28. P. Berrigan, "Letter to the Weathermen," in *The Berrigans*, ed. W. Van Etten Casey (New York: Avon, 1971), 210.

29. Fowler, *Stages of Faith*.

30. J. Leonard, *Private Lives in the Imperial City* (New York: Knopf, 1979), 29.

Chapter Six

1. S. Kierkegaard, *Concluding Unscientific Postscript*, trans. D. F. Swenson (Princeton, N.J.: Princeton University Press, 1941), 322.
2. J. Loder, *The Transforming Moment: Understanding Convictional Experience* (San Francisco: HarperCollins, 1981).
3. S. Parks, "Faith Development and Imagination in the Context of Higher Education" (Th.D. diss., Harvard Divinity School, 1980), 251.
4. Parks, "Faith Development and Imagination in the Context of Higher Education," 259.
5. D. M. Elliot and J. D. Guy, "Mental Health Professionals Versus Non–Mental Health Professionals: Childhood Trauma and Adult Functioning," *Professional Psychology: Research and Practice 24* (1993): 83–90.
6. V. Hugo, *Les Misérables*, trans. C. E. Wilbour (New York: Modern Library, n.d. [originally published 1862]).
7. S. Silverstein, *The Giving Tree* (New York: HarperCollins, 1964).
8. F. Flagg, *Fried Green Tomatoes at the Whistle Stop Cafe* (New York: McGraw-Hill, 1987).
9. J. Jacobs, personal conversation, Nov. 1984.

Chapter Seven

1. C. Wright, "Homage to Paul Cézanne," *The New Yorker*, 18 Dec. 1977, 36–37.
2. Homer, *The Odyssey*, trans. R. Fitzgerald (New York: Anchor Books, 1963), 210–211.
3. J. Herman, *Trauma and Recovery* (New York: Basic Books, 1992).
4. Homer, *The Odyssey*, 215.
5. H. Melville, *Moby Dick* (New York: Library of America, 1983 [originally published 1851]), 1329.
6. D. Henahan, "Music View," *New York Times*, 15 July 1990, p. 21.
7. W.R.D. Fairbairn, *Psychoanalytic Studies of the Personality* (London: Routledge & Kegan Paul, 1952), 66.
8. Fairbairn, *Psychoanalytic Studies of the Personality*, 66.
9. J. Manganiello, personal conversation, Nov. 1986.
10. J. Lehrich, personal conversation, Apr. 1989.
11. P. Chayefsky, *Marty* (CBS/Fox Video, released by United Artists, 1955).

12. S. Parks, personal conversation, June 1991.
13. C. Dickens, *Great Expectations* (New York: New American Library, 1963 [originally published 1860]).

Chapter Eight

1. H. Melville, *Moby Dick* (New York: Library of America, 1983 [originally published 1851]), 1318.
2. Melville, *Moby Dick*, 1329.
3. J. Herman, *Trauma and Recovery* (New York: Basic Books, 1992).

Resources for Researchers

1. R. Higgins, "Psychological Resilience and the Capacity for Intimacy: How the Wounded Might 'Love Well'" (Ed.D. diss., Harvard University, 1985), 261–313. See also: American Psychiatric Association, *Diagnostic and Statistical Manual, 3rd Ed.* (Washington, D.C.: 1980); A. Hartman, "A Basic T.A.T. Set," *Journal of Projective Techniques and Personality Assessment 34* (5); W. Henry, *The Analysis of Fantasy* (Melbourne, Fla.: Krieger, 1973); A. Hewer, "Structural Developmental Assessment" (unpublished manuscript, 1982); R. Kegan, *The Evolving Self* (Cambridge: Harvard University Press, 1982); L. Lahey and others, "The Guide to the Subject-Object Interview: Its Administration and Analysis (Cambridge, Mass.: The Subject-Object Research Group, 1988); R. Moos, "Assessment and Impact of Social Climate Scales," *Advances in Psychological Assessment*, no. 3, ed. P. McReynolds (San Francisco: Jossey-Bass, 1979); R. Moos, J. Clayton, and W. Max, *The Social Climate Scales: An Annotated Bibliography, 2nd Ed.* (Palo Alto: Consulting Psychologists Press, 1979); R. Moos and B. Moos, *Family Environment Scale Manual* (Palo Alto: Consulting Psychologists Press, 1981); H. Murray, *The Thematic Apperception Test* (Cambridge: Harvard University Press, 1943); G. Vaillant, *Adaptation to Life* (Boston: Little, Brown, 1977).
2. Higgins, "Psychological Resilience and the Capacity for Intimacy," 261–313.
3. Higgins, "Psychological Resilience and the Capacity for Intimacy," 261–313.
4. Higgins, "Psychological Resilience and the Capacity for Intimacy," 261–313.

5. G. Vaillant, *Adaptation to Life* (Boston: Little, Brown, 1977).
6. J. K. Felsman and G. Vaillant, "Resilient Children as Adults: A Forty-Year Study," in *The Invulnerable Child*, ed. E. J. Anthony and B. Cohler (New York: Guilford Press, 1987), 289–314.
7. Higgins, "Psychological Resilience and the Capacity for Intimacy," 261–313.
8. Higgins, "Psychological Resilience and the Capacity for Intimacy," 261–313.
9. Higgins, "Psychological Resilience and the Capacity for Intimacy," 261–313.
10. Kegan, *The Evolving Self*.
11. G. Vaillant, "An Empirically Derived Hierarchy of Adaptive Mechanisms and Its Usefulness as a Potential Diagnostic Axis," *Acta Psychiatrica Scandinavica 71*, supplementum no. 319 (1985): 171–180.

Index